Rose of the South

Mrs. Rose O'Neal Greenhow

Rose of the South

The Life of Rose Greenhow: Confederate Spy

My Imprisonment and the First Year of Abolition Rule at Washington

Mrs. Rose Greenhow

With a Short Biography of Mrs. Greenhow

by W. G. Beymer

LEONAUR

Rose of the South
The Life of Rose Greenhow: Confederate Spy
My Imprisonment and the First Year of Abolition Rule at Washington
by Mrs. Rose Greenhow
With a Short Biography of Mrs. Greenhow
by W. G. Beymer

FIRST EDITION IN THIS FORM

First published under the titles
My Imprisonment and the First Year of Abolition Rule at Washington
and
Mrs. Greenhow

Leonaur is an imprint of Oakpast Ltd
Copyright in this form © 2023 Oakpast Ltd

ISBN: 978-1-916535-62-6 (hardcover)
ISBN: 978-1-916535-63-3 (softcover)

http://www.leonaur.com

Publisher's Notes

The views expressed in this book are not necessarily
those of the publisher.

Contents

I RESPECTFULLY DEDICATE THESE PAGES
TO THE
BRAVE SOLDIERS
WHO HAVE FOUGHT AND BLED
IN
THIS OUR GLORIOUS STRUGGLE FOR FREEDOM.

ROSE GREENHOW.

LONDON: NOV. 6, 1863.

CHAPTER 1

Introduction

Whether a faithful record of my long and humiliating imprisonment at Washington, in the hands of the enemies of my country, will prove as interesting to the public as my friends assure me it is to them, I know not. It is natural for those who have suffered captivity to exaggerate the importance and interest of their own experiences; yet I should not venture upon publishing these notes and sketches merely as a narrative of indignities heaped upon myself personally. It is hoped that the story may excite more than a simple feeling of indignation or commiseration, by exhibiting somewhat of the intolerant spirit in which the present crusade against the liberties of sovereign States was undertaken, and somewhat of the true character of that race of people who insist on compelling us by force to live with them in bonds of fellowship and union.

I had been long a resident of Washington before the secession of the Confederate States, and, from my intimate acquaintance with public men and public measures under the old government, had peculiar and exceptional means of watching the progressive development of the designs of these leaders of opinion in the Federal States, which, as I had long foreseen, would necessarily end in forcing on a separation.

Much of my information upon this subject had been derived from the intercourse of society in the Federal capital; and would therefore have been unsuitable to be made public, if the relations of the North and the South had continued as they used to be—subjects of political discussion and party contest. But the Federal leaders have now carried the matter far beyond this point. After repeated and intolerable aggression upon the rights of these States—accompanied and aggravated by an insulting tone of moral superiority, until a union with such communities was no longer to be endured by any high-spirited people— they at length stirred up a furious and desolating war. For two years

9

a torrent of blood has flowed between their people and my people.

The noble State of Virginia, with which I am most nearly connected, has been devastated by hosts of barbarous invaders—always overthrown indeed in the field before Southern valour, but always destroying and plundering where they found the country unprotected; whilst my own dear native State of Maryland has been subject to a still more stinging and maddening oppression, in the utter destruction of all her liberties, and in the establishment of a brutal and vulgar military despotism, which has reduced the gallant old State to the debased condition of Poland or Venetia; and such 'order reigns in Baltimore,' as that moral death which tyrants call 'order' in Warsaw or in the beautiful City of the Sea.

To me, therefore, the days of my former abode in Washington seem to belong almost to another state of being. That time—when I, in common with all our people, looked up with pride and veneration to the banner of the stars and stripes—appears to be low with the years before the Flood. I look back to the scenes of that period through a haze of blood and horror. Those men whom I once called friends— who have broken bread at my table—have since then stirred up and hounded on host after host of greedy invaders, and precipitated them upon the beloved valleys where my kindred had their peaceful homes

Many who were dear to me have been slain, or maimed for life, fighting in defence of all that makes life of value. Instead of friends, I see in those statesmen of Washington only mortal enemies. Instead of loving and worshipping the old flag of the stars and stripes, I see in it only the symbol of murder, plunder, oppression, and shame! and, like every other faithful Confederate, I dwell with delight on the many glorious fields where this dishonoured standard has gone down before the stainless battle flag of the Confederacy.

In short, two years of terrible war, equivalent to an age of quiet life, have passed through the existence of us all, leaving a deep and ineffaceable track. Between us and those former friends there is a gulf deep and wide as eternity; and under these circumstances I have felt myself at liberty to be much more unreserved in the narrative of my personal recollections: suppressing, in fact, nothing which I thought would be either interesting or useful to my Confederate countrymen—except only when reserve was dictated by self-respect, or by the duty of avoiding disclosures which might compromise the safety of certain Federal officers, whom I induced without scruple, as will be more fully seen in the following pages, to furnish me with information, even in my captivity, which information I at once communicated with pride and pleasure to General Beauregard, then commanding the Confederate forces near Washington.

Whatever may be thought of the conduct of these Federal officers in betraying to an avowed enemy secrets material to their own Government, it will readily be admitted that after having made this use of them I should not have been justified in naming them, or affording a clue by which they could be discovered.

If, in detailing conversations which passed either with me or in my presence, before or after my arrest, I may be thought to have exhibited too great bitterness, it is hoped that the circumstances under; which I found myself may plead my excuse. It will be seen that I was well aware from an early period of the dark designs of the Abolition leaders at Washington, and that while they were holding publicly the language of patriotic zeal for the constitution and the law, they were already meditating, and preparing, all the dreadful scenes of lawless outrage and spoliation which have since that time rendered their names odious to the whole world.

It was well known to me what fate they were reserving for my own native State, and what diabolical agencies they were setting to work over all the country, both to destroy the Confederate States and to crush out the liberties of the North. The chief projectors of all these horrors, too, were well aware that I knew their plans and machinations intimately; and that, weak woman as I was, I possessed both the means and the spirit to throw serious obstacles in their way. Hence the keen and jealous surveillance by which my every motion was observed and noted, even long before my arrest. Hence, also, the useless series of torments and provocations to which I was subjected—the changes in my place of imprisonment, and the many attempts to entrap me into a betrayal of myself or the Confederate cause.

Hence the long and wearisome captivity, to break my spirit, or goad me into undignified bursts of indignation—in all of which I trust I may flatter myself that they signally failed. Satisfied thoroughly of the justice and sacredness of our great cause, and thinking only of the gallant struggle into which my kindred had thrown themselves, I was enabled, not only to 'possess my own soul' and keep my own; counsel, but also to establish and maintain a continuous correspondence with Virginia, and reveal certain contemplated military movements of the enemy in time to have; them thwarted by our generals.

For this I do not desire to take any special I credit in the eyes of the public. I only performed my duty, and have already been gratified by the thanks of those who best can judge of the services which I; endeavoured to render; and the matter is mentioned here merely as one of the reasons why it has been thought that a narrative furnished by one who enjoyed such opportunities of observation maybe I found not uninteresting.

It may be that the language which was sometimes extorted from me in conversation, or some of the remarks now found in my book, are more bitterly vituperative and sarcastic, than in ordinary times, and upon ordinary subjects, would be becoming in the personal narrative of a woman. Those who may think so are only entreated, before they judge, to endeavour to imagine themselves in my position—subject to the stinging indignities of a Washington prison, having to encounter sometimes the vicious taunts of vulgar guards, sometimes the treacherous warnings or counsels of politicians pretending to be my friends; a little daughter, too, always before my eyes, torn from the peaceful delights of home, and the flowery path of girlhood, and forced to witness the hard realities of prison-life, and hear the keys grating in dungeon locks. No wonder if my nature grew harsh and more vindictive, and if the scorn and wrath that was in my heart sometimes found vent by tongue or pen.

It was, above all things, when I thought of my own State of Maryland—where sleep the manes of my ancestors—that I burned with indignation in my prison. While the great State of Virginia, with her strong river frontier of the Potomac, was enabled to bid defiance to the utmost efforts of her enemies, it soon became evident that Maryland, penetrated by great bays and rivers, and with her very heart opened up to the naval forces of the enemy, would be, for the present at least, overpowered, and prevented from casting her lot openly and decisively with her sister States. I knew also that every genuine child of Maryland cherished in their souls but one feeling—one burning desire to share the destiny of their section, and to perish, if need be, in the glorious struggle; and could well imagine how so proud and refined a people would suffer and chafe to see themselves treated as vassals and serfs by a race they have always despised.

Yet the men were not so deeply to be pitied. They had always at least the resource of flinging themselves across the border, joining the Confederate service, and thus either opening a way to the redemption of their country, or at any rate meeting her oppressors on many a battlefield, and wreaking a righteous vengeance upon their heads.

But the women of Maryland—the far-famed, delicately-nurtured, and universally-courted ladies of that fair State—they, whose slightest notice in days gone by was so dearly prized by Northern men—they, so essentially Southern in taste, and style, and association—to see their country ruled by hordes of the despised Yankees, and their haughty city tamed and cowering under the insolent sway of the coarsest of all human creatures!—to know that '*the tinkling of that little bell*' at the State Department could tear the maiden from her mother's arms, to be dragged to the pollution of a Yankee prison! The thought was often almost maddening; and it may well be that my profound sympathy with my people has coloured with a deeper tinge of gloom my views of the whole field of action.

At all events, I have endeavoured in this sketch of my captivity to discharge a great duty. That duty was to contribute what I myself have seen and known of the history of the time. If the exposure therein made of the Yankee character, in the first year of its luxuriant and rampant development (after long compression in a condition of inferiority), shall add to the feeling of execration for such a race of people, and deepen the universal gratitude at the happy change which has severed us from them, and made it still more and more impossible that we can ever submit to any kind of political association with them again, then my poor narrative will not have been written in vain.

CHAPTER 2

On to Richmond!

On Friday, August 23rd, in Washington City—the metropolis of this once free and. happy land, the proud boast of which was that life, liberty, and property were protected by the law—I was made a prisoner in my own house, and subjected to an ordeal which must have been copied from the days of the Directory in France.

My blood boils when I think of it. But, for the benefit of all who may feel an interest in the subject, I will give a circumstantial account of an act which should shed renown upon the distinguished authors of it.

It is necessary for my purpose to make a brief *résumé* of the incidents of the few months preceding. I might even go back to the advent of the *Scotch cap and cloak*, but will content myself with an event quite as remarkable in the reign of the Abolition '*Irrepressible conflict chief*,' whose shadow now darkens the chair of Washington.

As the allusion to the '*Scotch cap and cloak*' may not be generally understood, I deem it advisable to furnish information on that head, as a means of explaining the *modus operandi* by which the Abolition leader entered the national Capitol.

He had been elected President by a strictly sectional majority, not having received one vote in the States south of Mason and Dixon's line—the great geographical line dividing North and South—arriving thereby at the very point in our political destiny which Washington, in his 'farewell address,' had foreshadowed as a cause for the dissolution of the Union.

During the heated sectional contest which resulted in the election of Mr. Lincoln by the Abolition party, they openly proclaimed '*the higher law doctrine*,' and announced their determination, regardless of constitutional guarantees, to deprive the South of her sovereign equal rights, and to reduce her to a state of vassalage; for a feeling of bitter jealousy had been festering and strengthening in the Northern mind against her, on account of the superior statesmanship and intellect, which had always given her pre-eminence in the councils of the nation, and in the legislative assemblies.

In order to carry into effect this hostile determination to destroy the political importance of the South, they had seized upon what they conceived to be the vulnerable point in our domestic institution—well knowing that they could enlist the fanatical aid and sympathy of those who were ignorant, save theoretically, of that institution, and of the benign and paternal manner in which it was conducted in the South; having in view no object themselves of ameliorating; the condition of the servile class, but to exterminate or drive them out, in order that their own pauper population might secure to themselves the superior advantages which were everywhere in the South monopolised by the slave population.

Denunciations were levelled against us by the poorer classes of the North as '*a pampered aristocracy,*' for the reason they gave '*that a poor white man at the South was not as good as a negro.*' And the negroes, I must confess, always arrogated to themselves this social superiority, for the bitterest insult they could offer each other was, '*You are no better than a poor white Yankee!*'

The Abolition party were not, however, prepared for the firm and dignified bearing of the South, at the result of an election strictly sectional and avowedly subversive of the Constitution; and they believed, according to their own established precedent, that mob law would take the matter in hand, and summarily dispose of the candidate elect, or prevent his inauguration.

Excited and absurd discussions and plans were made at Washington and other places as to the means by which he should reach the capital. Lincoln had, however, formed a plan of his own, and, having far more reticence than had been ascribed to him by his partisans, executed it whilst these discussions were going on, and suddenly appeared at Washington, at six o'clock in the morning, under the disguise of a '*Scotch cap and cloak,*' announcing himself with characteristic phraseology in the apartments of his sleeping Committee of Safety at Willard's Hotel with—'*Hillo! Just look at me! By jingo, my own clad wouldn't know me!*'

On the morning of the 16th of July, the Government papers at Washington announced that the 'grand army' was in motion, and I learned from a reliable source (having received a copy of the order to M'Dowell) that the order for a forward movement had gone forth. If earth did not tremble, surely there was great commotion amongst that class of the *genus homo* yclept military men. Officers and orderlies on horse were seen flying from place to place; the tramp of armed men was heard on every side—martial music filled the air; in short, a mighty host was marshalling, with all the 'pomp and circumstance of glorious war.' 'On to Richmond!' was the war-cry. The heroes girded on their armour with the enthusiasm of the Crusaders of old, and vowed to flesh their maiden swords in the blood of Beauregard or Lee. And many a knight, inspired by beauty's smiles, swore to lay at the feet of her he loved best the head of Jeff. Davis at least.

Nothing, nothing was wanting to render the gorgeous pageant imposing. So, with drums beating and flying colours, and amidst the shower of flowers thrown by the hands of Yankee maidens, the grand army moved on to the land of Washington, of Jefferson, of Madison, and Monroe; whilst the heart-stricken Southerners who remained, did not tear their hair and rend their garments, but prayed on their knees that the God of Battles would award the victory to the just cause.

In fear and trembling they awaited the result—hoping, yet fearing to hope. Time seemed to move on leaden wings. Imagination sounded in their ears the booming camion, and many a time their hearts died within them at the sickening delay. Few had the hope which filled my own soul, or shared in its exultant certainty of the result. At twelve o'clock on the morning of the 16th of July, I despatched a messenger to Manassas, who arrived there at eight o'clock that night. The answer received by me at mid-day on the 17th will tell the purport of my communication—

'Yours was received at eight o'clock at night. Let them come: we are ready for them. We rely upon you for precise information. Be particular as to description and destination of forces, quantity of artillery, &c. (Signed) Thos. Jordon, Adjt.-Gen.'

On the 17th I despatched another missive to Manassas, for I had learned of the intention of the enemy to cut the Winchester railroad, so as to intercept Johnson, and prevent his reinforcing Beauregard, who had comparatively but a small force under his command at Manassas.

On the night of the 18th, news of a great victory by the Federal troops at Bull Run reached Washington. Throughout the length and breadth of the city it was cried. I heard it in New York on Saturday,

16

20th, where I had gone for the purpose of embarking a member of my family for California, on the: steamer of the 22nd. The accounts were received with frantic rejoicings, and bets were freely taken in support of Mr. Seward's wise saws—that the rebellion would be crushed out in thirty days. My heart told me that the triumph was premature. Yet, my: God! how miserable I was for the fate of my beloved country, which hung trembling in the balance!

My presentiments were more than justified by the result. On Sunday (21st) the great Battle of Manassas was fought, memorable in history as that of Culloden or Waterloo, which ended in the total defeat and rout of the entire 'Grand Army.'

In the world's history such a sight was never witnessed: statesmen, senators, Congress-men, generals, and officers of every grade, soldiers, teamsters—all rushing in frantic flight, as if pursued by countless demons. For miles the country was thick with ambulances, accoutrements of war, &c. The actual scene beggars all description; so, I must in despair relinquish the effort to portray it.

The news of the disastrous rout of the Yankee Army was cried through the streets of New York on the 22nd. The whole city seemed paralysed by fear, and I verily believe that a thousand men could have marched from the Central Park to the Battery without resistance, for their depression now was commensurate with the wild exultation of a few days before.

On the afternoon of that day, I left New York for Washington, where I arrived at six o'clock in the morning of the 23rd, in a most impatient mood. Even at that early hour friends were awaiting my arrival, anxious to recount the particulars of the glorious victory. A despatch was also received from Manassas by me—

Our President and our General direct me to thank you. We rely upon you for further information. The Confederacy owes you a debt.
      (Signed)   Jordon, Adjutant-General.

My first impulse was to throw myself upon my knees and offer up my tearful thanks to the Father of Mercy for his signal protection in our hour of peril.

During my journey from New York the craven fear of the Yankees was manifested everywhere. At Philadelphia most of the women got off. I was advised to do so by Lieutenant Wise, of U. S. A. (son-in-law of Edward Everitt), as he said, 'It was believed that the rebels of Baltimore would rise, in consequence of the rout of the Federal Army.'

I laughingly replied, 'I have no fears; these rebels are of my faith. Besides, I fear, even now, I shall not be in time to welcome our President, Mr. Davis, and the glorious Beauregard.'

He sneeringly replied, 'that I should probably see those gentlemen there in irons.'

I received a scowl also from Mr. Winter Davis, who was a passenger from New York, and had been loud mouthed and denunciatory against the South during the journey. I observed, however, that he and Lieutenant Wise got off at Philadelphia, deeming 'discretion the better part of valour.'

A large force was distributed throughout Baltimore, and it was even difficult to thread one's way to the train on account of the military, who crowded the streets and the depot. Thence to Washington seemed as one vast camp, and on reaching the Capitol, the very carriage-way was blocked up by its panic-stricken defenders, who started at the clank of their own muskets. After a hurried *toilette* and breakfast, I went up to the U. S. Senate, where I saw the crest-fallen leaders who, but a few days before, had vowed 'death and damnation' to our race. Several crowded round me, and I could not help saying that, if they had not '*good blood*,' they had certainly '*good bottom*,' for they ran remarkably well.

For days after the wildest disorder reigned in the Capitol. The streets were filled with straggling soldiers, each telling the doleful tale, and each indulging in imaginary feats of valour, which would throw into the shade the achievements of *Coeur de Lion*, Amadis de Gaul, or Jack the Giantkiller.

Even senators entered into this scramble for stray laurels, for several assured me (Wilson and Chandler) that it was their individual exertions alone which had prevented the entire 'Grand Army' from precipitating itself pell-mell into the Potomac; and they were really indebted to the discretion of a subordinate officer, that the alternative had not been forced upon them. A telegraphic order had been sent to Washington by General M'Dowell, to cut the draw of the Long Bridge, 'as Beauregard and Johnson were hotly pursuing him with fresh troops.' This bridge spanned the Potomac just opposite Washington, and was the only means of crossing the river at that point.

Crimination, and recrimination, now became the order of the day, and everybody shrank from the responsibility of the forward movement. The commanding general, Scott, said, '*I didn't do it, for I was not ready.*' The Political Directory said, '*We didn't do it—it was that old dotard Scott, whom we will remove.'* President Lincoln said, *'I didn't do it—by jingo, I didn't!'* And so, in the end, the world was about as well informed as to who ordered the advance of the Grand Army as 'who killed Cock Robin.'

About this time, I met Mr. Seward, who assured me that *'there was nothing serious the matter,'* that I might assure my friends, upon his authority, that all would be over in sixty days. I answered him, 'Well, sir, you have enjoyed the first-fruits of the "irrepressible conflict."'

Seward had, a short time prior to his visit to England, in a speech delivered by him at Rochester, New York, as a bid for the nomination as President by the Republican party, made use of that remarkable expression of the *irrepressible conflict* between the white and black races, indicating, even at that early day, the policy to which he would commit himself in order to attain the object of his ambition—the Executive chair. At a later period, he endeavoured to explain this away, and in conversation with me said, 'If *heaven* would forgive him for stringing together two high-sounding words, he would never do it again.'

By-and-by things began to quiet down. The hirelings of the Government press exercised their ingenuity in mystifying the people. The countless hosts of the enemy were described (these, be it known, at no time exceeded twelve thousand actually engaged against the more than quadruple force of the invading army); their masked batteries and military defences threw into the shade the plains of Abraham, or even the fortifications of Sebastopol.

It would be idle to recount the gasconade of those who fled from imaginary foes, or to describe the forlorn condition of the returning heroes, who had gone forth to battle flushed with anticipated triumph and crowned in advance with the laurel of victory. Alas! their plight was pitiable enough. Some were described as being minus hat or shoes. Amongst this latter class was Colonel Burnside, who, on the morning that he sallied forth for the 'sacred soil,' is said to have required two orderlies to carry the flowers showered upon him by the women of Northern proclivities.

Meanwhile the muttered sound of the people's voice was heard from far and near asking meaning questions of the why and wherefore of the disasters It was like the rumbling of the distant thunder presaging the coming storm; and well the Abolition Government knew that, if this discontent was allowed to gather strength, it would hurl them from their present lawless eminence to the ignominy they merited.

The invaders had been taught to believe that a bloodless victory awaited them—that the 'All hail!' of the witches of Macbeth would greet them: and so possessed were they with the idea of their philanthropic mission as liberators of an oppressed people, '*bowed under the yoke of a haughty aristocracy*,' that many of their officers, particularly the famous New York 7th Regiment, took far more pains to prepare white gloves and embroidered vests for '*the balls*' to be given in their honour at Richmond than in securing cartridges for their muskets. When consulted on the subject I said, 'No doubt they would receive a *great many balls*, but I did not think that a very *recherché* toilet would be expected.'

The fanatical feeling was now at its height. Maddened by defeat, they sought a safe means of venting their pent-up wrath. The streets were filled with armed and unarmed ruffians; women were afraid to go singly into the streets for fear of insult; curses and blasphemy rent the air, and no one would have been surprised at any hour at a general massacre of the peaceful inhabitants. This apprehension was shared even by the better class of U. S. officers. I was urged to leave the city by more than one, and an escort offered to be furnished me if I desired; but, at whatever peril, I resolved to remain, conscious of the great service I could render my country, my position giving me remarkable facilities for obtaining information.

In anticipation of more fearful scenes, the inhabitants were leaving the city as rapidly as the means of transportation or conveyance could be obtained, and many even of the Federal officers sent their families to the North or other places of fancied security.

CHAPTER 3

Panic at Washington

At this time a number of Confederate prisoners, who had been taken in the first day's fight when our army fell back from Bull Run, were brought to Washington, and on passing Willard's Hotel were set upon by the crowd who usually congregated there, and pelted with stones and other missiles, which seriously wounded a number. In order to prevent the prisoners from being actually torn to pieces, a company of U. S. regulars had to be called out to protect them to their quarters, the old Capitol prison; and during the march to that point the soldiers had repeatedly to threaten to fire upon the mob, who pressed upon them with shouts and obscene revilings.

As soon as I heard of the circumstance, I went up to the prison to minister to the wants of our sufferers and found many with severe cuts and bruises. I was accompanied by my friend Miss Mackall, and had the satisfaction of not only being the first friendly face seen by them, but to know that I had arrived at the right time; for I found there an emissary of Lincoln—I had like to have said Satan—dressed in black, with a white neckcloth, who I afterwards learned was Mr. Commissioner Wood, one of the subscribers for Mrs. Lincoln's carriage and horses, and who had received his appointment in consequence thereof.

He was with great earnestness haranguing the prisoners, and trying to persuade them that they would all be hanged unless they took the oath of allegiance to the Abolition Government. I listened attentively to the man, who did not seem to relish the addition to his audience; and afterwards, as rapidly as I could, assured each group of prisoners that this man's threat was idle, and only for the purpose of intimidation, and for some false announcement to the world; that the Yankees were obliged to treat them as belligerents, and hold them as prisoners of war for exchange; that our Government would fearfully retaliate any violence against them, as we held an excess of prisoners of a hundred to one.

This satisfied them, especially the younger portion, who each refused the Yankee pardon on the terms proposed. I afterwards took the list of their various wants, and, in conjunction with high parties, whom it would be imprudent to name, supplied them with clothing and other needful things, food and beds and bedding inclusive, as the Yankees had made no provision of any kind, save the naked walls of a prison. There was an ample Confederate fund in Washington for this purpose. Mrs. Philips and family also exerted themselves in this holy work.

This lady was arrested in Washington at the same time that I was, and after a short detention was sent South. She then became a resident of New Orleans. During the reign of terror of Butler in that city a Yankee funeral passed her house, and she was seen to smile upon her balcony during the procession. For this *grave offence* she was dragged before him, and questioned as to her motive for doing so, to which she dauntlessly replied, 'Because I was in a good; humour.' She was condemned to three months' imprisonment, upon a barren island, under a tropical sun, with soldiers' rations, and subjected to other gross and brutal indignities, until the poor lady's health gave way, and her life became imperilled.

The representations and remonstrances of the medical attendant, who was more humane than his master, failed to procure any mitigation of the harsh sentence until the period had expired, when she was banished, an invalid for life. In the course of her examination before Butler, he said: 'I expect to be killed before I leave the South, by either you or Mrs. Greenhow;' to which she answered, 'We usually order our negroes to kill our swine!'

Mr. Charles Sumner was said to have been a complacent looker-on if not an actual participator in that chivalrous demonstration against unarmed prisoners. Mayhap his wrath was appeased by the sight of the bleeding victims, who could hold no correcting rod over his own coward shoulders.

A few days after an order was given to exclude all visitors, in which I was specially named. In spite, however, of the prohibition, I had no difficulty in communicating when I desired.

Soon after I passed into other hands my share in this good work; for more important employment occupied my time.

The Yankee Government and Yankee Congress were now exercised upon the subject of reorganising their shattered hosts. The military committee was specially charged with the task, and certainly grave efforts were being made to this end, the primary object being to mystify the people as to the past, in order to make them blind instruments in the future; for it was now truly a nation of subterfuges and humbugs.

At this time the solemn farce was enacted of admitting as U. S. senators the *bogus* members from Western Virginia. I was in the gallery of the Senate it the time, and happened to remark upon the proceedings to my own party, when a man sitting before me in the uniform of Lieutenant-Colonel of Yankee Volunteers, in company with a number of other officers, turned and said, 'That is treason; we will show you that it must be put a stop to; we have a government to maintain,' &c. This was the first effort of the kind to repress freedom of opinion which had come under my observation, and the beginning of that reign of terror for which we should be obliged to seek precedents in the age of a Nero or Caligula.

Yet I confess that it did not surprise me. I leaned forward and said deliberately, 'My remarks were addressed to my companions, and not to you; and if I did not discover by your language that you must be ignorant of all the laws of good-breeding, I should take the number of your company and report you to your commanding officer to be punished for your impertinence!'

Seeing me addressed by him, several gentlemen came forward, as also the doorkeeper, who said, 'Madam, if he insults you, I will put him out.'

To which I replied. 'Oh, never mind: he is too ignorant to know what he has done.' This defender of the faithful, meanwhile, played most vehemently with his sword, and I expected momentarily to have it drawn against me. His brother officers one by one withdrew, and left him alone in his glory.

A few moments after this scene a republican senator came up to the gallery to speak with me, and I related the circumstance, and advised him to go down to the Senate and move a revival of the alien and sedition law, as I supposed it would come to that, since armed ruffians were placed in the galleries to awe the crowd. This '*brave*' bore it as long as possible, and finally got up and went out. I saw this man once more, upon the occasion of my being summoned before the U. S. commission, after I had been some eight months a prisoner. He was standing in the doorway of the building in which the commission was held, as if he expected to see me; a look of triumph lighted up his face as his eye encountered mine. I could not resist the temptation of significantly passing my finger across my throat, and saying, 'Beware!'—as Balzac's story of the poor Marie Antoinette and Joseph Balsamo came to my mind.

This was destined to be a day of adventure. Quite an excitement was caused by a rumour that a battle was going on across the river. The Confederate forces were at that time in possession of Arlington Heights, the former residence of the venerable Park Custus, the grandson of Washington: from him it had come by inheritance to our own great General Lee. I went with my party to the portico of the Congressional Library, whence the best view could be obtained, and saw the smoke from the camp-fires gracefully curling up, and remarked, 'That is no battle. The rebels are cooking their dinners.'

A number of persons had crowded around and joined in the conversation. Someone proposed to send back to the Senate for Chandler, Wilson, and Foster, the heroic trio who had fled so valorously from the field at Manassas, spreading the news of the defeat. I objected on the score of humanity, as it was not right to give such a shock to their nervous systems, since neither of those senators had been able to stand the fire in their own pipes since that hapless Gilpin race.

Finally, I fell into conversation with a lank lean man, with a big nose and a pair of green spectacles, who asked me if I had ever witnessed a battle. I replied that I had experienced a *pronunciamento* in the city of Mexico. In the course of his remarks, he said that he would rather give up Washington than that it should be held by means of fortifications, but that Lincoln, Seward, and the whole set were cowards, and a great deal more which I considered useful information. I knew that this man was a senator, and fancied that it might be 'Jim Lane' of Kansas, he whom I have denominated as 'Balaam's Ass.' He said that he had seen me in the gallery of the Senate, and asked what I thought of the proceedings.

I related the attack on my liberty of speech, and wondered what sort of performance we should be treated to next, whether a tragedy or another farce; and, I confess, gave a most grotesque account of the speeches during the solemn mockery of the morning, expressing my surprise that more ingenuity had not been displayed to disguise the unconstitutionality of the act, to dismember and defraud a sovereign state of her territorial rights, individualising Trumbull's effort as one for which a schoolboy should have won a 'dunce cap.' I saw a suppressed

24

laugh all around, and that the person to whom I spoke seemed embarrassed, and finally fell back and spoke with a gentleman of my party.

This person came to me and said, 'Do you know that you have been talking to Senator Trumbull all this while?' I was quite as much amused at the *contretemps* as any of my hearers. But I should have considered it a reflection upon my good taste to have been previously cognisant of the fact, so assured Senator Trumbull that I had no idea that the subject of my criticism was the patient listener who stood before me—'But for once in your life you It have heard an honest opinion fearlessly expressed.' Abolitionist as he was, I must do him the justice to say that he behaved very well.

Humbug still continued the order of the day at Washington. Another cry was raised that the Capitol was again in danger. This time the programme was changed. The hero of Lundy's Lane and of Mexico was to be laid on the shelf, to all purposes superseded. But he still stood a mighty ruin in their way, propped by the lingering confidence of a nation, and no man was bold enough to say, 'This is not the right man for the place.' Cunning and; craft were the characteristic qualities called into requisition here. Seward, with Jesuitical skill, affected to support the weak old man, wishing to enact the fable of 'the monkey and the chestnuts.' But even his selfish policy had to yield to the tempest he had aided to raise.

As a preparation for what was to follow, Congress passed an 'act regulating the pay of the lieutenant-general in case of his resignation' or '*voluntary retirement*.'

Young America now became the theme of every tongue. The great battles of the world, both in ancient and modern times, were proved to have been fought by generals who were adolescent. Caesar, Hannibal and Napoleon were cited as examples, and even our own immortal Washington had many years deducted from his actual age when he fought the battles of the revolution.

The ears of the rabble were tickled by all this justice was lost sight of—and so a young chieftain was summoned to the field of intrigue. Nothing remarkable thus far had distinguished him above his compeers; but, touched by the magic wand of political expediency, he came forth full-fledged, with honours thick upon him. In a single day, from a subordinate position he became Major-General M'Clellan, the virtual head of the dictator's armies—whose policy of bestowing honours in advance differed widely from that of the greatest man of the present times, in the European world—Louis Napoleon—by whom grades were always conferred after the battle won, as witness Magenta, Solferino, &c. Subsequent to the rout at Manassas, President Lincoln promoted all the officers, many of whom were proved to have fled from the field in advance of their regiments.

Again, comes into bold relief the sycophancy of President Lincoln's proteges. All the military qualities of any age were unscrupulously purloined, to deck the hero of the hour. By degrees they fixed upon the great Napoleon as his prototype—I suppose from the fact that he is short, and rather inclined to corpulency, as was latterly the 'Little Corporal;' and, besides, sycophants are ever ready to discern what pleases best.

Under the auspices of the 'Young General,' the military are put in motion; hither and thither they are marched, and counter-marched; mysterious movement being his *forte*. He, however, set himself energetically to the task of reorganising and disciplining the demoralised rabble he was called upon to command.

General Scott, who at this time was still the nominal commander-in-chief, wrote a letter to the Honourable Henry Wilson, lauding his patriotic exertion, and urging him to accept military command, and commending his capacity for such position in very high terms. By a singular coincidence, M'Clellan urged the same gentleman '*to do him the honour to accept the position of chief of his staff.*' This proposition was made by M'Clellan in the reception-room of President Lincoln. I mention these incidents, to show the political bias of all parties at the time; that the Abolition star was in the ascendant, and that everybody fawned upon its chosen apostles.

M'Clellan also invited the Count de Paris and Duke d'Aumale to become members of his staff. Their acceptance was heralded with great circumstance, as this infusion of the aristocratic element into the Abolition ranks was regarded as a national triumph. Edifying accounts were given of their introduction to President Lincoln, and especially to Master Bob, the Abolition scion of royalty. They were amiable ladylike-looking young Frenchmen, better fitted from their appearance to assist in Mrs. Lincoln's educational scheme (thus treading in the footsteps of their Royal Ancestor Louis-Philippe, who taught French in Philadelphia) than to win laurels enough to disturb the equanimity of that wise and sagacious prince whom Providence has appointed to rule over France.

A commission of Brigadier-General was also tendered to Garibaldi.

Meanwhile the panic at Washington, instead of subsiding, received new impulse each day, from some extravagant rumours. A strong guard was stationed around all the public buildings. The redoubtable Jim Lane, of Kansas notoriety, and his band of ruffians, were quartered in the east room of the White House, for the protection of President Lincoln and his family. Sentinels paced to and fro in front of the house, and at six o'clock in the evening the gates were closed, and no one could enter without the countersign.

Everything about the national Capitol betokened the panic of the Administration. Preparations were made for the expected attack, and signals arranged to give the alarm. The signal was three guns from the provost-marshal's office, followed by the tolling of the church bells at intervals of fifteen minutes.

By a singular providence (for it would be wrong to ascribe these things to chance), I went round with the principal officer in charge of this duty, and took advantage of the situation. The alarm-guns of the Yankees were the rallying cry of a devoted band whose hearts beat high with hope. The task before them was worthy of all hazard, and our gallant Beauregard would have found himself right ably seconded by the rebels of Washington had he deemed it expedient to advance on that city.

A part of the plan was, to have cut the telegraph wires connecting the various military positions with the War Department, to take prisoners M'Clellan and several others, thereby creating still greater confusion in the first moments of panic. Measures had also been taken to spike the guns in Fort Corcoran, Fort Ellsworth, and other important points, accurate drawings of which had been furnished to our commanding officer at Manassas by me.

Quite an ingenious plan was adopted at this time to discover if the 'rebel' communication was uninterrupted. Young Doolittle, the son of the senator of that name, and clerk of the military committee, who was an occasional and useful visitor at my house, brought me a letter for Colonel Corcoran at Richmond, with the modest request that I would send it. I told him that M'Clellan's excessive vigilance had rendered communication almost impossible, but that he might leave it and trust to the chance. He called repeatedly to ascertain whether the letter had been sent; but I understood the motive, and was always very sorry that no opportunity had occurred. I need hardly say that during this period I was in almost daily correspondence with Manassas.

The Capitol, by this, had been made one of the strongest fortified cities of the world—every avenue to it being guarded by works believed to be impregnable. Thirty-three fortifications surrounded it. But this alone was not deemed sufficient. Extraordinary vigilance was exercised; market-carts and news boys were overhauled, to look for treasonable correspondence—every box was either a masked battery, or infernal machine—but, alas! without success, until a sudden inspiration seized them. The Southern women of Washington are the cause of the defeat of the grand army! They are entitled to the laurels won by the brave defenders of our soil and institutions! They have told Beauregard when to strike! They, with their siren arts, have possessed themselves of the plans and schemes of the Lincoln Cabinet, and warned Jeff. Davis of them.

The most skilful detectives were summoned from far and near, to trace the steps of maids and matrons. For several weeks I had been followed, and my house watched, by those emissaries of the State Department, the detective police. This was often a subject of amusement to me; and several times, when accompanied by my young friend Miss Mackall, we would turn and follow those who we fancied were giving us an undue share of attention. Still, I believed it private enterprise, originating with some philanthropist who had my well-being at heart; for I was slow to credit that even the fragment of a once glorious government could give to the world such a proof of craven fear and weakness as to turn the arms, which the blind confidence of a deluded people had placed; in their hands, for the achievement of other ends, against the breasts of helpless defenceless women and children. Nevertheless, it is a fact, significant of events to follow. Lawless acts of violence seldom stand alone; and the careful readers of the history of the last two hundred years will find numerous parallel cases.

No nation on the face of the globe has made such rapid strides to despotism as the Federal Government. The first acts of the Republican President were to violate the express provisions of the Constitution: those safeguards provided by the wisdom of our fathers for the protection of the rights of the citizen have been suspended, under the plea of military necessity. The law of the land has given place to the law of the despot.

The first act of the Republican Congress assembled in this city of Washington on the 4th day of July, 1861, was to legalise the acts of their President, thereby admitting that he, the chief magistrate of the nation, had been guilty of perjury and treason before God and man; for his oath of office had been, to support the Constitution of the

United States, and to administer the laws in accordance with its provisions. But instead of being impeached for his crimes, he was eulogised, and unlimited powers were conferred upon him.

A few voices were raised in protest in both houses of Congress. Breckenridge made a speech on the occasion which must transmit his name with undying honour to posterity; for it was the last cry of freedom ever to be heard in those walls, until they shall have been purged by fire and blood.

No voice of inspiration is needed to point where this nation is drifting. The crimes which have disgraced other lands, from the contemplation of which humanity shrinks appalled, will yet be enacted here. People do not sink at once from the height of prosperity, and power, and civilisation, to the lowest abyss of lawless despotism, without some spasmodic attempts at counteraction. But the systematic efforts at demoralisation will soon be apparent: the public taste will become vitiated; the voice of conscience will be smothered by the craving for excitement; fanaticism will assume the guise of patriotism, and under that sacred name the rights of civilisation will be trampled underfoot.

The guillotine was a most humane invention; but in the hands of a lawless mob became a fearful instrument of vengeance, and has damned to immortality its harmless inventor, who also perished by it. Mr. Lincoln and his Minister of State, Mr. Seward, have set at work the social guillotine; and I am but a poor prophet unless, in its evolutions, they also, become the victims; for they have inaugurated a mighty revolution, the bitter fruits, of which will be brought home to them.

It was the intention of the Abolitionists to arrest Breckenridge for treason immediately on the conclusion of his speech, had he afforded the slightest pretext for doing so. Several of the prominent; leaders had told me, 'that they had committed a blunder in ever having allowed him to take his seat.' I warned Mr. Breckenridge of his danger, and gave him the names of the parties who had spoken thus to me. He at once recognised his peril, and so re-worded his speech as to avoid the threatened danger, at which the Abolitionists were greatly chagrined.

Charles Sumner was anxious that a test-oath should be applied to those senators who were considered of doubtful loyalty to the Lincolnites, as had been already done to officers of the army; Colonel John Lee having the unenviable notoriety of being the first Southern-born officer who subscribed to this oath of allegiance to the tyrant.

It must not be supposed that the social element was neglected in these times of stern alarm. Mr. Seward was too new in his character of diplomatist to disregard so important a concomitant of success. He had recently returned from Europe—had basked in the smiles of Lord John Russell and the Exeter Hall clique—and had been taught by a charming diplomatic lady that a white neck-cloth was alone *comme il faut* at a dinner or evening party.

So, he took the Club House, made memorable in Washington on account of its proximity to the scene of that fearful Sickels tragedy, and commenced a series of entertainments, which were attended by a vast crowd of men in uniforms, and a sparse sprinkling of women, who, with few exceptions, were not of a class to shed much lustre on the Republican Court; for the refinement and grace which had once constituted the charm of Washington life had long since departed, and, like its former freedom, was now, alas! a tradition only.

We find, by historical observation, that nations as they begin to decline in morality and civilisation have always a morbid passion for pastimes and amusements which address themselves to the physical sense. France, in her days of revolution, had her saturnalia to the Goddess of Liberty—Mexico her bull-fights—and the Yankee nation her colossal reviews and mimic battles, at which President Lincoln, surrounded by his satellites, complacently assisted, as if the salvoes of artillery which rent the air in his honour could shut out from the ears of Heaven, as well as from his own, the wail of the widow and the orphan.

It is difficult to reconcile the frivolity of these people from the beginning with a sense of the perils which environed them. Mr. Seward, even after the direful rout at Manassas—when hecatombs of their dead lay manuring the sacred soil—persisted in saying '*There is nothing the matter!*' President Lincoln still said '*There is nobody hurt!*' even though he had reached the Capitol like an escape convict, under the disguise of a 'Scotch cap and cloak,' and continued for days to edify his visitors with an account of his ingenuity in eluding the supposed murderous snare which had been set for him—leaving his wife and children, however, with true Yankee chivalry, to encounter the dreadful fate from which he so exultantly described himself as having escaped.

'*Nobody hurt!*' and yet this same *unconstitutional* President pursues his evening drive under escort of an armed guard, which quite takes us back to the feudal ages. The sight pleased me, I confess, as a foreshadowing of the gathering tempest.

I wish I could present to the mind's eye a picture of Washington as it really appeared under the desecration of the Black Republican rule. Those of its former population who remained from necessity or other causes had disappeared entirely from the surface of society. A new people had taken their places, as distinct and marked in their characteristics as any barbarian race that ever overran Christendom, and who, in their insolent pride of conquest, speedily effaced every landmark of civilisation.

The city was filled to overflowing with greedy adventurers seeking office. Day after day, and month after month, the resistless tide, with black glazed carpet-bag in hand, came rolling in. I sometimes thought them the lost tribes of Israel, who, sniffing from afar the golden harvest, had pierced the confines of eternity and found their way over. Every thoroughfare—every public building—doorway, and corridor, and steps—were blocked up by these sturdy beggars, who came to demand the spoils of victory; and who, disdaining the accommodation of hotel or lodging-house, ate their meals out of those same black glazed carpet-bags, on the highways or byways, and slept like dogs in a kennel.

Add to all this the thousands of drunken demoralised soldiers who filled the streets, crowding women into the gutters, with ribald and obscene observations, and sometimes with more personal insult. It was even difficult to look from the windows without the sense of decency being shocked; and the public squares, which were once such favourite resorts, had now become the chosen places of debauchery and crime. The schools throughout the city had been closed, as it was no longer safe for children to go into the street.

Upon no class of the community did this total abnegation of all the laws, both human and divine, tell with such saddening effect as upon the free coloured population, especially the women, whose sober industrious habits of former days had given place, under the influence of the new order of things, to the most unbridled licentiousness, and who were to be seen at all public places bedecked in gorgeous attire, sharing the smiles of the volunteer officers and soldiers with the republican dames and *demoiselles*.

I have frequently received the answer, when I have sent to demand the services of a negro serving-woman, that she would not come, for the reason that she had an engagement to drive or walk with a Yankee officer.

I will gladly turn from the contemplation of this heart-sickening picture to the comedy of *High Life below Stairs* being enacted at the White House. Mrs. Lincoln, disregarding, or more probably being ig-

31

norant of, the conventional usages which have from time immemorial regulated the etiquette at the Presidential mansion, created much amusement and ridiculous comment upon the first public occasion after the assumption of her new dignity in the reception of the ladies of the diplomatic corps.

The custom at Washington is precisely similar to that practised at all other courts, that, as soon after the installation of a new chief as is practicable, the representatives of foreign nations accredited to the Government should be formally introduced by the Secretary of State, and a complimentary address delivered in their behalf by the *doyen*, or oldest member of the diplomatic body, which is answered by the President—all being arranged beforehand, even to the exchange of the addresses.

In like manner the ladies of the diplomatic corps, after due notification, are presented to the feminine representative of the White House.

This ceremony is always regarded as one of importance, second only to a presentation at St. James's or St. Cloud. The ladies in question, after due notification, presented themselves *en grande tenue* at the White House, where they were ushered very unceremoniously into one of the reception-rooms, and left in a most uncomfortable state of uncertainty as to the next step in the programme. After some time, and when speculation had well-nigh exhausted itself, a young woman, dressed in a pink wrapper and tucked petticoat, came bounding in, not making, however, the slightest recognition of the presence of the distinguished, visitors assembled, but stood balancing herself first on one foot and then the other, surveying them meanwhile with a most nonchalant air, and after having gratified her curiosity withdrew with as little ceremony as she had entered.

The surprised enquiry of the stranger ladies, 'Is this Mrs. Lincoln?' had scarcely subsided, when a small dowdy-looking woman, with artificial flowers in her hair, appeared. The first idea was that she was a servant sent to make excuses for the singular delay of Mrs. Lincoln. But she approached and addressed herself in conversation to the wife of a secretary of legation, and it gradually dawned upon the party that this was the feminine representative of the Black Republican Royalty, and they made the best of the awkward situation.

Mrs. Lincoln herself, however, not seeming to be aware that everything was not conducted in the most orthodox fashion, had instructed a little lady to inform Mme. Mercier that she was studying French, and would by winter be able to converse with her in that language. By this she has probably discovered that there is no royal road to learning.

I had a most graphic description of this scene from more than one of the victims of this first Republican Court ceremony, and only wish that I could give the picture with all its nicer touches. The young lady in the tucked petticoat was a niece of Mrs. Lincoln.

Owing to the fact of Mr. Seward being master of the ceremonies, Mr. Lincoln was a little less *bizarre* in his ministerial reception. But at the dinner given in honour of the occasion, when the different wines were served, and he was asked which he would take, he turned to the servant with most touching simplicity and said: 'I don't know: which would you?'

This anecdote is as well authenticated as the spilling of the cup of tea on Mrs. Masham's gown.

A distinguished diplomatist, in discussing the merits of the illustrious pair, said: 'He is better than she, for he seems by his manner to apologise for being there.'

President Harrison is said on his death-bed to have instructed the barber who shaved him, to carry out the provisions of the Constitution; and President Lincoln, much to the chagrin of his constitutional advisers, was in the habit of discussing matters of equal importance with his servants, or helps, as he termed them.

Mrs. Lincoln asserted with great energy her right to a share of the distribution of the Executive patron age. She had received as a present, from a man named Lammon, a magnificent carriage and horses, promising him in return the marshalship of the district of Columbia, one of the most lucrative offices in the gift of the Executive.

Mr. Lincoln had, however, determined to bestow the office upon another applicant, who had also paid his *douceur*, and who was in attendance, waiting to receive the commission which was being made out. Mrs. Lincoln came into the President's office, asked what commission it was that he was signing; and on being told, seized it from his hands, tore it in pieces, saying that she had promised it to 'Lammon', and he should have it, else her name was not Mary Lincoln.

Lammon of course received the commission, and the discomfited applicant reported this conjugal scene; and from that hour commenced the system of votive offerings at the shrine of Mrs. Lincoln.

It had been a custom at Washington to distribute the hay and grass, cut from the public grounds, to the poor and meritorious population of the city. It was a cheap and graceful charity on the part of the

Government, duly appreciated by the recipients; for, thus aided, many a poor widow was enabled to buy bread for her children, from the proceeds of milk from her cow. Mrs. Lincoln put a stop to this praiseworthy custom, and claimed it as one of her perquisites.

Commonplace and vulgar as these incidents may seem, they are, however, useful illustrations of the practical application of William M. Marcy's famous aphorism, *'To the victors belong the spoils.'* The anecdotes of Queen Christina of Sweden present more clearly the character and degree of civilisation of the people over whom she reigned than any laboured historical effort could have done; and no one would dream of describing a royal banquet amongst the Fejee islanders and omit the cold bishop on the side-table.

CHAPTER 4

Days of Trial

The digression in the last chapter has drawn me from my purpose of telling how I became a prisoner of State.

September the 6th was the first time since that eventful period that I had had access to pen and paper—all writing-materials having been hitherto withheld from me by order of the heads of the War and State Departments; and, as I knew not at what hour the act of grace might be rescinded, I felt inclined to make the most of it.

As I have said, on Friday, August 23, 1861, as I was entering my own door, on returning from a promenade, I was arrested by two men, one in citizen's dress, and the other in the fatigue dress of an officer of the United States Army. This latter was called Major Allen, and was the chief of the detective police of the city. They followed close upon my footsteps.

I had stopped to enquire after the sick children of one of my neighbours, on the opposite side of the street. From several persons on the sidewalk at the time, *en passant*, I derived some valuable information; amongst other things, it was told me that a guard had been stationed around my house throughout the night, and that I had been followed during my promenade, and had probably been allowed to pursue it unmolested, from the fact that a distinguished member of the diplomatic corps had joined me, and accompanied me to that point. This caused me to observe more closely the two men who had followed, and who walked with an air of conscious authority past my house to the end of the pavement, where they stood surveying me.

I continued my conversation apparently without noticing them, remarking rapidly to one of our humble agents who passed, 'Those men will probably arrest me. Wait at Corcoran's Corner, and see. If I raise my handkerchief to my face, give information of it.' The person to whom this order was given went whistling along. I then put a very important note into my mouth, which I destroyed; and turned, and walked leisurely across the street, and ascended my own steps.

A few moments after, and before I could open the door, the two men above described rapidly ascended also, and asked, with some confusion of manner, 'Is this Mrs. Greenhow?'

I answered, 'Yes'.

They still hesitated; whereupon I said, 'Who are you, and what do you want?'

'I come to arrest you.'

'By what authority?'

The man Allen, or Pinkerton (for he had several aliases), said, 'By sufficient authority.'

'Let me see your warrant.'

He mumbled something about verbal authority from the War and State Departments, and then both stationed themselves upon either side of me, and followed into the house. I rapidly glanced my eye to see that my signal had been understood, and remarked quietly, 'I have no power to resist you; but, had I been inside of my house, I would have killed one of you before I had submitted to this illegal process.'

They replied, with evident trepidation, 'That would have been wrong, as we only obey orders, and both have families.'

This scene occurred in much less time than is requisite to describe it. I took a rapid survey of the two men, and in that instant decided upon my own line of conduct; for I knew that the fate of some of the best and bravest belonging to our cause hung upon my own coolness and courage.

By this the house had become filled with men; who also surrounded it outside, like bees from a hive. The calmness of desperation was upon me, for I recognised this as the first step in that system of infamy which was yet to hold up this nation of isms to the scorn of the civilised world. This was the first act of the new co-partnership of Seward, M'Clellan, & Co.,—the strategic step, on coming into power, of the young general so lauded—an attack upon women and children, and a brilliant earnest of the laurels to be won on his march to Richmond.

I asked, after a few moments survey of the scene, 'What are you going to do?'

'To search,' Allen replied.

'I will facilitate your labours;' and, going to the mantel, I took from a vase a paper, dated Manassas, July 23, containing these words—'Lt.-Col. Jordon's compliments to Mrs. E. Greenhow. Well, but hard-worked'—the rest of the letter being torn off before it reached me, some ten days before, through the city post-office. I suspected its delicate mission, so kept it, from an instinct of caution, and had shown it to Major Bache, of U. S. A., Captain Richard Cutts, Wilson, of Massachusetts, and several others.

I threw it to Allen, saying, 'You would like to finish this job, I suppose?' He took it, discarding, however, the city envelope in which I had received it.

My cool and indifferent manner evidently disconcerted the whole party. They had expected that, under the influence of the agitation and excitement of the trying position, I should have been guilty of some womanly indiscretion by which they could profit.

An indiscriminate search now commenced throughout my house. Men rushed with frantic haste into my chamber, into every sanctuary. My beds, drawers, and wardrobes were all upturned; soiled clothes were pounced upon with avidity, and mercilessly exposed; papers that had not seen the light for years were dragged forth. My library was taken possession of, and every scrap of paper, every idle line was seized; even the torn fragments in the grates or other receptacles were carefully gathered together by these latter-day Lincoln resurrectionists.

My library, be it remembered, was *my sanctum*; it was there also that I gave lessons to my children, many of whose unlettered scribblings were tortured into dangerous correspondence with the enemy.

I was a keen observer of their clumsy activity, and resolved to test the truth of the old saying that '*the devil is no match for a clever woman!*' I was fully advised that this extraordinary proceeding might take place, and was not to be caught at a disadvantage.

I had received a note a few days before, stating that one of M'Clellan's *aides* had informed a lady in George Town that I was to be arrested, also that the name of the Honourable William Preston, U. S. Minister Plenipotentiary to Spain, who was at that time in Washington, stood in the proscribed list. He was warned by me in time to effect his escape.

Meanwhile I was a prisoner in one of my own parlours, not allowed to move, with stern eyes fixed upon my face, to read certainly what they did not find; for, although agonising anxieties filled my soul, I was apparently careless and sarcastic, and, I know, tantalising in the extreme. My servants were subjected to the same surveillance, and were not allowed to approach me.

Every effort was made to keep my arrest a secret. My house externally was quiet as usual; three sides of it, being surrounded by a high wall, screened the guard from observation. It was considered the headquarters of the Secessionists, and I being regarded as the head of the conspirators at Washington, a rich haul was anticipated. They reckoned without their host this time.

In despite of all their wisely taken precautions, the news of my arrest rapidly spread. At eleven o'clock I was taken prisoner—at about three o'clock my young friend Miss Mackall, and her sister, came to make enquiries; she had heard it in the city. As she entered, she was rudely seized by the detective, who stood concealed behind the door, and pushed forward, as was also her sister. They were terrified at the sight of the rude lawless men who were in possession of my once peaceful quiet home, The dear, brave-hearted girl put her head on my shoulder and wept, for she said, 'I did not know what they had done with you.'

I whispered,' Oh, be courageous, for we must outwit these fiends.'

But before I had succeeded in completely reassuring her, the detective called Captain Dennis approached and in a loud authoritative voice demanded her name and residence, as well as that of her sister We were all, after this, ordered to return to the back parlour, under escort of this Captain Dennis whose duty for the time was to watch me.

The work of examining my papers had already commenced. It was indeed a hard struggle to remain a quiet spectator of this proceeding, but nevertheless nerved myself to the task, as my object was to throw the detectives off their guard. I had no fear of consequences from the papers which had as yet fallen into their hands. I had a right to my own political opinions, and to discuss the question at issue, and never shrank from the avowal of my sentiments.

I am a Southern woman, born with revolutionary blood in my veins, and my first crude ideas on State and Federal matters received consistency and shape from the best and wisest man of this century, John C. Calhoun. These ideas have been strengthened and matured by reading and observation. Freedom of speech and of thought were my birth-rights, guaranteed by our charter of liberty, the Constitution of the United States, and signed and sealed by the blood of our fathers.

Mr. Calhoun had been the intimate friend of my husband, and often our guest, having remained several months at a time with us during his senatorial sojourn at Washington.

For many years, I had been honoured by a correspondence with him, and it was my privilege to sit by his bedside and minister to his wants during his last illness, and to treasure in my heart his words of wisdom; and when he died, I followed his remains, as one of his children, to his last resting-place—the Senatorial Committee of Arrangements, of which our honoured Commissioner to England, Mr. Mason, was one, having assigned me that position in the solemn pageant.

Mr. Webster walked by my side as we turned from the tomb, and, with tears trickling down his face, made use of these words: 'One of earth's princes hath departed—the purest, best, and greatest man I ever knew! He was a Roman senator when Rome was.' The same expression he had used in his eloquent oration of the morning. Mr. Clay, in his eulogy upon him in the Senate at the same time, said, 'He was my senior in everything but years.'

After the examination of my papers by Seymour, the most respectable and the only educated man amongst those detectives, he said, 'Well, madam, you have no reason to feel anything but pride and satisfaction at the ordeal you have gone through, for there is not a line amongst your papers that does not do you honour. It is the most extensive private correspondence that has ever fallen under my examination, and the most interesting and important; there is not a distinguished name in America that is not found here. There is nothing that can come under the charge of treason, but enough to make the Government dread and hold you as a most dangerous adversary.'

But to return to the sad relation of my wrongs. The search still went on. I desired to go to my chamber, and was told that a woman was sent for to accompany me. It did not even then flash upon my mind that my person was to be searched. I was, however, all the more anxious to be free from the sight of my captors for a few moments; so, feigning the pretext of change of dress, &c., as the day was intensely hot, after great difficulty, and thanks to the slow movements of these agents of evil, I was allowed to go to my chamber, and then resolved to accomplish the destruction of some important papers which I had in my pocket, even at the expense of life. (The papers were my cipher, with which I corresponded with my friends at Manassas, and others of equal importance.) Happily, I succeeded without such a fearful sacrifice.

The detective Dennis little dreamed that a few paces only stood between him and eternity. He rapped at my door, calling 'Madam! madam!' and afterwards opened it, but seeing me apparently legitimately employed, he withdrew. Had he advanced one step, I should have killed him, as I raised my revolver with that intent; and so steady were my nerves, that I could have balanced a glass of water on my finger without spilling a drop.

Shortly after the female detective arrived. I blush that the name and character of woman should be so prostituted. But she was certainly not above her honourable calling. Her image is daguerreotyped on my mind, and as it is an ugly picture, I would willingly obliterate it. As is usual with females employed in this way, she was decently arrayed, as if to impress me with her respectability. Her face reminded me of one of those india-rubber dolls, whose expression is made by squeezing it, with weak grey eyes which had a faculty of weeping. Like all the detectives, she had only a Christian name, Ellen. I began to think that the whole foundling hospital had been let loose for my benefit.

Well, I was ushered into my chamber, a detective standing on guard outside of the door to receive the important documents believed to be secreted on my person—nothing less, I suppose, than a commission of Brigadier-General from President Davis, upon the principle that, whereas President Lincoln had conferred that distinguished grade upon many who deserved to be old women, President Davis had, with characteristic acuteness, discovered qualities in a woman equally entitled to reward.

I was allowed the poor privilege of unfastening my own garments, which, one by one, were received by this pseudo-woman and carefully examined, until I stood in my linen. After this. I was permitted to resume them, with the detectress as my tire-woman.

During all this time, I was cool and self-possessed. I had resolved to go through the trying ordeal with as little triumph to my persecutors as possible. I had already taken the resolution to fire the house from garret to cellar, if I did not succeed in destroying certain papers in the course of the approaching night; for I had no hope that they would escape a second day's search. My manner was therefore assumed to cover my intentions. I was also sustained by the conscious rectitude of my purpose, and the high and holy cause to which I had devoted my life.

I felt that a people struggling to maintain their rights and to transmit unimpaired to their children the glorious heritage of revolutionary fathers, was under the protection of that Divine overruling Providence, which could carry me unscathed across the burning plough-shares spread for my destruction. With this conviction in my soul, I resigned myself to the law of the strongest, for I knew not what further trials were in store for me.

The orders were to entrap everybody who called at my house. Miss Mackall and her sister were already in durance. Mrs. Mackall, who came in pursuit of her children, was seized and detained, as also several other casual visitors. I know not, in fact, how many were taken into custody, for, as the evening advanced, I was ordered upstairs, accompanied by my friends, a heavy guard of detectives being stationed in the rooms with us.

A little later I had reason to regard it as a signal act of Divine mercy that those friends were sent me. As I have said, it was believed that all the Secessionists in the city were in communication with me, so everyone who called, black or white, was viewed as an emissary; a former man-servant of mine, and his sister, in passing the house, were made prisoners. The man was confined below stairs, and the young girl taken into the parlour, with only those brutal men as her companions. I was not aware of her being in the house until startled by a smothered scream.

My first idea was that some insult had been offered to my maid, but, being satisfied on that point, I tried to believe that my sense of hearing had deceived me. Still, I could not divest myself of the horrible fear, and after a while succeeded in sending someone down. The girl was found in a state of great alarm, from the rudeness to which she had been exposed, and was sent below to her brother; and I now began fully to realise the dark and gloomy perils which environed me.

The chiefs of the detectives having gone out, several of the subordinates left in charge now possessed themselves of rum and brandy, which aided in developing their brutal instincts; and they even boasted, in my hearing, of the *nice times* they expected to have with the female prisoners.

As every evil is said to be checkmated by some corresponding good, I was enabled by this means to destroy every paper of consequence. I had placed them where they could be found by me at any hour of the day or night, and was not slow to avail myself of the state of inebriation in which the guards were plunged. Stealing noiselessly to the library in the dark, I mounted up to the topmost shelf, took from the leaves of a dusty folio papers of immense value to me at that moment, concealing them in the folds of my dress, and returned to my position on the bed without my gaolers having missed me. The papers were much more numerous than I imagined, and the difficulty was how to dispose of them.

The chance of my friends being searched on going out (as they

41

were assured, they should do) at three o'clock, made me hesitate as to that method. I remembered, however, that, in the search of my person in the morning, my boots and stockings had not been removed; so, Miss Mackall concealed the papers in her stockings and boots. This proceeding of course occupied some time, but it was noiselessly accomplished in the presence of the guard. It was agreed between Miss Mackall and myself, that if, after leaving my room, she learned that her person would be searched, she should be seized with compunction at leaving me, and return to share the honours of the conflagration.

It is proper here to state that the mother of Miss Mackall was not cognisant of this, or any other circumstance calculated to have involved her in the difficulties surrounding me.

The guard, meanwhile, all unconsciously continued their conversation, which, under the influence of the ardent spirits they had imbibed, became heated and angry. I exerted myself to promote the discussion, and arrayed their different nationalities one against the other—they were English, German, Irish, and Yankee. (Two of the most insolent of these men an Englishman named Lewis, and an Irishman named Scully were, sometime after, apprehended in Richmond as spies, and condemned to death. On my arrival there they wrote to me to petition my intervention in their behalf.)

I reasoned that so unusual a circumstance as men wrangling in my house would warn my friends of the existence of an extraordinary state of things. It was a clear moonlight night, and fear, like death, had hushed every sound in that section of the city. It was a judicious conclusion, as I subsequently learned.

I must here record a circumstance which will go far to prove that a certain *gentleman in black* does not always take care of his own. The chief detective, Allen, having gone out on some other errand of mischief, on returning about nine o'clock encountered a gentleman who was at that time provost-marshal of the city, and who was about to call to make a visit at my house. Allen, being ignorant of or disregarding his official position, attempted to arrest him.

He ran, pursued by Allen, until he reached the provost's quarters, when, ordering out his guard, he arrested Allen, and held him in close confinement until the next morning, regardless of his oaths, or his prayers to be allowed to send a message to Lincoln, or Seward, or M'Clellan. By these indirect means Providence seems to have watched over and averted destruction from me.

Between the hours of three and four, on the morning of the 24th, my friends were permitted to depart, under escort of a detective guard, who were stationed around their houses for the following day.

After this I was allowed to snatch a few hours of repose, much needed after the mental and bodily fatigue of that most trying day. But I must also state that the two doors leading into my chamber were kept open, with a guard stationed inside of each.

On the morning of the 24th, at about eleven o'clock, my friend Miss Mackall, much to the surprise of the Yankee detective police, returned, and for several weeks shared my imprisonment.

For seven days my house remained in charge of the detective police, the search continuing throughout all that time, as also the examination of my papers and correspondence. The books in the library were all taken down and examined leaf by leaf. There would have been some wisdom in this the first day. Several large boxes, containing books, china, and glass, which had been packed for several months, were subjected to the like ordeal. Finally, portions of the furniture were taken apart, and even the pictures on the walls received their share of attention also. My beds even were upturned many times, as some new idea would seize them.

I now watched their clumsy proceedings free from anxiety, as I had, under their own eyes, sent off or destroyed all my papers of value.

The search still went on. My powers of observation became quickened to a degree which would have made me a valuable auxiliary to the honourable body, to whose care the Abolition Government had confided the lives and honour of helpless women and children.

Seemingly I was treated with deference. Once only were violent hands put upon my person—the detective, Captain Dennis, having rudely seized me to prevent my giving warning to a lady and gentleman, on the first evening of my arrest (which I, however, succeeded in doing), and as the birds escaped his snare, his rage grew beyond bounds, and he seized me with the spring of a tiger, and crushed my poor arm, which long bore the marks of the brutal outrage. The story of the hapless Queen of Scots was most feelingly called to my recollection. A strong effort was afterwards made to drive this from my mind, as if aught but the life's blood of the dastard could efface it.

My orders were asked for my meals, which I humoured as one of the necessities of my situation. But Lily and I were like the Siamese twins, inseparable. My pistol had been taken from me, and I had no means of defence, and for the first time in my life I was exposed to the dread of personal violence.

I had, however, the satisfaction, after a few days, of perceiving that even my lawless captors were rebuked into more quiet and reserve before me, although they still presumed to seat themselves at table with me, with unwashed hands, and shirt-sleeves.

The tactics of my gaolers changed many times. Occasionally, it seemed that my confinement was only nominal; all this, of course, was to throw me off my guard. The subordinates threw themselves in my way, as if disgusted with the task assigned them, and, with *hearts overflowing with kindness, and hands ready to be bribed,* discoursed most fluently upon the outrage committed in my arrest.

Two deserve especial notice. One was a burly Irishman, with smooth tongue, professing the religion of my ancestors, that of the Holy Catholic faith. He marvelled that so noble a lady should have been treated as a common malefactor; and, by way of still further showing his sympathy, he set himself to the task of making love to my maid, hoping by this means to possess himself of the important State secrets of which he believed her to be the repository.

Sentimental walks, and treats at confectionaries at Uncle Sam's expense, were a part of the programme. She, Lizzy Fitzgerald, a quick-witted Irish girl, warmly attached to me as a kind mistress, and knowing nothing which the severest scrutiny could elicit to my disadvantage, entered keenly into the sport, and, to use her own expressive words, '*led Pat a dance,*' and, under these new auspices, performed some very important missions for me.

The other, a canny Scotchman, whom they called Robert, expatiated, with tears in his eyes, upon '*the sublime fortitude*' I had exhibited on this my moral gridiron; and, seeking still further to commemorate the meek and lowly grace with which I had borne myself, asked me to present him with M'Clellan's report on the Crimea, with my autograph, for, he said, 'Madam,' choked with emotion, '*there is no telling what may happen*; and I would like to look at your name, and know that you had forgiven me.' His manner was touchingly pathetic, and very like what I should suppose Jack Ketch's to be, on asking for the *black cap after all was over.* These two men offered to take letters for me.

I learned, incidentally, that the provost-marshal's office was kept on the *qui vive* by the daily report of these proceedings, from which important results were expected to be derived.

During all this time I was never alone for a moment. Wherever I went a detective followed me. If I wished to lie down, he was seated a few paces from my bed. If I desired to change my dress, or anything else, it was obliged to be done with open doors, and a man peering in at me. That every sense of delicacy recoiled from this indecent exposure may well be imagined. But, alas! I had no alternative but to submit, for, when I remonstrated with the detective, Captain Dennis, I was met by the answer that it was the order of the provost-marshal, and that I was indebted to him that more disgusting severity had not been enforced.

General Mansfield had been superseded in the position of provost-marshal of the district of Columbia by Brigadier Andrew J. Porter, who was far more congenial, in his character and acquirements, with the *Satrap* and his minions, and not likely to entertain any conscientious scruples in the performance of any duty which might be assigned to him; and who seemed to have been equally fortunate in the selection of his own principal police-officer, Captain Averil, of the U.S.A., whose genius certainly lay in his new line of duty. He was ever on the alert to discover some new persecution for the unfortunates within his power, in order to testify his zeal and fidelity.

CHAPTER 5

Reign of Terror

Meanwhile, my private papers and letters were still under the process of examination, and were divided off into parcels, marked 'highly important,' 'political,' 'legal,' &c. according to the perceptive faculty of the examining parties, and borne off to the War Department.

There was one paper amongst them which I venture to assert will never be brought to light. It was a full and detailed account, so far as could be collected, of the appalling attempt of the Abolition party to poison President Buchanan, and the chiefs of the Democratic party, in Washington, at the National Hotel, a few days prior to the inauguration of President Buchanan.

This diabolical scheme was very near accomplishment, so far as regarded the life of President Buchanan, who was for a long time in a very critical condition, and it was only by the use of powerful stimulants that his constitution rallied from the effects of the poison. He told me that often during the day at this time he was obliged to drink several tumblers of unadulterated brandy, to keep himself from entire physical exhaustion.

This created great commotion in Washington, and various efforts were made to account for it in a natural way. One story was, that the rats, which were very troublesome, had been poisoned, and that they had fallen into the tanks which supplied the hotel with water. But the corporate authorities took the matter in hand, and instituted a very thorough examination; the tanks were all emptied of water, and no rats could be found; the sewers under and leading through the town were also opened, to see if any poisonous exhalations could come from them; and the corporation reported that there was no local cause for the epidemic. Everybody fled from the plague-stricken spot; and the hotel, which was one of the largest in the city, was closed.

At the same time, information of a very important character came to the knowledge of the authorities. A druggist of Philadelphia wrote to the Attorney-General (Caleb Gushing), at Washington, that, in his absence, an order had been received and filled by one of his subordinates for thirty pounds of arsenic, to be sent to Washington; that so unusual a quantity had excited his alarm; that, upon further enquiry, he learned that the express charge had been prepaid at Philadelphia for its transportation, which was likewise unusual. It was also found that the package had reached Washington by Adams & Co.'s Express, and had been called for and received by some unknown party.

To show the pertinacity with which the plot was followed up, Congress had made an appropriation for a *Major-Domo* of the White House, with a salary of $1,200. The person who had charge of Mr. Buchanan's rooms at the National was the applicant for the post, and was on the eve of receiving the appointment, when a gentleman from New York, arrived in post haste, in the night, roused up the private secretary of the President, and gave him information of importance. The applicant for the place of *Major-Domo* of the White House, after this, did not again present himself, but disappeared from the city.

Judge Black, the Attorney-General of the United States, under Mr. Buchanan, whose statements corroborated the above information, told me also that he had obtained a clue to the whole plot, but that Mr. Buchanan would not allow the affair to be pursued, because of the startling facts it would lay open to the world, and that he shrank from the terrible exposure.

I considered it a great weakness on his part to have forbidden the investigation, as it might have averted the John Brown raid, and many other acts of the '*Irrepressible Conflict*' party. Between fifty and sixty persons fell victims to this wholesale poisoning experiment.

A very large sum had been offered for my cipher. This extraordinary sum had stimulated the zeal of the *employés* of the Government to a very remarkable degree. I had, of course, too much control over myself to afford any indication of my knowledge of what they were seeking, but affected ignorance and unconcern.

The tables were filled with fragments of old letters, and scraps in cipher, in several languages, from early morn till late at night. For seven days they puzzled over them. I had no fear. One by one they had allowed the clue to escape them, and for what remained Champollion himself would have required a key. Only once was I frightened. Miss Mackall, who, like myself, was always on the alert, abstracted from a heap of papers a sheet of blotting-paper, upon which was the whole of my despatch to Manassas on July 16—another evidence that Providence watched over me as an humble instrument in a glorious cause.

I was at this time kept perfectly well posted with regard to matters outside, and sometimes received valuable information through the inadvertent conversation of my gaolers. I had been already notified that several of my despatches had been betrayed into Seward's hands by a spy of the name of Applegate; that a Cabinet Council had been convened, assisted by Scott and M'Clellan; and that several Republican officials had been summoned, amongst the number Wilson of Massachusetts, as being implicated by my information. The despatches created consternation. The whole Abolition Government were at this time shaking with fear of the advance of our glorious army, and their children were even hushed to sleep with the cry, 'Jeff. Davis is coming.'

I had deemed it important that the political intrigues then going on at Washington should be clearly understood by the Confederate Government; and as I might almost be said to have assisted at Lincoln's Cabinet Councils, from the facilities I enjoyed, having *verbatim* reports of them as well as of the Republican caucus, I was thoroughly competent to the task of giving a faithful synopsis of their deliberations.

One of the despatches referred to was a long letter to President Davis, describing in detail the intrigues to get rid of Scott by the temporary elevation of M'Clellan, in which was repeated a conversation I had held with several members of the New York Press, as an indication of the temper of the times, upon a proposition they had under discussion, of uniting to dethrone Seward and Cameron, and the reasons *pro* and *con.* for leaving Seward where he was; that his time serving policy was less conducive to unity and strength; that he would never inaugurate any new measures; that if the faction which seemed strongest cried for the abolition of slavery, or renewed guarantees for its protection, he would lend himself to it, or to anything else which could tend to his advancement; that his genius lay in his faculty of drawing to himself all the advantages of any successful measure, and of shuffling out of the way of an unpopular one; that Bennett, of the *New York Herald*, had understood him perfectly, and had said of him, in reply to my remark that 'Seward was the only statesman amongst the Black Republican party,'

'He has not the first principle of a statesman: he is a miserable political charlatan, and has been the advocate of every unconstitutional measure in this State from Anti-rentism down to Abolitionism. He has not blood enough in him to entertain an honest opinion on any subject, but wishes to be a great

48

man, and will truckle to anything for power,' that the Chevalier Wikoff
had gone to Seward and repeated to him some portion of this conversation, and that he (Seward) had reddened to the roots of his hair,
but had appointed an hour to receive him, for the discussing certain
propositions he had to make on the part of the New York Press, on
the *peace question*: that the *chevalier*, after this conversation, came to
me and proposed that I should give him a safe-conduct to General
Beauregard, with a recommendation that he would forward him to
Richmond, from which city he could write a peace letter: that Mr.
Seward favoured the idea. He then said, '*Suppose you go to Manassas, and
let me go under your protection.'*

I said, 'That would be impossible.'

He replied quickly, '*Oh! I have arranged all that with Seward.'*

I said, 'You misunderstand me: your reputation is so bad, that no
lady would travel in your company.'

That, unabashed by this, he then said, 'But will you give me a letter which will take me through to Richmond? *I will be willing to go
blindfold, and be put in a cage after I get there, so that I may write the letter.'*

To which I replied, 'I have no authority to grant your request, and,
so far from giving you facilities for carrying out your wishes, I should
consider President Davis derelict in his duty if he did not cause any
man to be hanged who would do what you propose;' that peace now,
upon any other basis than separate independence, was out of the question; and that, if he had any desire to aid in the accomplishment of that
desirable end, he had better, through the New York papers, endeavour
to enlighten the minds of the people on the subject; that we of the
South had been driven to draw the sword in self-defence, &c. I told
of Cameron's peculations, which were not then generally known—of
M'Clellan's plans for reorganising the army—in short, of all that was
proposed, or being done by the Yankees.

The second despatch was entirely in cipher, but contained du-
plicate drawings of some fortifications and weak points, which they
complimented as being equal to those of their best engineers—*as well
they might*; besides information of importance, in case our army advanced on Washington. My letter was pronounced '*a very able produc-
tion*'. I had at least the satisfaction of knowing that Lincoln and the
assembled wisdom of Abolitionism did justice to the zeal with which
a Southern woman executed her patriotic duty.

Their fears elevated me to a most dangerous eminence, and they
deliberated whether I should not be publicly tried for treason, and

made an example of. The effort to obtain my cipher was with the hope of establishing direct evidence against me, such as would be available in court upon a public trial, and as a justification to the world for their extraordinary proceedings, for which there had been no precedent, in a civilised age, save in France during the Revolution.

My social position was such, that they did not dare follow out the suggestions of their first excited consultations in disposing of me; for in their own ranks, I had many devoted friends, who openly expressed their admiration of the position I took under the circumstances of danger and difficulty which environed me.

Mr. Davis directed me, in a despatch received at this time, to give up the cipher, if I could thereby obtain any advantage. This discretionary instruction of the President left me free to follow my own judgment, and destroy it, for reasons vital to me, and fraught with hazard to others, actually engaged and still unsuspected.

My despatches were all written and received at this time under a *nom de plume*, and Yankee cunning and ingenuity had, even at this early day, exhausted itself in efforts to inveigle me into an admission or recognition which, would compromise me or my friends. They had had the infamy to circulate a report that, for a large sum, I had engaged to desert my cause and betray my party. But I thank God that they did not succeed in shaking the confidence of my friends, which was an important object.

That I could have made my own terms with them can easily be seen from the importance they attached to my capture. They had the effrontery to insinuate to me, through their subordinates, that a '*graceful concession*' on my part would be most cheerfully responded to by the Government. And when I replied that if this was in furtherance of the report they had set in circulation—an attempt to bribe me—my only response would be that, for weal or woe, I had cast my lot as God and nature directed, and that their whole bankrupt treasury could not tempt me to betray the meanest agent of our cause.

I was asked if I knew that my life was in danger, and that probably, to *save my neck*, I might answer differently, to which I replied that the life of anyone is in danger when in the power of lawless scoundrels. Beyond that I had no fears, for their own cowardice protected me, as they knew ample retaliation would follow an attempt on my life.

On Thursday, the 29th, the Yankee Government went through the farce of offering to hire my house and furniture. I asked to be allowed to see a lawyer for consultation, and was told that they would not grant me that right. I then answered that, as a prisoner, I was not competent to any legal act, and that I declined all negotiations with them; that they had already ruined, and destroyed, and stolen all that I valued in the house, and that they might continue to hold it by the same lawless tenure—that of brute force—as I would not become a party to my own robbery. This I said to Quartermaster Howard, who came on the part of the Government, and, to do him justice, he appeared heartily ashamed of his mission.

General Butler was with Cameron and other officials, in the provost-marshal's office, when Captain Howard went to report the result of his mission, which he did in terms complimentary to me, coupled with the remark that he felt like tearing the straps from his shoulders, from a sense of mortification at the part he was forced to play as he stood before the noble woman. Butler said, If the Government will take my advice, and consign that *haughty dame* to my care at Fortress Monroe, I warrant to put her through an ordeal which will no longer endanger the loyalty of our officers, &c. &c.

Verily, a Roman tyrant made a consul of his horse, but Lincoln has exceeded him in enormity by making of Butler the beast a military governor.

My object in seeing a lawyer was of course not with the idle hope of protecting my property. But up to this time the *habeas corpus* had not been suspended, and I wished to force the issue between the civil and military authorities, as a means possibly of arresting the coming evils. I was informed by the man Allen that I knew my rights too well, and that the Government did not intend to afford me the means of asserting them.

I did, however, in spite of their vigilance, succeed in sending a message and note to Judge Black (late Attorney-General of the United States) and to the Honourable E. J. Walker, requesting them to call upon me. But those grave legal gentlemen, influenced by prudential considerations, or sympathy with the inquisitorial hierarchy, gave no heed to my request, and I was thus left in the hands of an unscrupulous cunning enemy, with only my own judgment to guide me.

To show the utter recklessness of the Abolition Government, and the extraordinary means they temporarily resorted to, to infuse valour into their de moralised ranks, it was now authoritatively published that our great and good President had died in Richmond a few weeks after the Battle of Manassas. He was said to have died of a slow fever, brought on by great mental anxiety, and compunction at the share he was supposed to have had in bringing about the revolution; that he had breathed his last sigh at twenty minutes to six in the morning; that his attending physicians and family and friends were present; that his mind was clear, and that he solemnly exhorted his friends to renew their allegiance to the United States, and to do all in their power to put down the revolution.

The flags were reported to be at half-mast at Arlington Heights, Manassas, and all other points in our possession, and that minute guns were fired during the day. This account went through the whole North, and was the cause of immense rejoicing, for our President had filled them with fear and dread, in proportion to the confidence and veneration with which he had inspired every Southerner.

On Friday morning, the 30th of August, I was informed that other prisoners were to be brought in, and that my house was to be converted into a prison, and that Miss Mackall and myself, and little girl and servant, were to be confined in one room. After considerable difficulty and consultation with the Secretary of War, another small room was allowed for my child and maid, with the restriction, however, that I should not go into it, as it was a front room, with a window on the street. Subsequently my library was also allotted to me.

My parlours were stripped of their furniture, which was conveyed into the chamber for the use of the prisoners. By this time, I had become perfectly callous. Everything showed signs of the contamination. Those unkempt, unwashed wretches—the detective police—had rolled themselves in my fine linen; their mark was visible upon every chair and sofa.

Even the chamber in which one of my children had died only a few months before, and the bed on which she lay in her winding-sheet, had been desecrated by these emissaries of Lincoln, and the various articles of *bijouterie*, which lay on her toilet as she had left them, were borne off as rightful spoils. Every hallowed association with my home had been rudely blasted my castle had become my prison. The law of the land had been supplanted by the higher law of the Abolition despot, and I could only say, Lord, how long will this iniquity be permitted?

But I stray from my story. Soon armed men filled the house, the clank of whose muskets resounded through it like the voice of doom. I was confined to my chamber, at the door of which two soldiers stood, musket in hand.

The commotion below told me that other prisoners were arriving.

They were the Philips family Mrs. Philips, and her two oldest daughters, and her sister Miss Levi. A silent greeting, *en passant*, was all we were allowed to exchange. These ladies had been arrested the day after I was, and were subjected to the like, if not greater indignities, from which the presence of the husband and the father could not protect them; and now they were dragged from their own homes, the mother from her little children, several of whom were infants of tender age; her house ransacked, her papers overhauled, without finding anything to base even a suspicion upon—the only circumstance against her really being, that she was a Southern woman, and a lady, scorning association with the '*mudsills*' whom the upheaving of the revolution had brought to the surface of society.

Another prisoner was to be confined in the room adjoining mine. A heavy bar of wood had been nailed across the door between, so as to prevent all communication. She was brought in late at night; her deep and convulsed sobs broke on the stillness of the hour. I sat by the door, and heard the officer in charge call her name. It was Mrs. Hasler, of whom I had some previous knowledge; but, had she been a stranger, her hapless lot would have established a claim to my sympathy.

I had sent to this person's house, the night of my arrest, to warn her, but found her house already in charge of soldiers, and my messenger barely escaped arrest. I was, of course, intensely anxious to let her know that she was in my house, and to communicate with her. She had been accredited to me as a reliable messenger by Colonel Jorden; had successfully served in that capacity several times; and it was through her means (most innocently, however) that my despatches had been betrayed into the hands of the Government. Special care was taken to prevent this prisoner and myself from communicating, as they hoped through her to establish direct evidence against me.

The morning after her arrival I diverted the attention of the guard, whilst Miss Mackall slipped into her room, and warned her to deny all knowledge of me—which was, however, limited to the fact of her having been an agent of communication.

Poor woman! she had been most infamously used—dragged from her own lodgings to a station-house, where she had been kept for a whole week, lying on a dirty straw-bed, without sheets or pillow, amidst the lowest and most disgusting class of the community; and her nervous system had been completely shattered by it.

All intercourse between the prisoners was interdicted. Had we been adjudged to the condemned cell more rigorous measures could not have been enforced.

Miss Mackall was allowed to see her mother and sisters only in the presence of an officer. Intercourse thus restricted afforded but little pleasure. Still, it was a link between us and the outer world, which had not been appreciated at its full value until we were deprived of it.

It must not be supposed that I have related all the incidents which occurred in these first days. Under the eyes of the detective police, I had received and answered despatches from my friends. Amongst them had been the order from my President to give up my cipher, upon specified contingencies. I am restrained, by prudential considerations, from mentioning many, and where the parties only escaped by the stupidity of my gaolers.

The efforts of the Black Republicans had been persistently to make the term Secessionist one of disgrace and reproach, and although they had with great assiduity courted the few Southern families who remained, there was no language too coarse for them to use in describing Secessionists—always, of course, assuming that the person addressed had too much self-respect to be thus classified. Every social element was brought to bear against the unhappy Southerner; ties of blood and kindred were arrayed in dread hostility, those who remained upon the Abolition side affecting to think that their family *escutcheons* had been tarnished by the misguided members who advocated the Southern cause, and constitutional liberty. No one suffered in this respect more than myself, for many members of my immediate family sided with the despot, and held high official position under him.

The detective police, who had hitherto had charge of me, now gave place to the military guard selected from one of the volunteer companies—the Sturgis Rifles, who hitherto constituted M'Clellan's body guard. A lieutenant and twenty-one men were detailed for this valorous duty.

The detective police, on resigning their charge, were very anxious that I should not be apprised of their true characters. They had assumed to be officers of the United States Regular Army, and deluded themselves with the idea that I had not discovered the wolf under the sheep's clothing. My wish had been to foster this delusion by every means in my power, as I thereby gained some advantages; and I very reluctantly allowed myself to be enlightened on the subject by some enthusiastic young officers, who cherished the hallucination that honour still lingered under the old livery of the United States.

The officer in charge of my prison, Lieutenant Sheldon, was directed by Captain Averil, U.S.A., chief of the provost-marshal's corps, to encourage me to write letters, which were to be subjected to the inquisitorial examination. Of this fact I was, however, to be kept in ignorance. To the honour of Lieutenant Sheldon, he did not lend himself to the plot. I availed myself, however, of the privilege of writing, and have certainly to thank this most sagacious captain for having afforded me the means of communication.

I was at this time seized with a taste for tapestry-work. The colours necessary for its prosecution came to me through the provost-marshal's office, wound in balls, with simply a memorandum, by which I could always know the original arrangement of colours. I had made a vocabulary of colours, which, though not a very prolific language, served my purpose. My letters, above all things, puzzled these 'wise men of the East,' who finally came to the conclusion that, 'for a clever woman, Mrs. Greenhow wrote the greatest pack of trash that was ever read.'

By way of justifying this opinion, I will submit a specimen of my epistolary efforts:—

'Tell Aunt Sally that I have some old shoes for *the children*, and I wish her to send someone *down* town to take them, and to let me know whether she has found any charitable person to help her to take care of them.' My immediate correspondent was of course ignorant of the true meaning. But, carried to that respectable old lady, 'Aunt Sally,' she read it thus:—'I have some important information to send across the river, and wish a messenger immediately. Have you any means of getting reliable information?'

Of course, my versatility of mind was exercised to vary the style and character of these effusions, so as not to attract attention to them, and I am glad to state that in this effort I was eminently successful.

Miss Mackall, although not a prisoner, was subjected to most of the restrictions in this house of bondage, the freedom originally allowed her being, as I rightly judged, for the purpose of ensnaring others. These clumsy tricksters could not comprehend the sacrifices which a woman will make in the performance of a duty which commends itself alike to her judgment and feelings. I could have escaped the snare set for me, but I should thereby have done great injury to our cause. Few would have ventured, after such an example of timidity, to furnish the necessary information, or encounter the odium of being supposed to sympathise with the *rebels*.

I felt it to be my post of duty whatever danger threatened, and that I at least would cast no reproach upon my party in going through the trying ordeal; that every woman's heart, throughout the South, would make my cause their own; and that, so far from intimidating, the knowledge that one of their sex was suffering for the same faith, in the prisons of the tyrant, would nerve the most timid to deeds of daring.

The idea of the Yankees at first was to hold me up conspicuously before the eyes of the public as a terrible example and a warning. In this they signally failed, for I became, even amongst their own people, an object of interest. And one of their own papers, the *New York Times*, some months later, said:

'Had Madam Greenhow been sent South immediately after her arrest, as we recommended, we should have heard no more of the heroic deeds of Secesh women, which she has made the fashion.'

On the 7th of September my child was taken very ill. In consequence I wrote to Provost-Marshal Porter, asking that my family physician might be allowed to visit her. With *characteristic humanity* he refused, and proposed to send me one of his own creatures, whom I declined to receive, preferring to trust her life to the care of the good Providence which had so often befriended me.

A few days after, a Dr. Steward was introduced. He was a vulgar, uneducated man, bedizened with enough gold-lace for three field-marshals; and endowed with a considerable degree of modest assurance. He evidently expected, by affected *bonhomie*, to overcome my repugnance to his visits; but he reckoned without his host, for, if my confessor had come to me under such auspices, I should think that the devil had been tampering with him, and refuse to receive him.

The routine of my prison-life was constantly varied by some new device, on the part of my captors, to obtain legal evidence against me. They had already subjected me to an ordeal little short of the '*celebrated question*' of the Spanish Inquisition, by a total disregard of all the laws of decency. Every feeling of the woman had been shocked and outraged, and they now sought to act upon my nervous system, by dark insinuations and threats against my life and reputation. My papers had been examined with a minuteness bordering upon the farcical.

Letters were found from most of the gifted and great in our Southern land, whom they now branded as traitors; copies of some of my own letters, also, both before and after Lincoln's ill-fated elevation, expressing in earnest language my appreciation of the coming dangers, and, in some instances, warning my correspondents to 'take time by the forelock.' These, however, added no link in the chain of evidence, but only served to magnify in their eyes my mental ability, and consequent capacity to injure them, and redouble their anxiety to convict me.

The despatches already in their hands, and which had caused them to tremble even in the midst of their armed *Hessians*, at best would be but circumstantial evidence against me; and my connection with these even would have to be established upon the testimony of that double spy, Applegate, whom Cameron had sent in that capacity to Manassas, under the pretext of obtaining the body of his brother; and this man I could have proved to have been in the pay of our army, and had furnished some valuable information.

Mr. Seward, in spite of the obfuscation of his perceptive faculties, retained enough of his legal acute ness to know that, in so grave a matter as trial for treason, the charge must be sustained by two respectable witnesses, and that any case made out against me, upon the evidence before them, would have been dismissed from every court in Christendom. I did not shrink from this trial; and when repeatedly warned that it might take place, said, 'Let it come. I will claim the right to defend myself, and there be rich revelations.'

The Government having come to the sage conclusion that Mrs. Hasler was one of my agents, hoped, through her credulity or fears, to obtain additional testimony against me. With this object, the spy Applegate was brought to see her. She received him with unsuspecting confidence, and drank in with greedy ears his marvellous tales. He complained bitterly of having been searched and badly treated, before he was allowed to see her, and exhibited his torn hat in evidence. His great object, he said, was to fall upon some plan of communicating with me, as he had information of importance for me, and asked her if she could communicate.

This programme had been all arranged at the provost-marshal's by General Porter and his subordinate knaves; Captain Averil being entitled to the suggestion of *tearing the hat.*

I had been warned of all this in advance, but had not thought it advisable to apprise Mrs. Hasler of it. She could not commit herself further to this man than she had already done; neither had I any apprehensions concerning myself, as she knew nothing, having simply acted as agent, on several occasions, for the transmission of despatches, of the purport of which she was as ignorant as the mail boy of the contents of his bag.

It was proposed to confront this worthy agent with me, but his own fears rendered abortive every effort of this kind. He lived in mortal dread of his life, and when *a friend of mine* went to see him, in order to obtain for me some information, he found him double-locked in his room, with a pistol lying on either side of him. He soon after left the city, lest he should pay the penalty of his crimes.

★★★★★★★★

This man, Applegate, was subsequently chief of the detective police at Memphis, where it is said he did a good business by restoring to their masters, at 200 dollars per head, the negroes stolen by General Sherman, who was then in command at this place.

★★★★★★★★★★

This incident, as well as others which had preceded it, will convince the Abolitionists that, although they held me in close confinement, my system of espionage was more perfect than their own.

This Dr. Stewart was, I fancy, destined to be my *bête noire*. He said that he was ordered by Provost-Marshal Porter to make a daily inspection of my sanitary condition. His vanity was enlisted in this. He wished to be able to say, in the course of his morning rounds, 'I have just been to see the rebel prisoner Mrs. Greenhow, and she says so and so.' I had no idea of permitting this, and therefore told him that I did not desire to receive his professional visits, as I was perfectly well, &c. He wrote a prescription for Miss Mackall, in English, every word of which was misspelt, and signed himself '*Brigand Sargent*' I laughingly mentioned the circumstance of a physician's writing a prescription in other than Latin.

By some means my remarks reached him; so, on the repetition of his visit on the following day, he addressed me with 'Good morning, Mistress Greenhow; is there anything *Materia Medica* can do for you today?' Recalling forcibly to my mind the story of the Irishman:— '*Parlez-vous Français?—Oui.*—Then lend me the loan of a gridiron.'

I now told *Materia Medica* that his visits were intrusions on my privacy, offensive to me, and requested that they might be discontinued. It will hardly be credited that after this I should have been subject to the annoyance again. On the day succeeding he came in as usual, with unblushing effrontery, not even deigning to knock at my door. I took no notice of him, but sent for Lieutenant Sheldon to take charge of my formal protest against the continuance of the outrage. This he did, making also verbal representations which relieved me from further *sanitary inspection*.

58

About this time a stable in the rear of my *whilom home*—my prison—caught on fire, through the neglect of some drunken soldiers by whom it was occupied. It created the wildest alarm; the whole of the provost-guard, headed by Captain Averil, rushed to the scene of action, and surrounded the house. The following morning the Government organ contained an account of a very daring attempt at rescue of the rebel prisoners (with a diatribe against me personally), of so resolute and desperate a character that it had to be repulsed at the point of the bayonet.

This veracious statement was concluded by a high compliment to the intrepidity and courage of Captain Averil, for having defeated this *imaginary* effort to defraud justice, which was furnished, I was told, by himself.

Somewhere about the 8th of September, the Honourable Edwin M. Stanton, accompanied by Judge-Advocate Colonel Key, came to see Mrs. Philips and family, to make arrangements for their being sent South on parole, which was effected a day or two afterwards.

Mr. Stanton came also to see me. I had, of course, no idea of the position he was subsequently to hold in the Abolition Cabinet; *neither had he at that time.* After some preliminary conversation, he asked me what I had done to bring down the wrath of the Abolitionists upon my head, I answered, I had been guilty of *lèze-majesté,* and hence my incarceration; in fact, that I knew not the charge, and, for the purpose of ascertaining it, and forcing the Government to a consideration of my case, I now wished to employ him as my counsel, to obtain a writ of *habeas corpus.*

This he declined, accompanied by expressions of high appreciation and proffer of service in any other way—to which I of course attached no value. I had previously applied to Judge Black, Attorney-General under Mr. Buchanan, and to the Honourable R. J. Walker, both of whom I had known intimately; and this last effort convinced me that no Northern man had the courage or the desire to attempt to stem the tide of Northern usurpation, which was destined to sweep like an avalanche over the land, destroying civil liberty, and establishing in its stead an irresponsible military despotism.

I felt now that I was alone, and that the wall of separation from my friends was each hour growing more formidable.

A new grievance was also put upon me. Miss Mackall, who up to this time had remained with me, was, on the 25th of September, abruptly taken away, and all intercourse or communication with me interdicted. So, rigid had become the rules that persons were warned, under penalty of arrest, from walking or driving by the prison. A police-officer dogged eternally poor Lily's footsteps, which so harassed and annoyed her, that she often prayed for the protection of her prison-life.

Wearily and heavily now passed the days and weeks. Another plan was also adopted to reduce me to submission. My food, which up to this time, though plain and often uneatable, had been sufficiently abundant, was now so reduced in quantity and quality, as to be inadequate often to satisfy the cravings of hunger. My child, as well as myself, suffered greatly under this new infliction. I wrote to Provost-Marshal Porter, protesting against this inhumanity, but he turned a deaf ear to my remonstrance; and my little Rose (who was allowed to play on the pavement, under escort of a guard) was often indebted to the kind friends who sent her food whilst there, that she should not cry herself to sleep from hunger.

Those Yankee descendants of the Pilgrim Fathers had improved upon the ancestral practice of *burning and hanging and quartering* their enemies, by *quartering* and starving theirs.

An outrage was now perpetrated, more foul, more galling to me as a woman, than any which had preceded it. A woman of bad repute, known and recognised by several of the guard as such, having been seen in the streets of Chicago in the exercise of her vocation, calling herself Mrs. Onderdunk, was brought to my house, and placed in the chamber of my deceased child adjoining mine. For what object I know not, but this woman was allowed unrestricted intercourse with me, the order being given that our meals should be served together.

Here again my thanks are due to Lieutenant Sheldon; for so soon as the character of the woman became known to him, he restricted her to her apartment, in which she frequently received Mr. Frederick Seward, Undersecretary of State; Mr. Webster, Private Secretary of the Secretary of State, and other persons officially connected with the Government.

It might have been supposed that my former social position, and that which members of my immediate family still held in the Federal city, would have protected me from this attempt to degrade me. But surprise will cease when the character of this people has been exhibited more clearly, and the unscrupulous and demoralising influences, brought by them to bear amidst the social relations of life, exposed.

Under the system established by Mr. Seward, of the secret police, a spy was in every household. These were often selected from the higher classes of society, as witness Mrs. —— and Mrs. —— of Baltimore, and Mme. —— and Mrs. —— of Washing ton City. By such means the sanctity of home was invaded; every unguarded expression uttered within its sacred precincts was sure to reach the ears of the secret police—those Thugs of America, who, less merciful than their Eastern prototypes (who warned their victims of their coming fate by a knife stuck in the wall), entered the houses and the chambers of women and children at the dead of night, dragging them from their beds, and, regardless alike of tears and prayers, forced them to assume their garments under the eye, and often amidst the scurrilous jests, of their rude and licentious agents. One young girl, to my knowledge, died from the shame and horror of this ordeal.

And yet this people, with the deep damnation of their acts before them, dare to proclaim their mission to be, the upholding of the Constitution, and the restoration of the Union. I often wonder that the thunderbolts of heaven do not strike them as they utter the sacrilegious lie.

Their leaders now, in all private circles, when they deemed themselves secure, unblushingly announced their real determination to abolish slavery. Sedgwick, of New York, one of their most intelligent members of the Lower House, told me 'that he did not care a rush for the flag; that that was a claptrap for the ignorant;' and that if 'he thought that by this war the old Union could be restored, with its constitutional guarantees for slavery, that he would not vote a dollar or a man. No,' he said, 'it was for universal emancipation his party fought, and they were now strong enough to declare their true policy.'

The Honourable Henry Wilson said, 'The country had been ruled long enough by Southern aristocrats, and that his party would enforce their principles at the point of the bayonet; and as to Maryland, they had put the iron heel upon her, and would crush out her boundary lines.'

Baker, of Oregon, one of President Lincoln's most confidential advisers, and United States senator, said, in a conversation which I held with him at the time of the pretended attempt to reinforce Fort Sumter, in answer to a remonstrance of mine on the subject, 'It is true a great many lives may be lost, and we may not succeed in reinforcing Fort Sumter. But the President was elected by a Northern majority, and they are now becoming dissatisfied; and the President owes it to them to strike some blow by which he will make a united Northern party.'

Dickerson, of Rhode Island, said, 'that if the rebellion could not be sup-

pressed in any other way, he was for the abolition of slavery, as a certain means of reducing the South to a state of vassalage.'

I state these conversations, and I might add many more to the list, in order to show that even at this early day, when the initiatory step in the revolution had scarcely been taken, all affectation was thrown aside as to the real object of the war—that of subjugation of the South by means of general emancipation of the slaves.

Mrs. Hasler was at this time released, upon taking the oath of allegiance, and making a full confession of all she had done or knew. I was heartily glad of it. She had paid dearly for a momentary impulse, her sympathy or connection with our cause being confined to the transmission of a few letters. For this she was imprisoned two months in solitary confinement, and it required the stern faith of the martyrs of old to withstand the ordeal of our Lord Abraham the First. But even this was not done as an act of justice to the victim, whose health had become seriously impaired, but by the kindly exertions of a lady who exercised as potential an influence over the wily Secretary of War, Simon Cameron, as the celebrated Madame du Barri did over the grandfather of Louis XVI.

It would be impossible to record the daily, hourly, petty annoyances to which I was exposed. Every article of clothing which went to the laundry had to be examined by the corporal of the guard, in presence of the officer of the guard. Upon one occasion the corporal of the guard, on sending out some article of clothing for one of the prisoners, neglected this duty, for which he was tried, degraded to the ranks, with imprisonment for thirty days, and loss of pay for three months.

Thus, it will be seen that, whatever repugnance may have been felt by an officer in the performance of this task, it was obligatory upon him by order of the provost-marshal, who seemed to have had some original ideas on the subject of the transmission of treasonable communications, although none on the subject of decency. The provost-guard was set in commotion one day, headed by Captain Averil, on account of a sprig of jessamine having reached me without going through the usual examination.

CHAPTER 6

Olla Podrida

The Abolition Government had been for some time amusing the minds of its credulous subjects with a new scheme for the annihilation of the South. The greatest naval expedition since that of Philip II. for the subjugation of England, because good Queen Bess turned a dull ear to his matrimonial scheme, was being fitted out, and, regardless of lucky or unlucky synonyms, it was also called. 'The Great Armada.'

Every invention of modern science was employed in arming and equipping this vast fleet, so as to insure the greatest amount of death and devastation to our unhappy doomed Southern land. Twenty thousand picked troops were sent as a part of the expedition, and, most terrible of all, Burnside was to command it—going South to look for his hat and his boots which he had lost at Manassas.

It would be idle to record the anxieties which possessed me, as day by day I followed, through the *New York Herald*, the progress of the preparation, and final equipment, and embarkation of the men.

The destination of this formidable *armada* now became an affair of vast moment, and I revolved in my mind the various means by which this *essential* information could be obtained. Accident favoured this thirst for knowledge better than any plan, however well arranged, could have done.

We are told that Jove nods sometimes; and Mr. Secretary Seward, who in the morning is the most reticent man in the world (admirably illustrating Talleyrand's famous axiom, that language is given to conceal thought), is, after supper, and under the in fluence of the generous gifts which the gods provide, the most genial and confidential. I have often had occasion to admire the confidingness of his nature on these occasions, and wondered if the judgment of the world was correct in ascribing to him the character of a subtle schemer and tortuous intriguer.

It was upon one of these festive occasions, when the mind of the great statesman had become properly attuned, and his thoughts soared above the sordid materialism which fettered his genius during the plodding methodical business hours, that he addressed himself to the task of indoctrinating a distinguished Foreign Representative, whose views, I am sorry to say, were not dissimilar to his own, as to the utter hopelessness of the Southern cause, and assuring him that in thirty days (a favourite period of his) the rebellion would be crushed out demonstrating this melancholy fact by describing in detail this '*invincible armada*,' and the devastating course it was predestined to take.

This important information was conveyed to me by *my little bird*. Mayhap it was the bird sent out from the ark, and did not return, and now came back to me with better than the olive-branch. I leave this as an antiquarian speculation. But being satisfied by other means of the accuracy of the intelligence, I lost no time in preparing one of those *peculiar square despatches*, written in *that cipher* for which a very large amount had been offered, and, with a prayer to Almighty God for its safe delivery, committed it to my faithful bird, and sent it across the waters to General Beauregard, to be forwarded to our great and good President at Richmond.

I might describe, if I chose, the danger that my *poor bird* passed over, and how it at one time took refuge in the dovecot of the enemy, and other things of startling interest; but this would indicate the course of the heaven-sent messenger, and jeopardise the future.

I learned at this time that Dr. Gwin, formerly United States Senator for *California*, was in Washington, a prisoner, although at large, and I desired very much to communicate to him verbally some details which would have been useful to our Government, but which I did not dare write, as it would have compromised the safety of a friend whose position was one of prominence under the Yankee Government. I wrote a note to Dr. Gwin, stating this fact, and that I could arrange with perfect safety a personal interview. I laugh now at the description of the doctor's terror on receiving my note, and his earnest appeal for God's sake not to attempt to communicate with him, for he was surrounded by the detective police, &c. He had not learned that therein was his immunity to do seemingly impossible things.

The equinoctial gales had now set in, and the wailing, shrieking, and howling of the tempest, as it swept along, fell on my ear like the soft cadences of sweet music.

The Abolition fleet had been a little too tardy in its movements to reap the full benefit of the equinoctial blast; still it was considerably damaged, several vessels being stranded. A large number of horses, and quantities of ordnance stores also, were thrown overboard, thereby causing considerable delay before the *great armada* finally set forth upon its devastating errand. Meanwhile my despatch reached Richmond.

I was very much startled one day, somewhere about the 1st of October, at receiving a proposition from a Yankee officer to aid in effecting my escape. The first idea that flashed upon me was (for I confess that my bump of caution had been largely developed by the events of the last few months), that this was a trick to ensnare some of my friends, or for the purpose of affording a pretext for conveying me to a Northern prison. Whatever my suspicions were, I deemed it politic to give no indications of them, so I responded to the proposal as if I believed it made in good faith, and opened communication with a friend on the subject, warning my friend *secretly*, however, of my suspicions, and giving instructions as to the programme to be followed.

All things worked admirably. The real objects which I had in view (and which I refrained from stating, for reason that it might afford an imprudent indication) having been effected, I threw grave obstacles in the way of the accomplishment of the heroic feat, and it was finally abandoned, from seeming want of resolution on my part to undertake it.

I can hardly tell now how my time was passed. I had gone through the heat of midsummer into the autumn, the severity of my imprisonment increasing all the while my food so uneatable, that for days I had lived upon crackers and cheese. I was not even allowed to take exercise in the yard; and was credibly informed that a proposition was discussed as to whether my windows should not be nailed up, so as to deprive me of light, as a means of forcing me into the terms of the Government.

During all this period I was shut out from all intercourse or communication with my friends. The interdict was absolute: no one was allowed to see me. Even the religious consolation which is accorded to the lowest criminal in the Christian countries of Europe was denied me. Several members of the Holy Catholic clergy applied to see me, and were repulsed with great rudeness at the provost-marshal's, as being *'emissaries of Satan and Secesh.'*

I wrote to enquire whether the provost-marshal had made a wholesale compact with the Devil, by which my child and maid were to be given over to destruction, as well as myself—reminding him that there was no *monopoly* in contracts with the *Gentleman in Black* (the system of corrupt monopoly of Government contracts was at this time being loudly denounced), and asking that the privilege might be accorded them of going to church. This was granted for the ensuing Sunday, and occasionally afterwards, but always under escort of a guard, whose orders were to sit in the same pew and allow no communication with anyone.

One morning, as I opened my chamber-door to pass to the library, I saw the detective, Allen, dragging an old lady up the stairs, who had great difficulty in ascending, even with his assistance. It was the venerable mother of the martyr Jackson; and I honoured her grey hairs as being his mother more than if a diadem had circled her brow. She was placed in the room adjoining mine, the bar of wood having been removed after the last occupant left. The guard, however, were not aware of this fact, and I was amused as I heard the detective double the guard, and order that no one was to communicate with the prisoner.

I cautiously opened the door between our apartments, and mounted over a divan which stood across the entrance. She sprang forward at seeing one of her own sex. I rapidly cautioned her, by pointing to the door leading into the hall, placed my finger on my lips, and softly approached her, when the venerable lady folded me in her arms, and gave me the information which I have stated above as to who she was. I then knelt at her feet, and she rapidly poured into my ear tales of the outer world. She told me that she had been dragged from her bed at midnight; that she had been only allowed to throw a loose gown over her nightdress, and that even in the presence of her captors, and was thus brought forth.

My heart bled to see this noble woman of eighty years subjected to such an ordeal. But she proved herself worthy of being the mother of her brave son. She recounted to me the heart-rending history of his ruthless murder, and how his body had been pinned to the floor by the demons, and kept there for many hours for them to gloat over, until his heartbroken wife with her own feeble hands dragged it forth for Christian burial.

She told me also of the heroic deeds of our brave soldiers, which filled my heart with pride and thankfulness, and I bowed my head in her lap and said, 'Mother, give me your blessing!' And the old matron's words of 'God bless you and give you sustaining strength, my child!' seemed to inspire me with new courage for what was to come.

Soon the officer of the guard returned. The terrible bar was placed in the door, and I did not again enjoy the privilege of speaking with the mother of Jackson, neither was I allowed to minister to her comfort. She was kept in a room without fire or lights, the weather being very cold, until about twelve o'clock at night, when she was released.

Jackson had been one of the first victims of this war of aggression. He was a resident of Alexandria, Va. Before the occupation of that city by the Yankee forces, a marauding party under Ellsworth, a New York fireman and *desperado*, strayed into Alexandria one morning, about daylight, when Ellsworth, seeing the Virginia State flag floating from Jackson's house, detached himself from his party, and rushed into the house to tear it down.

Jackson was roused from sleep in time to kill the daring ruffian who had thus violated his rights, and was himself murdered a short time afterwards, under circumstances of great barbarity, by the remainder of the gang, who then spread themselves through the city, plundering and committing outrages upon women of respectability. For this four of their number were condemned to be shot, but their escape was subsequently connived at by the authorities.

A few days after this, a Miss Poole or Stewart was brought in.

On the 16th day of November, I received a visit from my sister, Mrs. James Madison Cutts, and my niece, the Honourable Mrs. Stephen A. Douglass, accompanied by Colonel Ingolls, U. S. A.—the permit to see me making the presence of an officer during the interview obligatory, and limiting it to fifteen minutes. I had been so ruthlessly debarred communication with my kind, that I had long since arrived at the conclusion, that all human kindness had taken flight, along with my brethren of the South, and left this Godforsaken city of Washington, with its unfortunate *détenue*, at the mercy of the merciless Abolitionists.

Colonel Ingolls earnestly recommended my '*graceful submission*' to the Government, and kindly offered to mediate in my behalf with Secretary Seward.

I declined this amiable counsel and proffer of aid as inconsistent with my own feelings and derogatory to my honour.

I had now been three months a prisoner, with no charge preferred against me, or reason assigned for the illegal act; and I determined to address a respectful letter to Mr. Seward, the Secretary of State, on the subject, hoping to obtain some elucidation of a matter certainly of personal interest to me. This I did on the 17th of November. I also

67

sent a copy of this letter to my friends at Manassas, with no idea or intention, however, of its ever being given to the public, and I confess that at first, I was deeply chagrined at the circumstance. But when I afterwards knew the anger and annoyance of the Abolitionists at having the secrets of their prison-house laid bare, I became perfectly satisfied of the superior wisdom of my friends in giving it publicity. As a part of my story, I subjoin the letter:—

Washington: November 17, 1861.
398, 16th Street.

Hon. Wm. H. Seward, Sec. of State.

Sir—For nearly three months I have been confined a close prisoner, shut out from air and exercise, and denied all communion with family and friends.

"Patience is said to be a great virtue," and I have practised it to my utmost capacity of endurance.

I am told, sir, that upon your *ipse dixit* the fate of citizens depends, and that the sign-manual of the ministers of Louis XIV. and XV. was not more potential in their day than that of the Secretary of State in 1861.

I therefore most respectfully submit that on Friday, August 23rd, without warrant or other show of authority, I was arrested by the detective police, and my house taken in charge by them: that all my private letters and papers of a life-time were read and examined by them: that every law of decency was violated in the search of my house and person, and by the surveillance over me.

We read in history that the poor Marie Antoinette had a paper torn from her bosom by lawless hands, and that even a change of linen had to be effected in sight of her brutal captors. It is my sad *experience* to record even more revolting outrages than that, for during the first days of my imprisonment, whatever necessity forced me to seek my chamber, a detective stood sentinel at the open door. And thus, for a period of seven days, I, with my little child, was placed absolutely at the mercy of men without character or responsibility; that during the first evening a portion of those men became brutally drunk, and boasted in my hearing of the *nice times* they expected to have with the female prisoners, and that rude violence was used towards a servant girl during that first evening. For any show of decorum afterwards practised towards me I was indebted to the detective called Captain Dennis.

In the careful analysis of my papers I deny the existence of a line that I had not a perfect right to have written or to have received. Freedom of speech and of opinion is the birth-right of Americans, guaranteed to us by our charter of liberty—the Constitution of the United States. I have exercised my prerogative, and have openly avowed my sentiments. During the political struggle I opposed your Republican party with every instinct of self-preservation. I believed your success a virtual nullification of the Constitution, and that it would entail upon us all the direful consequences which have ensued. These sentiments have doubtless been found recorded among my papers, and I hold them as rather a proud record of my sagacity.

I must be permitted to quote from a letter of yours, in regard to "Russell of the *London Times*" which you conclude with these admirable words: "Individual errors of opinion may be tolerated, so long as good sense is left to combat them."

'By way of illustrating *theory* and *practice*, here am I—a prisoner in sight of the executive mansion—in sight of the Capitol, where the proud statesmen of our land have sung their pagans to the blessings of our free institutions. Comment is idle. Freedom of speech, freedom of thought, every right pertaining to the citizen, has been suspended by what, I suppose, the President calls a *"military necessity."* A blow has been struck by this total disregard of all civil rights against the present system of government far greater in its effects than the severance of the Southern States. The people have been taught to contemn the supremacy of the law, to which all have hitherto bowed, and to look to the military power for protection against its decrees. A military spirit has been developed which will only be subordinate to a *military dictatorship*. Read history, and you will find that the causes which bring about a revolution rarely predominate at its close, and no people have ever returned to the point from which they started. Even should the Southern States be subdued, and forced back into the Union (which I regard as impossible, with a full knowledge of their resources), a different form of government will be found needful to meet the new developments of national character. There is no class of society, no branch of industry, which this change has not reached, and the dull plodding methodical habits of the past can never be resumed.

You have held me, sir, to a man's accountability, and I therefore claim the right to speak on subjects usually considered beyond a woman's ken, and which you may class as *"errors of opinion"* I offer no excuse for this long digression, as a three months imprisonment, without formula of law, gives me authority for occupying even the precious moments of a Secretary of State.

My object is to call your attention to the fact, that during this long imprisonment I am yet ignorant of the causes of my arrest; that my house has been seized and converted into a prison by the Government; that the valuable furniture it contained has been abused and destroyed; that during some period of my imprisonment I have suffered greatly for want of proper and sufficient food. Also, I have to complain that more recently a woman of bad character—recognised as having been seen in the streets of Chicago as such, by several of the guard—calling herself Mrs. Onderdunk, was placed here in my house in a room adjoining mine.

In making this exposition, I have no object of appeal to your sympathies. If the justice of my complaint and a decent regard for the world's opinion do not move you, I should but waste time to claim your attention on any other score.

'I may, however, recall to your mind that but a little while since you were quite as much proscribed by public sentiment here, for the opinions and principles you held, as I am now for mine. 'I could easily have escaped arrest, having had timely warning. I thought it *possible* that your *statesmanship* might prevent such a proclamation of weakness to the world as even the fragment of a once great Government turning its arms against the breasts of women and children. You have the power, sir, and may still further abuse it. You may prostrate the physical strength, by confinement in close rooms and insufficient food. You may subject me to harsher, ruder treatment than I have already received; but you cannot imprison the soul. Every cause worthy of success has had its martyrs. The words of the heroine Corday are applicable here: *"C'est le crime qui fait la honte, et non pas l'echafaud."* My sufferings will afford a significant lesson to the women of the South, that sex or condition is no bulwark against the surging billows of the *"irrepressible conflict."*

The "*iron heel*" of power may keep down, but it cannot crush out, the spirit of resistance in a people armed for the defence of their rights; and I tell you now, sir, that you are standing over a crater whose smothered fires in a moment may burst forth.

It is your boast that thirty-three bristling fortifications surround Washington. The fortifications of Paris did not protect Louis Philippe when his hour had come.

In conclusion, I respectfully ask your attention to this my protest, and have the honour to be, &c., &c., &c.,

Rose O'N. Greenhow.

CHAPTER 7

New Trials

The contest between the different divisions of the Abolitionists for the spoils was now carried on with quite as much heat and bitterness as had ever characterised the discussions of the two great sectional parties upon the vital questions of constitutional rights.

M'Clellan had been brought forward as a necessary expedient for the removal of Scott, without any idea, however, of foisting him permanently upon the party. But he had taken root amidst the less ultra portions of it, and, from having been a tool in the first place, now stood defiantly at the head of a party of his own, who clamorously supported his pretensions.

The Abolition Government did not, however, at this time desire to crush; they merely wished to clip the wings of the eaglet they had hatched, to prevent his soaring too high. His mission had been only half accomplished. General Scott, although virtually suspended from all power, still stood legally as Lieutenant-General of the Republic and Commander-in-Chief of its armies—their blandishments and slights had alike failed in inducing him to retire. He still held on, his vanity in some degree blinding him to the humiliation of his position.

Nominally commander-in-chief, he merely served to confuse the war councils by the exercise of his undoubted prerogative—that of originating, or approving military measures; and he had the mortification of seeing his recommendations very generally disregarded, which was the more remark able, from the fact of their being always of the most aggressive character towards the South; General Scott never having forgiven that section for rejecting him as their candidate for President in 1853.

The state of irritation in which he was kept at this time, brought on a prolonged attack of the gout, and the scenes which often took place were described as ludicrously tragical for the younger officers, who were obliged to approach him officially.

He had in reality no friends. His arbitrary manner had chilled the growth of affection, even in his days of power, and those who had endured his arrogance for personal advantage, now that his star was set, addressed themselves to other patrons; and the old hero, who had borne himself loftily on a hundred battlefields, but who had at last sullied the glory of his proud deeds by ranging himself under the Abolition banner, to trample under foot human rights, was now reaping the bitter fruits, in the contempt and indignity of the party for whom he had foresworn his birth-right. Wolsey's celebrated monologue was doubtless often recalled to his memory, for truly in his *extremity had he been left to the mercy of his enemies.*

The political cauldron at Washington at this time presented a curious spectacle. Fremont had already been brought forward as a rival to M'Clellan. He was supported by the more violent of the Abolitionists, with Francis P. Blair as his sponsor, who, skilled in all the tortuosities of political intrigue, was admirably adapted to the position, and perhaps was the only living, man who could have galvanised Fremont from the condition of obscurity into which he had collapsed, after his defeat as the Republican candidate for President in 1857.

Whilst the feud raged with all imaginable bitterness between the friends of the different partisan chiefs, M'Clellan was devoting himself, with a zeal worthy of a better cause, to the task of producing and organising an army out of the chaotic elements at his command; and I often looked on with sickening heart, at the energy and talent displayed by him, in surmounting the difficulties which beset him in the performance of his Herculean labours.

It has been long since determined as the first great rule for a commander, that he should acquaint himself thoroughly as to the capabilities of his army. It was this knowledge of his subordinates which distinguished Napoleon above all others. And M'Clellan seems, in this instance, to have been guided by the example of this illustrious man, and to have studied well the motley mass composing the grand army.

His conclusion was not very flattering—for he decided that their nervous organisation was incompatible with bayonet charges, and hand-to-hand encounters. Hence, he decided to make the war hereafter an artillery duel, as the only chance of success against *the dare-devil Southern chivalry, who were born to the use of arms.*

To this end he devoted all his energy and influence. The workshops of the North were set in motion, and science and skill were employed, to construct the most terrible projectiles and guns of largest range; and all for the purpose of forcing upon the *unappreciative* rebels the blessings of fraternal intercourse.

Perhaps never before in the world was so large an amount of ammunition destroyed in reviews, sham battles, and royal salutes. It was, however, a military necessity to accustom the men, as well as the horses, to stand fire. Scarcely one of these martial games went off without some accident, resulting in the loss of life, from the unskilful use of the terrible playthings. Intense satisfaction was, however, felt that the rebels had not these scientific adjuncts, and, in the next engagement, would be *hors de combat*.

I speak *ex cathedrâ* on this head, as I had the good fortune of having had *minutes* of M'Clellan's private consultations, and often extracts from his notes.

Mr. Seward at this time certainly established his claim to be considered the most adroit schemer of the day, and possessed in a rare degree the faculty of making the passions and prejudices of others sub serve his own ends.

This was demonstrated by his skilful management of the two great parties who were contending for military supremacy. His sliding scale was so admirably adjusted, that it was difficult to determine which party he favoured; and the truth was, he really attached himself to neither. No principle of his was involved in the fanatical crusade, only over-towering ambition; and, whichever party was likely to be the strongest, with that party will he ultimately throw himself. His bump of caution was also largely developed. He had raised the whirlwind, and he wished to shelter himself from the dangers of the '*irrepressible conflict*' until its fury had been spent.

The State Department, with its myriads of secret police, was a safe anchorage for the time being, as from thence he could ply the trade of the assassin or high way robber without paying the penalty of his crimes; for, by *the tinkling of that little bell* at the State Department, the citizen, north, east, or west, was at his mercy. Who will question the wisdom of the South, if even at the price of blood she resisted this unholy usurpation? Besides, if these measures should afterwards prove to have been unwise, and likely to interfere with any ulterior policy, which the chapter of accidents might develop, or political expediency recommend, he had always the *rail-splitter* for a scapegoat, as he of course was only acting by poor Lincoln's orders, who, by the way, was still under the tutelage of this man of varied parts, learning the polite usages of society.

The last vestige of civil and constitutional rights had been swept away. The *habeas corpus* was suspended throughout the dominions of Abraham the First; and the opinion of the venerable Chief Justice Taney, that eminent jurist and pure patriot, sustaining the legal tribunals, was set aside, and derided as an 'old woman's story.' The Legislature of Mary land, in the exercise of its sovereign prerogative, was prorogued, and the chief members of it conveyed to a Northern *bastille*; and the elections which subsequently came off were carried by driving from the polls, at the point of the bayonet, the legal voters, and substituting in their stead the hireling soldiers who infested every portion of the State: thus carrying out to the letter Senator Wilson's boast, *'We have set the iron heel on Maryland, and will crush out her boundary lines.'*

The city of Baltimore especially suffered in this onslaught against the laws of God and man. Her citizens were subject to the vilest indignities, the most prominent of whom were sent to someone of the strongholds of the tyrant, to be held, in many instances, as hostages for the good behaviour of their friends.

In despite of all this, with the city under the Federal guns, and the threat of being razed to the ground fulminated against her, and troops stationed throughout every portion of her—Baltimore has vindicated her claim to be called the unterrified, and, regardless alike of bribes or threats, her people have remained true to their instincts of honour and fealty to the South, and at peril of life, and liberty, and property, have ever extended their bountiful hand to shelter and assist their brethren in their hour of need. May Heaven cast its protecting shield over the noble generous city of Baltimore, and may she ere long be welcomed as one of the proudest gems of the Confederacy!

My own lot was now dismal enough. I felt almost as one who had passed the confines of eternity, and was looking on from another sphere upon the phantasmagoria in this. I seemed to hold no visible connection with the world. My friends and relatives were denied access to me, unless they belonged to the Black Republican ranks; and these were too prudent to risk their popularity by often availing themselves of the privilege, and only then under the pressure of that public opinion, which delighteth to decry their neighbours, for acting precisely as they would have done under similar circumstances.

Every means was employed which petty malice could devise to annoy me. It had been argued at first that, accustomed as I had been to a great deal of society and a very active life, to immure me in solitary imprisonment, without air or exercise, would soon reduce even my rebellious nature to submission. But, failing in this calculation, they now sought eternally some invasion of the few privileges left. For instance, in going from my chamber to the library, I would be often turned back until the officer in charge could go to the provost-marshal's, and my poor little girl was circumscribed to a few feet in front of the house, with an extra guard detached to watch her; and although I paid for my own laundry, it was often two or three creeks before I could send out my clothes. I was also obliged to buy my own lights, as the Government refused to allow me any.

Lieutenant Sheldon had been ordered under arrest, upon the charge of taking out communications for me, but was released by order of Seward.

My poor friend, Miss Mackall, with whom I kept up uninterrupted communication, in spite of all the vigilance, was untiring in her efforts to see me. In turn she implored every member of the Cabinet, and finally went to Lincoln, whose reception of her was characteristic of the man. He told her *'that she had had too much of my teachings already—that I had done more to damage, and bring his government into disrepute, than all the rest of the darned rebels together; and by G—d she should never see me again, if he could help it.'* This was fatally prophetic. I, however, sent him word that whilst he was engaged in the undignified task of reviling a prisoner, and that prisoner a woman, I was far more philanthropically occupied in making a new disguise for him to quit Washington in.

The dear girl was, however, almost heartbroken, for she loved me well, and made a last appeal to Provost-Marshal Andrew J. Porter, who, improving upon his master's brutality, indulged in a philippic against me, and concluded by rudely saying *'that he wondered why he had not already arrested her.'* She left him in tears, sobbed bitterly the way home, retired to her bed, from which she never after rose.

Lily wrote me that same evening a full account of the above, which reached me through my *medium* unsuspected. She grew rapidly worse, and in little more than a week from the above period she was dying. Throughout her illness she prayed to see me, and, a few hours before the fatal event, was so earnest in her prayer—saying, that *'she could not die happily unless she was gratified'*—that, although late at night, her mother sent to the provost-marshal. His reply was that he had not the authority to grant the permission, and that it rested with the Secretary of State, Seward. Thereupon I wrote to Seward, asking the privilege of visiting my dying friend, subject to any restriction he might impose. His reply was forwarded to the provost-marshal, a copy of which was sent me:—

The provost-marshal will please inform Mrs. Greenhow that, in consequence of her correspondence with the general commanding the armies now besieging Washington, her request to visit the house of Mrs. Mackall cannot be complied with, as it would be an interference with military arrangements, &c.
(Signed)   Wm. H. Seward.

And so, my darling faithful friend was laid in her grave, and the cold earth shut out her beautiful loving face for ever from my eyes. I could not then weep; but I prayed that the God of Justice would, in his hour of need, deny the heartless '*charlatan*' that mercy which he, dressed in his brief authority, had denied to me.

Captain Averil's congenial services in the Police Department were at last rewarded by promotion, which transferred him to a new field of action, and he was succeeded by Captain M Millen, whose gentlemanly conduct afforded a striking contrast. On assuming his position, he wrote me a most respectful and kind letter, offering any service not inconsistent with his duty as an officer of the United States; and, although his acts were always guided by the most fastidious loyalty to his own Government, he was ever delicate and deferential in the performance of his disagreeable duty.

He was severely reprimanded on more than one occasion for being too lenient—in other words, too gentlemanly—and finally my letters, received or written, which had been submitted to him for examination, were transferred to the detective Dennis, who, in order to seem vigilant in proportion to his former stolidity, returned me the simplest note, as being offensive to the *canaille* of the provost-marshal's office.

I was about this time, the last of November, quite ill, from the close confinement and insufficiency of food. Dr. M Millen, a brother of Captain M Millen, was allowed to attend me, and he ordered that more palatable and nutritious food should be supplied me, which was done for a few days; but on discovering that it was furnished at the cost of Lieutenant Sheldon, I refused to receive it, and got on as well as I could upon crackers and cheese, which my faithful maid would contrive to procure for me.

I shall ever retain the most grateful recollection of Dr. M Millen's gentle humane kindness, as well as that of his brother Captain M Millen. The conduct of these two formed a striking contrast to the bestial natures by whom I had been surrounded, and who had control of my liberty and life.

Dr. M Millen was never but once after this allowed to visit me, and then in the presence of an officer, and his conversation strictly limited to his medical enquiry and prescription. An idiosyncrasy common to the Abolition dynasty was, that I exercised some spell over all who approached me, whose natures were not brutalised.

The peculations of Simon Cameron, the Secretary of War, had now assumed such colossal dimensions, and the onslaught against him by those who had not been so favoured by opportunity were so bitter, that the Government at Washington were seriously embarrassed. They had been, of course, aware of all this for months. Hence it was not peculation, but the inconvenience of the discovery and consequent publicity, which now disturbed Mr. Lincoln and his Ministry; and a reasonable doubt may here be expressed as to whether the whole Government were not committed to practices equally nefarious.

Mr. Seward had in the beginning, upon the formation of the Cabinet, made the appointment of Cameron a *sine quâ non*; so, he still sustained him with great warmth. Cameron, although an uneducated man, of mediocrity of intellect, was gifted with wonderful accumulative faculties; but, unlike most men who are endowed with this peculiar talent, he dispensed his money with a princely hand for the attainment of his ends, and there is no doubt but that the astute Secretary of State, Mr. Seward, had often experienced the benefit of the financiering talent of his friend.

One of the charges made and substantiated against Cameron was, that he had drawn pay and rations and equipment for 86,000 men more than had ever been mustered into the service, and that in every contract made by the War Department, whether for purchase of munitions of war or clothing for the soldiers, his profits had been upon a like gigantic scale.

Cameron's friends had claimed for him, in the original cast of the Cabinet, to be made Secretary of the Treasury, as affording the widest scope for the expansion of his genius. But the north-eastern wing of the Abolitionists, headed by Sumner and Wilson, opposed this with great vehemence, indulging in animadversions not very flattering, and brought forward Chase in opposition, when a very animated contest began between the partisans of each, the conclusion of which it was difficult to foresee.

From an unexpected quarter of the House, however, a pacificator arose 'to pour oil upon the troubled waters' of Abolitiondom. Mr.
Wigfall, of Texas, a United States senator, in his place said, addressing
himself to Mr. Cameron—who was also a senator—'Hearken unto
the counsels of thine enemy. It is said that you are about to assume the
portfolio of the Treasury Department. It is a mistake. With war comes
the necessity for large supplies and big contracts. I would advise you
to take the War Department, as best suited to you,' and fortified his
advice by erudite and apt quotations.

Whether Mr. Cameron was influenced by this well-timed advice
I know not; but it is a remarkable coincidence that his claims to the
first position were soon after withdrawn, and he subsided quietly into
the War Department.

A Congressional Committee was appointed to investigate these
and other malpractices against the National Treasury. But long before
they had fairly entered upon their labours, Cameron had been sent
as Minister Plenipotentiary to the Court of Russia. The Government
by this act showed as reckless a disregard for international courtesy, as
for its own national dignity, and manifested, more clearly than vol-
umes could have done, the character it was hence forward to maintain
amongst the nations of the earth.

For here was a man—driven ignominiously from the councils of
the nation by the force of public opinion, for the meanest form of corruption—sent as a representative of that nation, at one of the haughti-
est Courts of Europe. The Government itself entertained doubts of his
reception; and Cameron did not set out on his mission until they had
received satisfactory assurances on the subject.

CHAPTER 8

Fremont and Other Things

Fremont, in his administration of the department of the West, appears to have followed closely the precedent established by the Apostolic Simon in the War Department. Charges of an astounding nature were sent on to Washington against him of malfeasance in office—in short, the old California charges of peculation, favouritism in the giving of contracts, and general reckless extravagance. He had also proved himself to be utterly incompetent in a military point of view; and this even his most zealous partisans were obliged to admit. Consequently, his removal was loudly demanded.

No one who has followed the course of this adventurous aspirant for fame, will be surprised at any phase of his destiny. And as he has been brought forward conspicuously before the eyes of the world, it may not be amiss to give a slight sketch of his origin and antecedents.

Like many of the soldiers of fortune whose names have been emblazoned on the scroll of fame in the Old World, he is entitled to the *bar sinister* on his shield. Fremont *Père* was a French dancing-master, and taught the graceful art in the city of Richmond, about the year 1812 or 1814, to most of the *belles* and *beaux* of that period. The celebrated Miss Maria Mayo—afterwards Mrs. General Scott—was one of his pupils, and my husband, as a little boy, had the benefit of his instruction.

This worthy son of *la belle France* was not content with the golden harvest he could legitimately reap in the exercise of his professional skill, but essayed his talents in another field, and soon made himself master of the situation, and bore off in triumph a Mrs. Pryor, the wife of an old and respectable citizen of Richmond, who, by the way, took a most philosophical view of the domestic calamity, and, instead of pursuing with fire and sword the enterprising Frenchman, left him in peaceful possession of the truant fair, and took to himself a more congenial helpmate. The romantic pair had winged their flight to Charleston, in which city he resumed the practice of his profession; and our hero, John Charles Fremont, was the fruit of this auspicious conjunction.

Some of the citizens of Charleston took great interest in young Fremont, who was educated at their expense and afterwards sent to West Point, where he graduated, without, however, giving any indications of extraordinary capabilities, and was, some years afterwards, appointed as assistant to Mr. Nicholet, in his scientific explorations and surveys; and here even he was regarded more for his methodical industry than for genius. He was a good draftsman, and, after Mr. Nicholet's death, was employed to work out the result of his labours, which he did with accuracy and skill. Fremont had meanwhile married the daughter of the Honourable Thomas Hart Benton, who after a few years assumed his guardianship, and launched him on his career.

By Benton's influence he was sent to explore the route across the Rocky Mountains to California, arriving there as the war with Mexico broke out; and there is no doubt that in the illegal and high-handed measures of which he was guilty, and the extraordinary assumption of power by him, he but acted strictly under the instruction of Benton, who expected himself to be sent to Mexico with vice regal powers, as he happily said in the Senate, with '*the sword in one hand, and the purse in the other.*'

This scheme was exploded too soon for success, and the bitter denunciation of it by all parties in the Senate convinced the Administration that it was useless to propose it for their ratification. But the failure, from whatever cause, drew upon the administration of Mr. Polk the antagonism of Benton from that period.

The failure of Benton's scheme operated very injuriously upon Fremont. The commander of the department of California, General Kearney, who was a most generous and high-toned officer, at first remonstrated with him upon the illegality of his proceedings, but failing to produce any effect, suspended and sent him to Washington under arrest for trial, where he arrived more with the air of a hero than one charged with high crime and misdemeanour.

★★★★★★★★★★

General Kearney died some years since at St. Louis from the effects of disease contracted in Mexico, and must not be confounded with the Yankee General Phil. Kearney, who was killed in Virginia on attempting to escape, after having given up his sword as a prisoner of war.

★★★★★★★★★★

The court convened at Washington for the trial of Fremont was composed of officers of the highest grade, General Kearney being himself president of the court. Since the days of Warren Hastings, perhaps no court had ever been invested with so much interest. It was crowded each day by high officers of the Government and other friends of the accused. Colonel Benton was allowed extraordinary latitude in the defence, and at times browbeat or threatened the various members composing the court, or the witnesses.

In short, the whole power of the Administration was employed to screen the criminal, and even private courtesies to the members of the court by those connected with the Government were discouraged. I was severely remonstrated with by a high official, upon the occasion of receiving General Kearney and the other members of the court at dinner.

Notwithstanding the extraneous pressure brought to bear upon it, the court maintained a dignified impartiality in the exercise of its judicial functions, giving the accused the benefit of all that could be adduced in his favour, and not deterred by the array of power and influence from pronouncing judgment according to the proofs before them. So, after an arduous and exciting trial, which lasted several weeks, the court found Fremont guilty upon every specification, and recommended that he should be severely reprimanded, and struck from the rolls of the army. The evidence, which is on file in the War Department at Washington, was so conclusive, and the charges of so flagrant a character, that the sentence was obliged to be confirmed. Mr. Polk subsequently, however, reappointed him: but Fremont refused to accept the executive clemency, knowing that he would be tabooed by the army.

Shortly after he returned to California, and on her admission as one of the States of the Federal Union, he was selected by the Governor as one of the persons to represent her in the United States Senate. He drew the short term: consequently, his legislative functions were only exercised for the space of three or four months, and so little did he impress the people, as to his capacity for the political arena, that although he sought, with great pertinacity, the renewal of the honour, he was never after able to achieve it.

Fremont had managed, during his first military sojourn in California, to *establish a claim* to the celebrated Marriposa Grant; and he now proposed to build an *adobe* house upon a portion of it, and to settle himself there as a *ranchero*. It was at this time that I saw him in San

Francisco, and spoke with him upon the subject. He seemed really to long for the primitive life he had marked out, and confessed himself utterly unsuited for the part he had been appointed to play upon the world's great stage—in which opinion I heartily concurred.

He did not long, however, enjoy his Arcadian existence, Messrs. Palmer, Cook, & Co. being the evil spirits who tempted him from his retirement to the turmoils of life again.

The above-mentioned firm of Palmer, Cook, & Co. were bankers of San Francisco, and the *bonâ fidé* proprietors of the Marriposa, owning three-fourths of it, whilst Fremont represented one-fourth, subject to heavy mortgages upon it, for moneys advanced by them.

The Marriposa was certainly a most royal demesne, of incalculable mineral wealth; but, like the treasures described in Aladdin, locked in the bowels of the earth, until the skill of the magician was employed to draw them forth.

It was too vast and costly an undertaking for individual enterprise, and it was consequently resolved by the parties interested to enlist European capitalists in the plan for working the mines, and otherwise developing its resources. Companies were formed in England to that end, which were to be chartered, and stocks issued, &c. It was scarcely secondary in magnitude to the famous Mississippi scheme.

Fremont was supplied with ample funds, and sent to Europe as the agent of the *projet*; and, in order to give *éclat* to his mission, these speculators resolved to nominate him as the Republican candidate for the Presidency, having no end in view but the inflation of their *bogus* stock, and ultimate pecuniary advantage.

Not content with the political *prestige* they had given him, those able financiers resolved to make him also appear as the richest man in the world. Circumstantial statements of his daily income, of an incalculable amount, were published simultaneously in New York, Paris, and London. Rare gems, of great size and value, were said to be found in the mineral regions of the Marriposa—amongst them, emeralds of such remarkable beauty, as to throw into the shade the crown jewels of Europe. These were advertised as having been set for Mrs. Fremont. In short, the Monte Christo of Dumas' creation was not the possessor of such countless riches as was this agent of a wholesale swindling firm.

Meanwhile the Abolitionists resolved to accept the candidate which chance had furnished them, to try the strength of their party, of which they had no approximate idea. Charles Francis Adams (now United States Minister to England) had been nominated with that object some years before at Chicago, but the result had demonstrated such a lamentable minority, that no prominent man was willing to risk his prospects of future success, by allowing his name to be used. Consequently, the whole strength of the Abolition party, by way of experiment, was concentrated upon Fremont; and, although the constitutional party triumphed in the election of their candidate, they were filled with dismay and grave misgivings for the future, at the formidable front which the *higher law* party presented, who, in their turn, were surprised at their own strength. And from that hour the Federal Government was doomed, and James Buchanan destined to be the last President of the United States. It was after this defeat of the Abolitionists, that the terrible poisoning scheme was attempted.

The Marriposa humbug exploded, and Fremont was dropped by the party who had temporarily used him, and suffered to relapse into poverty and obscurity, until the revolution again brought him upon the surface.

The current of my story has been somewhat impeded by this long narrative. Fremont's removal from the command of the department of the West had been determined on at Washington. Mrs. Fremont came on herself to take counsel of F. P. Blair, and, if possible, delay the execution of the sentence. But the exertions of that clever lady produced no visible effect in her husband's favour, although they fired the zeal of her ancient servitor and friend, who redoubled his exertions, but also fruitlessly.

Blair laboured under the hallucination, that his own posthumous fame was indissolubly connected with that of Thomas Hart Benton, and that this was in some way mysteriously associated with the fulfilment of Benton's prophecy as to Fremont's future greatness. Hence, he laboured to bring about its accomplishment, even though he encountered the antagonism of his own sons, who violently opposed Fremont—regardless of the injunction, that a house divided against itself must fall.

Blair had also a private score to settle with the Southern chivalry. It had been by the influence of the Southern members of the democratic party, that he had been deprived of his position as Government organ, and consequent loss of the splendid pickings from the national crib. So, in order that he might wreak his vengeance upon that section, he was willing to tear down the walls of the temple itself.

Mrs. Fremont was treated with but scant ceremony by the authorities at Washington. After many days of delay, she addressed a short but haughty note to President Lincoln, demanding an answer to her communication, in order, as she stated, 'that she might return to her husband and children;' and the reply which this elicited from President Lincoln, was as curt as her own. So, she returned West from her bootless mission at Washington, and was received at St. Louis with regal honours—a carriage and four awaited her, in which she was escorted by a troop of cavalry, with bands of music and bonfires, to her husband's quarters. So said the veracious chroniclers of the triumphal entry.

Meanwhile the fiat had gone forth, and Halleck was appointed to the management of the department of the West, which Fremont had so lately mismanaged, having, however, greatly the advantage over his predecessor, in being of the genuine Abolition party.

Edwin M. Stanton had been appointed to succeed Cameron in the War Department. The Abolition Congress was again in session, and its work of proscription renewed. General Scott held on with a tenacity only equalled by that of Daniel Webster during President Tyler's administration. But he was just now the fifth wheel to the Abolition wagon, and seriously clogged their movements, and they resolved to adopt measures for the accomplishment of his removal, which even they had shrunk from save in the last extremity. So, charges of treason were trumped up, and articles of indictment actually prepared. This last feather broke the camel's back, and he succumbed.

The first step accomplished, it was determined to indulge the old man's avarice to the extent of their power. The public mind was prepared for what was to follow by daily statements of his sinking health, which alarmingly increased.

> His resignation was prepared. Lincoln and his Cabinet attended at his lodgings to hear it read, which being received, Lincoln, "*standing*" read to him the gracious act, securing to him for life his pay, and all the perquisites he had hitherto enjoyed.

After this, General Scott took a solemn leave of Lincoln, and eulogised his patriotism *as second only to Washington's*. That same afternoon he departed for New York, and gave his parting benediction to 'the young general, who, with his staff, *in a pelting rain, accompanied him to the train, all dressed in black, like the Knight of the Raven Plume.*'

Mr. Secretary Seward and Mr. Secretary Chase—with the mockery of honour—accompanied him to New York. Telegrams from each stopping-point gave desponding accounts of the health of the illustrious exile from power and place. At last, he reached New York, *saw only Mr. John Van Buren*, and embarked, after a few days, for France. Arriving there in due course of time, he seized upon the pretext of the Mexican and French *imbroglio*, and returned, in the next steamer but one, to New York, where he lives in elegant state upon the price of his honour—*sic transit*. (This account has been almost entirely taken from the Government organ.)

The public were for a little while amused with the rumour that the defunct hero was to be sent as special ambassador to Mexico, but that, of course, was only a *canard*.

The espionage over me was now greater than at any previous period. Life was almost unendurable; an undefined nameless terror was stealing over me of something more dark and terrible than I had yet been exposed to. This feeling may be appreciated, when it is remembered that I was a defenceless woman, in the hands of a party which had shrunk from no crime to carry out its ends. I was constantly assailed in its papers; and some of my former friends and connections sought, instead of protecting me, to palliate and excuse the cowardly attacks.

My anxiety was not allayed by receiving a secret communication to be on my guard, '*as an infernal plot was hatching against me;*' at the same time enclosing extracts from Abolition papers, stating that I '*had lost my mind, and that it was rumoured that the Government intended to remove me to a private lunatic asylum.*' My blood freezes even now, when I recall my feelings at the reception of this communication, and I wonder that I had not gone mad.

My equanimity was by no means restored at this time by the announcement that the Surgeon-General of Pennsylvania Volunteers, and several others, desired to pay their respects to me. I received him with smiles on my lips, and fear and hate in my heart. (I do not remember the name, as my journal was at a later period taken from me.) But he was very courteous, and apologised for intruding upon me, by saying that '*he had been most desirous of seeing a lady who had become so celebrated in the eyes of the world.*' Our conversation was spirited, and upon the all-exciting topics of the times, in which I bore my part as an uncompromising rebel; and, although the frightful idea was ever present, that this man had been probably sent for the purpose of dooming me to a madhouse, I jested lightly, defiantly, with him.

Finally, he said to me, 'Do you never find your mind giving way under this close solitary confinement?'

86

I replied, 'Do you see any indications of aberration of mind?'

He answered, 'Madam, you fill me with admiration and astonishment, not only by your cheerfulness, but from the wonderful knowledge you have of what is going on! I had never believed that any person could rise so superior to surrounding circumstances. For I know,' he continued, 'that the Government has placed such an estimate upon your capacity, as to resort to measures of unusual harshness in your imprisonment.'

'Well,' I said, 'Doctor, I defy their skill to thwart any purpose of mine; and so far from succumbing, I never felt my mind clearer or more capable of mischief against your government than at this moment.'

The visit, after some further conversation, terminated; and I know not whether I was indebted to this gentleman, but I heard no more of the mad house scheme.

The officer of the guard, Lieutenant Sheldon, was not now allowed to hold personal communication with me. The guard were set as spies upon each other, and upon him. They were ordered not to speak to me or answer questions, under penalty of severe punishment. One day a guard, by name Hebburn, gave me some ordinary information. Miss Poole, hearing him, sent for the corporal of the guard, and reported it. The poor man was dealt with very harshly in consequence.

She also reported that my little child received some communication for me on the pavement, which was untrue, and the poor child was, from that time, doomed to as severe imprisonment as I now endured. (Lieutenant Sheldon subsequently informed me that Miss Poole had made this statement.)

This was, perhaps, my hardest trial—to see my little one pining and fading under my eyes for want of food and air, without the power to avert the terrible doom which seemed impending. The health and spirits of my faithful maid also began to fail, and I felt often tempted to exclaim, 'My God, let this bitter cup pass from me!'

The winter had set in with unusual severity, and the heavens seemed in accord with the gloom of my own destiny. By reason of the inclemency of the weather, I was now deprived of my only remaining pleasure—that of receiving from *afar* the stealthy greeting of friends— stealthy for the reason that if seen to wave a hand towards my prison, arrest was sure to follow; the reign of terror being now at its height. No one, unless under similar circumstances, can realise the extent of this deprivation.

I remember, some years ago, when I was very young, being invited to meet the celebrated Italian exile Gonfallonieri, who had been a victim of Austrian despotism, and was for many years in solitary confinement as a state prisoner. No knowledge from the outer world ever reached his dungeon. Empires had changed their destiny, and kings had fallen. The great Napoleon had ended his mortal career at St. Helena. Charles X. had been hurled from the throne of France, and Louis Philippe reigned in his stead. Of this he knew nothing until he reached New York, a prisoner no longer, but exile from friends and fatherland.

I wept as I listened to his sad recital, and thanked God that my destiny had been cast in a land where crimes like this could never be committed.

I did not then foresee that the scourge of Black Republican rule was to come upon us, and sweep from the New World every vestige of civil rights and freedom, as had been often done in the Old.

M'Clellan, from having been lulled into a false security by the flatteries lavished upon him to that end, began now to realise all the difficulties of his position. The insensate cry of 'On to Richmond!' was again raised, and his judgment sought to be overruled as to the means by which that *feat* was to be accomplished.

M'Clellan had laboured hard to make his army the best appointed, and best disciplined, in the world; and, considering the heterogeneous materials he had to work upon, he certainly had effected marvels. The programme which he had marked out for himself was fully in accordance with the wisdom and foresight he had displayed in other respects. He under stood thoroughly the morale of his army, and that his only hope of success in invading the South was by overwhelming numbers.

But Seward and the other *Sachems* of Abolitiondom did not intend that M'Clellan should reap the substantial fruits which the success of his plans would have placed within his grasp. The object for which he had been inflated to his present eminence, had been fully accomplished. General Scott had as completely passed away from the public mind, as if his funeral dirge had been already sung. So, these '*carpet warriors*,' who had already slain their thousands by the stroke of their pens, addressed themselves seriously to the work of checkmating M'Clellan, and would, had they dared, have removed him from his ill-starred eminence.

M'Clellan had, however, succeeded in gaining the confidence, as I have said before, of a large party. It is true that he had done nothing, so far, to establish a claim to high consideration, having as yet performed no deeds of valour to entitle him to his laurel wreath, although his achievements in Western Virginia, in the early part of the campaign, had been absurdly exaggerated, as an excuse for his undue elevation. The popular voice, nevertheless, was in his favour, and cried loudly that he should be retained to carry out his programme.

His soldiers were attached to him, and any attempt to suspend him would have been attended with hazardous results, until that army had been again demoralised by the hardships and exposure of another unsuccessful campaign.

Had M'Clellan possessed the moral courage at this time to have boldly stated *his ultimatum*, and given in his resignation in case it was not complied with, he would have triumphed temporarily over his adversaries, who were not prepared to push things to this extremity. They still believed Washington to be threatened by Beauregard, and, amidst the feasting and revelry of the Capitol, they were tremblingly alive to the idlest rumour of an advance. The fortifications were being hourly strengthened and extended, and large quantities of provisions and other stores were distributed in the basement of the Capitol, and public buildings, and throughout other portions of the city, in preparation for a siege.

The public archives had been removed to Philadelphia in the beginning of August, a short time after the battle of Manassas, when the panic was at its height, thereby creating great fright in the city of brotherly love, as the *sealed yellow cases*, in which those important State papers were conveyed, were supposed to be the Yankee dead from the disastrous plains of Manassas. So not only were the imaginations of the Philadelphians disturbed by the fear of the grim ghosts of the unassoilzied dead, but pestilence also; and, in order to allay the excitement consequent thereupon, it became necessary to make an official announcement of the character of the freight contained in the *yellow cases*.

Unimportant as this incident may seem, it is still a part of the record of the days of panic.

CHAPTER 9

Diablerie

As if for the purpose of annoying me at this time, the few short and unsatisfactory letters which I sent through the provost-marshal's office were, upon one pretext or another, objected to. Upon one occasion I wrote to a friend to '*tell Cousin Lucy that I had firm reliance upon Divine Providence:*' That was returned to me, with a note stating that '*all names must be written in full, and no ambiguous expressions used.*' I thereupon, by way of protest, wrote to suggest that the provost-marshal should issue a printed circular, prescribing the formula to be used by prisoners, as I was gifted with no faculty to divine what he might consider *ambiguous*; that the only expression which could possibly be *incomprehensible* to him was that wherein I had expressed my reliance on *Divine Providence*; and that he recalled to my mind a circumstance which had occurred in a much more civilised land than this.

The British Parliament having, some years ago, instituted a commission to enquire into the moral condition of the colliers, a learned divine, who formed part of that commission, reported on his return, in evidence of their state of moral ignorance, that on going to one of the largest collieries he asked, '*Does anyone know Jesus Christ HERE?*' That the question reverberated through the pit, and the answer came thundering back—'*No; we don't know him. He don't work here.*' A similar response would probably be elicited from the provost-marshal's office, as to a question of '*Divine Providence.*'

An order was also issued from the State Department, prohibiting me the purchase of the newspapers, or my being informed of their contents. This was in consequence of the publication of my letter to Mr. Seward. The utmost consternation prevailed as to the means by which it had reached Richmond, as it was not intended that the secrets of the prison-house should be blazoned to the world.

The *New York Herald* published my letter, with the following editorial critique:—

Mrs. Greenhow's Indignant Letter to Mr. Seward—We are indebted to the Richmond "Whig" for the pungent letter which we publish today of Mrs. Rose Greenhow to Mr. Seward, touching her late imprisonment in her own house in Washington, as a Secession emissary. Having been released and sent over into Secessia, she doubtless furnished a copy of the letter in question to the journal from which it is extracted. (I was not released, however, until more than six months after this period.) It is just such a philippic as one would expect, under the circumstances, from a spirited, dashing, active, and fearless female politician of the South Carolina school of Secession malignants. She complains bitterly of the rude and offensive behaviour of her gaolers; but she forgets that men thus employed are very seldom remarkable for the refinements and accomplishments, graces and gallantry of the fashion able circles of Washington.

She discourses fluently but flippantly upon the freedom of speech, and upon her right to exercise it, and upon the cruel tyranny of her imprisonment; but she forgets that while at large in Washington she was a dangerous agent of a hostile army besieging our national capital. Grant all the personal rights of freedom of speech and action which Mrs. Greenhow demands, in the midst of this great rebellion, and we may as well abolish our armies, and turn over the country to unrestrained ruffianism; for under this system of liberty we should all be at the mercy of ruffians and robbers.

In those gay Secession circles which ruled the Court and Cabinet at our Federal city under the diluted rose-water administration of Mr. Buchanan, Mrs. Greenhow was a bright and shining light. She had no doubt shared with that brilliant and charming coterie, of which Mrs. Slidell and Mrs. Gwin were the ruling spirits, that splendid Secession idea of the easy occupation of Washington by Jeff. Davis, his camp, Cabinet, Congress, and Government, and that under this new regime the fascinating coterie afore said, including Mrs. Greenhow, would be exalted to a higher and an indefinite reign of beauty and glory. Mr. Seward, however, interposed like an evil magician, and with a wave of his powerful wand destroyed all these beautiful castles in the clouds. And so, we can excuse this piquant and pungent letter of Mrs. Greenhow. Even the great Napoleon, philosopher as he was, when cooped up at St. Helena could not refrain from scolding.'

On the 20th December, the Judge-Advocate, Colonel Key, came to call upon me. I had seen him several times before. There was a certain *laissez-aller* about this officer very offensive to me. He was, or affected to be, very deaf, as an excuse for approaching very near in conversation. The second time I saw him, he attempted to take my hand, as he said, '*to find out whether I had ever done any work.*' I withdrew it, saying that my head had laboured more than my hands.

Upon this occasion, however, his manner was respectful and earnest. He expressed anxiety to serve me; said that he had thought my imprisonment *impolitic*; that he was opposed to the policy of imprisoning women; and that, although he came now without being officially empowered to speak with me on the subject of my release, he was free to tell me that he had held conversations with some of the heads of the Government on the subject, and that they were greatly embarrassed to know what to do with me.

I answered, 'Oh, yes. They dare not hang me; are afraid to release me; and would like to encourage me to escape, in order that they might catch me and spirit me away'—having in mind the effort made a short time previous to induce me to attempt to escape.

He smilingly continued: 'The Government have come to the conclusion that it is of no use to attempt to make terms with you; that between you and them it is, *Do your worst to the end of the war; and the only way left is to treat you as the British Government did Smith O'Brien—banish you.*' He then said quickly, 'What terms would you be willing to subscribe?'

My heart beat wildly, for even that chance gleam of freedom agitated me. I, however, crushed down the impulse—for I saw that he was watching me very narrowly—and answered, 'None, sir. I demand my unconditional release, indemnity for my losses, and restoration of my papers and effects.'

He said, 'These last I cannot undertake, for I know that your papers will not be given up; and all the effects of rebels will be confiscated. I may not,' he continued, 'be able to accomplish anything in regard to your personal freedom, as there is a very strong influence against you. But I think you had better let me make the best terms I can.'

I replied, 'Freedom is sweet; and, although I have suffered much, there are many things dearer to me, and I will not compromise a principle even though I am detained as a prisoner for the war—the sentence, I learn, already pronounced against me.'

He inclined his head, and then spoke of still greater hardships to which I might be exposed, and professed himself greatly interested in my situation. I told him that I would require time to think over all he had said, and that I was at the present wholly unprepared to terminate a conference upon the subject, and that I would desire him to call again. He requested me to write to him through the provost-marshal's office, as he could not venture to call otherwise, as it would subject him to the suspicion of Southern sympathies. This will serve as another illustration of that iron despotism which forbade even the exercise of ordinary humanity. This man was a native of Maryland, and paid the penalty of treason to his State by the suspicious vigilance of his new masters.

On Christmas-Day Mrs. Douglas sent, through the provost-marshal's office, a large cake and other little tokens to my little girl, which made her very happy and bright. Lieutenant Sheldon also, by a stretch of authority, allowed her to go out and join in the festivities of the day at the houses of several of her young friends. Other tokens of respect and affection reached me through less *orthodox* channels; and so, if the day was not a happy one, it was at least marked by no disagreeable incident—as if to contrast it with the dark ones immediately to follow.

On the 26th, I received a note by *my little bird*, warning me that an attempt would be made to remove me to a Northern prison that a telegram had been sent to Fort Warren, to hold in readiness a room for me there. At the same time, I was assured that I should be rescued in case this was done that my friends only awaited my orders—that my prison was watched by them day and night, and signals agreed upon, &c.

My house, which had been transformed into a government prison, now became a sort of Mecca. Strangers visiting Washington thronged to see the residence of so 'noted a rebel,' and the newspapers pandered to the greedy curiosity to know something of my habits and tastes. The apartments of the unfortunate Marie Antoinette were not more thoroughly scrutinised, or her occupations for the weary hours given with more minute details, than were mine.

The house was called Fort Greenhow. Photographs of it appeared in several of their illustrated papers, and their mimic *Punch, Vanity Fair,* devoted a number to me, wherein, with very heavy wit, it proved that I, a simple woman, had out witted Seward, and discomposed the whole Yankee nation.

Coarse abuse was ofttimes levelled against me, which they took care should reach my ear. These cowardly vituperations passed harmlessly by, as I had a proud consciousness of superiority, and regarded them as testimonials in favour of my devotion to the cause of my country's freedom.

Other prisoners were from time to time brought in, and generally of the lowest class, with the exception of Mrs. Eleanor Lowe, an English lady, whose son was in the Confederate service, and the Posey family of Maryland, who were most estimable people. These were, however, only detained for a few days, upon suspicion of giving signals to the Confederate Army across the Potomac.

On the 30th of December, a woman named Baxley was confined as a prisoner. She was arrested on the *Truce* boat, by reason of her garrulous boasting of having gone to Richmond to obtain a commission for her lover, one Dr. Septimus Brown, of having nuts from President Davis's table, and of instructions to open communication with my prison; being also, as she said, the bearer of a letter to me. All this, I need scarcely say, was the result of a disordered imagination, although it afforded a pretext for what was to follow. The conduct of this woman on arriving at the prison confirmed the impression entertained at the time of her arrest, of her being *non compos mentis*. She raved from early morn till late at night, in language more vehement than delicate. I was an involuntary listener to her cries and imprecations, and pity and disgust were often strangely commingled. My chief care was to prevent my child from hearing much that was unfit for her ear. But I felt the horrors of my position hourly increasing.

Occasional excitement was now produced in the prison by the real or affected faints of Miss Poole and this Mrs. Baxley—the premonitory symptoms being a loud cry, and heavy fall upon the floor of one or other, followed by the call of the sentinel on duty, of 'Corporal of the guard, No. 3!' This individual usually rushed to the rescue, accompanied by two or three of the stoutest sentinels, bayonet in hand—the officer of the guard bringing up the rear, with the judicial gravity of Sancho Panza, conspicuously flourishing a brandy bottle, that being the masculine panacea for all the ills of life.

On the 29th, I wrote again to the Honourable Wm. H. Seward, thinking that he had had time sufficient to digest the contents of my first letter, which, in consequence of its publication in the *New York Herald*, and other papers, formed the subject of conversation in all circles in Washington. Friend and foe united in ascribing to it a degree of literary merit to which it had no claim. I was amused at the various criticisms passed upon it by the *refined ladies* of President Lincoln's Court. They were horrified that I should have spoken so plainly of the infamies to which I had been exposed, although their sensibilities were not shocked at the fact that, in a Christian age, a lady should have suffered these outrages—only that she should proclaim them. This is but a fair sample of the morality of the 'New Regime.'

On the morning of the 5th of January, as I attempted to pass from my chamber to my library, I was startled, but not surprised, at finding a double guard stationed at my door, with instructions not to allow me to quit my chamber until Lieutenant Sheldon had returned from the provost-marshal's. Since the evening of the 26th, I had seen indications of some new tactics. The detective police had been in constant attendance for four or five days. Consequently, I was prepared for any extraordinary display of their inventive genius.

Miss Poole had been allowed unlimited range of the house at all hours of the day or night. This concession was purchased by surveillance over me. My child had been closely confined upon her representations, as was also my maid, and the attempt of several of the guard to communicate information to me had been likewise reported. All knowledge of the outer world which now reached me was in writing. Her room adjoining mine made it impossible for me to speak to anyone.

The newspapers reached me sometimes, in spite of the rigid prohibition. I, however, was obliged to destroy them as soon as read, for fear of their discovery bringing harm to those who furnished them.

The 'Government Organ,' which I received at this time, contained an article headed 'Daring attempt to rescue the dangerous rebel, Mrs. Greenhow.' It went on to say that, on the 27th, a cake had been brought to my house by a suspected party; that on examining it, a large number of Treasury notes were found concealed in it, together with a note describing a plot for my escape and conveyance into Virginia, the money sent being to bribe the guards; that so dangerous a person as I was should be conveyed to a place of greater security, and that the Government had determined to remove me to some one of the Northern bastilles, out of reach of my sympathising friends.

This was so absurd that, in spite of the danger it foreshadowed, I could not help being amused by it. I could now understand why double guards had been stationed all around the house, an additional force having been detailed for the purpose, and for several nights they had been under arms, with double cartridges served out to them. It was, of course, all for the purpose of giving plausibility to the cake story, and justification for the acts of villainy in contemplation. I had defied and exposed their infamous secret police system, every member of which hated me, and they now resorted to this clumsy device as a means of gratifying their malignant spite, as well as to inspire me with a wholesome dread for the future.

It is difficult to estimate properly the extent of the power and influence wielded by this corrupt organisation. It had so acted upon the nervous fears of Lincoln, Seward, M'Clellan, & Co., by the discovery of murderous plots which existed by virtue of their inventive genius only, as to acquire complete ascendency over them. A detective guard was appointed for the protection of each. The chief of police took precedence of everyone in obtaining audience, and had access to the representatives of the Government at any hour of the day or night. And there was no officer of the Government too high to dread their influence. General Stone, of the old United States Army, owed his arrest and disgrace to these creatures. In fact, they now were the power behind the throne, and their very names inspired terror, and were whispered with livid lips by the trembling victims within reach of their power.

The sound of my own voice now appeared strange to me, and I often read aloud, that I might not lose the power of modulating its tones.

I felt that a crisis in my destiny was rapidly approaching. On the evening of the 4th an order was given that the prisoners should not leave their quarters after six o'clock. This had clearly no reference to me, as I never went beyond my own apartments; but it confined Miss Poole to hers, whereupon she had one of those remarkable fainting fits which I have described before.

The officer of the guard now returned from the provost-marshal's, and the corporal came to announce to me that the prohibition had been removed, and I was at liberty to go to my library. I breakfasted with my child, and seated myself at my usual occupation for this hour—that of giving her lessons. By this time, I learned that a guard had been stationed inside of Miss Poole's room. I was very much shocked, for I could not imagine what the unfortunate woman had been doing to have brought this severity upon herself. I attempted to enter my chamber, and was told that I could not go into it. Hearing the sound of men's voices within, I readily comprehended that Mr. Seward's secret police were at work, in order to obtain the copy of the second letter I had written to him a few days before. But, as in the first instance, my copy had gone out simultaneously with the original, which was held back until that object had been accomplished.

I returned to the library, and destroyed all the papers which I feared to fall into their hands.

In about two hours the officer of the guard came to the library, looking as pale as marble, followed by the corporal and two of the guard, all armed—the officer having on his belt and sword, and the others with musket and bayonet. Looming in the distance were the shadows of those evil spirits, the detective Allen or Pinkerton, with several of his satellites. The officer of the guard touched his hat and said, 'Mrs. Greenhow, will you please walk downstairs?' I arose, and, after glancing around without speaking, obeyed. I believed that the detectives thought that I would resist, and therefore came prepared with brute force to execute their will, and I was resolved to give them no advantage over me by losing my temper.

But none can tell the effort it cost me to control myself. The most brutal of the guard had been selected for this morning's work. I was detained about an hour out of my apartments, when I was notified that I could return to them. I was fully prepared for what was to follow. The north window of the library had been sealed and nailed up, and my journal and every scrap of paper had been taken from my writing-desk and table; and, upon examining my wardrobe, I found that several valuable articles of clothing had been abstracted. Whether this had been done by the detectives or the guard, I am not prepared to say.

On the morning of the 6th, I sent to the officer of the guard to demand pen, ink, and paper; also, that I might be allowed to purchase the newspaper. He returned for answer that General Porter had ordered that I should not be allowed to have either. I sent a second time, to say that I wished to write to the Judge-Advocate, Colonel Key. Thereupon he sent me a single sheet of paper, and pen and ink. I wrote that same day to Colonel Key, stating that I was now prepared to hear what he had to say to me further upon the subject of my release. With a courtesy very remarkable for an *employé* of the Abolition Government, he came immediately on the receipt of my note, but appeared embarrassed and ill at ease.

He told me that circumstances had occurred since I last saw him which made him fear that he had lost all power to serve me. He asked me what proposition I had to make. I replied that in my last interview I had defined my position, and stated my *ultimatum*. He said it had been spoken of to send me North, but that it had been objected to on the ground that I might institute legal proceedings against the Government, which would give them some trouble. I replied, 'Which I should most unquestionably do.' He said, unfortunately the publication of my letter to Seward, and another couched in terms of still greater bitterness, had aroused great indignation against me, and he questioned whether the subject of my release would be now entertained.

I replied that I did not question his sincerity, as he had given me a strong reason—in the fact that he was going with M'Clellan into Virginia—in support of it; but I very much doubted whether the parties who had authorised him to speak on the subject with me had been honest originally in their intentions, but had rather designed through that means to obtain some indications from me. I then related the late domiciliary visit to which I had been subjected. Upon this he made no comment, but alluded enigmatically to the power arrayed against me, and left me, saying that he would return in a short time, after consultation with parties whom he would not name. He did return in about two hours, and gave me the very consolatory information that, on account of the '*dangerous extent of the knowledge I possessed,' it was deemed inexpedient to release me.* He refused to tell me whose influence had been exerted against me; but I already knew that it was Seward and M'Clellan, 'instigated by the detective Allen.'

CHAPTER 10

Record of Facts

From the rough notes in my possession, I am enabled to supply a copy of my letter to Seward of December 27th. By a fatality which it would not be safe to explain, the copy which I sent out never reached the hands for which it was designed:—

> Hon. Wm. H. Seward, Sec. of State, U.S.
> Washington, 398 Sixteenth Street.
> December 27.

Sir,—I wrote to you some five weeks since, and I am not surprised at receiving no response to my letter—for where all law is set at defiance, it is not to be supposed that the rules of good breeding shall be adhered to. Neither am I astonished that a letter addressed to the Secretary of State, containing a grave appeal to his humanity against gross outrages, should form the subject of conversation amongst his subordinates in their drunken orgies in bar-rooms and hotels. This new era has inaugurated new customs.

Aut Caesar aut nullus is said to be your motto. My object in addressing you is to bid you pause in this your onward march—to survey the ruin you have already wrought—and, if there be one latent spark of philanthropy still dormant in your soul, to kindle it in the cause of suffering humanity. For this cruel war lies at your door, and not at that of my brethren of the South.

In order to refresh your memory as to the errors you have committed, it is necessary that I should make a brief summary of the history of the past. We all know of the crusade which for years has been waged against the institutions of the South—beginning at Exeter Hall in England, re-echoed at Faneuil Hall in Boston, and from thence spreading like a pestilence throughout the whole North. The best talent was employed to decry the institution of slavery. Romance-writers exercised their inventive genius to draw thrilling pictures of its horrors. The pulpit lent its powerful aid, and fulminated the thunders of the Church in terms of burning eloquence, until a feeling of fanaticism was aroused rarely equalled in fury, and men rose to power only as they favoured the madness of the hour.

The political party at the North seized upon this fanatical element as a means for the realisation of its ambitious aspirations. All of its extraordinary assumptions were accepted as an integral of the *Chicago Platform*. You, Sir, were thrown aside as not being deeply enough committed to the John Brown raid (although you had subscribed to the Helper book) to be trusted as the standard-bearer, and a more facile chief chosen. And the battle-cry was—not the triumph of the Constitution, or the preservation of our glorious Union but— "Down with the institution of slavery in the South!" as a means to subjugate that section.

'Well, Sir, the battle was fought and won, by an overwhelming sectional majority in favour of the *"higher law"* party. The constitutional or Southern party, at the head of which stood Mr. Davis, the present President of the Confederate States, said, "Wait! Whilst a single plank of safety remains, let us stand by the government established by the wisdom of our fathers."

Congress met. The Southern members of took their seats, solemnly impressed with the obligation upon them to do all in their power to settle the questions at issue whilst there was yet time. Separate appeals were made to the dominant party, in both houses of Congress, and all the inevitable consequences of a failure to compromise the difficulties upon a firm basis were placed before them in strong but temperate language.

Various acts of legislation were attempted, such as the Crittenden resolutions, &c., but all voted down by your party. During the discussions upon these momentous questions, the Southern members participated with a gravity and freedom from excitement commensurate with the importance of the crisis it foreshadowed. Did the Abolition majority heed their cries for justice? No! The calmness of the Southern party was regarded as the paralysis of fear, and jeers were levelled at them, and threats made that if they did not "submit" to be ruled with a good grace, "their State organisations should be taken from them, and governors put over them from Massachusetts or Illinois." (From speech made in the Senate, by Senator Baker, of Oregon.)

And thus, the winter passed on, in vain and futile efforts upon the one side, and insolent and arrogant threats on the other.

You, Sir, when appealed to from your place in the Senate as the acknowledged Premier of the new President, for some declaration of policy calculated to allay the excitement, replied that, *"in two or three years, when this eccentric movement shall have passed away, you might favour some measure of compromise"*

The forbearance of the Southern party was not yet exhausted. On the 4th of March, President Lincoln took his seat, and they still hoped that he would recognise the gravity of the impending crisis, and give some guarantee which might allay the popular excitement. But he treated the matter with unbecoming levity—affected to see nothing extraordinary in the state of the country—proclaimed that *"there was nobody hurt"*—although he had reached the Capitol in disguise, and was inaugurated in the presence of an armed force greater than had ever assisted at the coronation of an Autocrat of the Russias.

Meanwhile, the Peace Congress, which had assembled in the city of Washington, was still sitting, and its session was consumed in unproductive discussion, carried on by the Abolitionists in a spirit of violence and intolerance never witnessed before, save in the National Assembly of France during the Reign of Terror. It finally adjourned without the agreement to a single measure of compromise, and the Southern members of it returned to their homes, with the conviction on their minds that there was nothing left for them but the unconditional surrender of their rights, or the last and final appeal of nations—to arms!

With a foresight worthy of imitation, South Carolina had already passed her ordinance of Secession.

The Virginia Convention had commenced its session in the city of Richmond on the 13th day of February. The ablest men in the State had been selected to represent her in that august body, and their deliberations were conducted with the patriot ism and wisdom of the councils of '76. They foresaw the devastating war which was before them—that Virginia was destined to be the battlefield—and, in the exercise of their solemn duty, they were impelled, in the name of common humanity, to do all in their power, short of the sacrifice of national honour, to delay the catastrophe until the passions of men had had time to cool, and in the hope of the sober reaction to follow. Hence, a majority of the Convention favoured the armed neutrality of the State, and opposed the ordinance of Secession.

Your party were well advised of the temper of the Convention, and determined to precipitate matters; for they had no wish for a peaceful solution of the difficulties, and resolved to kindle the torch of civil war at once. Your President was induced by yourself and the other ultra leaders to issue his proclamation, calling for 75,000 men for the defence of the Capitol. In one hour after this proclamation reached Richmond, the ordinance of Secession was passed.

Your cry that "the Capitol is in danger" was responded to with alacrity; but your soldiers, on reaching Washington, were surprised to find everything peaceful and quiet, and men and women pursuing their usual avocations, as if the tocsin of alarm had not been sounded throughout the land, and no hostile demonstration visible anywhere.

"Why is this?" they asked. "For what have we been summoned from our families and homes?" It was but the first step in your programme of lawless usurpation. You had boldly seized the power which the Constitution had vested in Congress alone. And it was no part of your plan that men should analyse your acts. One of your most trusted councillors, Baker, of Oregon, declared to me that your President was elected by a Northern majority—that they were becoming dissatisfied, and it was necessary that he should strike some decided blow in order to make a united Northern party.

It was with this end in view that the attack on Fort Sumter was planned, in order to force upon South Carolina the initiatory step of resistance; and you deliberately doomed to destruction the brave but misguided men who composed the garrison of the fort—for your ships lay outside of the bar, with orders not to go to her relief—and when Anderson, fathoming your intent, surrendered after having held an untenable post as long as the rules of military honour required, deep disappointment was felt by your Government at Washington that the whole garrison had not been sacrificed, in order that you might parade the blood of the victims, along with the insult to the national flag, as a rallying cry. And it was seriously debated amongst you as to whether Anderson should not be tried as a traitor. But it was necessary, in order to carry out your programme, that he should play the hero. It is a fact worthy of note, however, that he was thence forward deprived of all command.

Your cry that the national flag had been outraged, was answered by a howl from the Abolition hordes of the North; and so, for the time your object was accomplished, and a united North presented her formidable front.

It is your boast that you have 700,000 men in the field for the subjugation of the South. I do not doubt but that you can raise a million—for all your industrial resources are paralysed, your factories are idle, your commerce destroyed, and your people want bread. It is this which has filled your ranks, and not patriotism.

You have, Sir, brought about a mighty revolution, whose tide is even now surging towards your own homes. You have suspended the law throughout the land, and, by your secret police, hold the assassin's knife at the throats of your own people. The mist of fanaticism, which makes them for the present but blind instruments in your hands, will pass away; and he who raises the whirlwind does not always ride upon it into a harbour of safety. So far, what have you achieved by this total disruption of the entire social system, with your vast armies and the expenditure of untold millions? Nothing but to make Washington a safe and pleasant abiding place for President Lincoln and his Cabinet.

You cannot conquer us, Sir. A nation armed in the defence of her rights is under the protection of God. In every encounter we have demonstrated our superiority, and driven your countless legions, with all the appliances of modern warfare in their favour, disastrously from the battlefield.

You may seek to overwhelm us by still greater numbers, and lay waste our land from the Potomac to the Gulf of Mexico; and if our men fall in the defence of our rights and our firesides, our women will take their places, and die with their natural protectors—for already they know what mercy they have to expect from the "*irrepressible conflict*" party.

We may not successfully compete with you in the open field, but we will then defeat you by stratagem. And beware lest you drive us to secret organisation, or you in your day may experience that the vengeance of man is swifter than that of Heaven. No, Sir, you cannot subdue a people endowed with such a spirit of resistance; and, although we may yet wade through oceans of blood, we will achieve our independence, or leave our whole Southern land one howling wilderness, and a monument to all future time of the crimes of your party.

Oh, Sir, let this terrible lesson suffice. Let the wail of the widow and the orphan throughout this wide land touch your heart, and give us peace ere the gulf be widened between us. Give us peace ere you have trailed that once proud emblem of our former greatness at the feet of our arrogant hereditary foe. Do this, and the crimes you have already committed may be forgotten, and I could find it in my heart to forgive the evils you have inflicted upon me.

I have the honour to be, &c. &c. &c.

Rose O'N Greenhow.

This letter was written prior to the surrender of our commissioners, Mason and Slidell, and I cannot be supposed to have been very solicitous that Mr. Seward should uphold the dignity of Yankeedom. Neither did I expect that he would; for I knew that his cowardice would shrink from assuming the responsibility of the acts of his agent, Wilkes, at the same time that his casuistry and cunning would afford a plausible mask for the real feelings which guided his decision.

Contempt and defiance alone actuated me. I had known Seward intimately, and he had frequently enjoyed the hospitalities of my table, and at a time when few had the moral courage to countenance him. Upon his return from Europe, shortly after the miserable fanatic John Brown had paid the penalty of his crime, Mr. Seward was dining at my house with a large party, amongst whom were Mr. and Mrs. Charles Francis Adams.

An unfortunate allusion was made to some circumstances connected with the affair at Harper's Ferry, when Mrs. Adams launched out into a panegyric on John Brown—calling him that '*holy saint and martyr,*' turning her glance full upon me at the time—to which I replied, in a clear and audible voice—for it may be supposed that this conversation silenced all other—'I have no sympathy for John Brown: he was a traitor, and met a traitor's doom;' and, turning to Seward, I remarked, 'I think you evinced very good taste in repudiating all connection with John Brown in your speech a few days since in the Senate.'

In reply, he said:—

I remember to have met him once, and but once only. He called on me about some matter of business, the nature of which I don't now recollect. He struck me as a wild and visionary man, erratic in his ways, and singularly striking in his appearance. But, at the same time, in our brief interview, he impressed me with the conviction that he was a bold, truthful, and honest man, but eccentric to a degree bordering on an unsettled state of mind. I was at this time busy with my preparations for going to Europe, and necessarily crowded with affairs, and the interview entirely passed from my mind until this unfortunate occurrence, in which I have been sought to be implicated, and which clearly proves the correctness of my original suspicion as to the unsettled state of his mind.

Colonel George Magruder remarked that his conduct at Harper's Ferry had not sustained Mr. Seward's impression of his character, as it proved that he was not free from fear, from the vice of lying, and of robbery, and of theft. Seward replied, in an indifferent tone, 'I knew nothing about him—only saw him once for a few moments—and the impression was very much weakened by the new scenes through which I have since passed.'

The conversation at this point diverged, and Seward aided me with great skill in directing it into a new channel. Mr. Adams, who was sitting on the other side of me, remained perfectly silent.

I should have shrunk from the most distant allusion to these incidents, had they not become matters of public notoriety. President Buchanan spoke to me on the subject, to which I replied, 'Do you keep spies in my household?' I was very much vexed, for I had hoped that the social gatherings of so humble an individual as myself would have escaped observation.

He said, 'How you talk! I have heard it spoken of by five or six persons, who all greatly commended your spirit and independence. And you have my most hearty approval.'

Honourable Henry D. Wilson, of Massachusetts, told me also that the Black Republicans blamed Mrs. Adams very much, and thought the demonstration on her part *very ill-timed.* A few days after I encountered Mr. Seward, and he approached me, saying, I have just been writing to our friend Lady N———, and have told her that in all Washington you were the only person who had the independence to give a mixed dinner party' (alluding to the strong social lines of division which were then drawn between the Southern and Northern parties).

I replied, 'And you may also add, that I am so well satisfied with the result of that experiment that I shall not try it again.'

Perhaps, had he fathomed my real object, he would not have been so grateful to me for the social countenance. At this early day I saw foreshadowed what was to follow, and I desired to obtain a thorough insight into the plans and schemes of those who were destined to become the prominent actors in the fearful drama, in order that I might turn it to the advantage of my country when the hour for action arrived. To this end I employed every capacity with which God has endowed me, and the result was far more successful than my hopes could have flattered me to expect. I had verbatim reports of every caucus, of every Cabinet Council, beginning with the hasty conclave convened on the morning of Lincoln's unexpected arrival in masquerade at Willard's Hotel; with piquant additions of private anecdotes of the distinguished pair, in which Mrs. Lincoln was described as boxing the ears of a buxom chambermaid who inclined too amiably to receive the salute of her illustrious spouse.

Seward, at this time, verily believed in the fulfilment of his own predictions, that all things would be restored to quiet in thirty days. Like the ostrich, which buries its head in the sand at the approach of danger, he had wrapped himself in his self-sufficient pride, which, aided by *his increased convivial habits*, made him see all things through the mirage of his own mind. His coadjutors entertained the same belief, although based upon different grounds. With the vast power of the Federal Government in their hands, and with no constitutional scruples as to its use, they believed that they had the means to corrupt so large a proportion of the prominent men of the South, that it only required them to use this *moral suasion* at will, to bring about the desired result.

They had already employed it with such success as to make them confident of the future. Scott had been won to their support, through this nefarious influence; Crittenden and Holt had been successfully tampered with, each bribed by the same bait—a seat on the Supreme Bench—which was never designed to be given to either. Charles Sumner actually recorded his vote in caucus in favour of Crittenden. Crittenden told me that he expected to receive the appointment. I asked a member of that caucus, 'Wilson, Will they give it to him?'

'*I rather think not,*' was the reply; '*but we will hold out the bait to them until they can't retreat.'* The recreant renegade Stanley, of North Carolina, who had some years before been defeated as the Abolition candidate for Governor of California, was bought to betray his native State by being made Provisional Governor thereof. Other conspicuous instances I might cite; but this record belongs to the historian, whose duty it is to brand those traitors for all time with the mark of Cain, rather than to this simple record of my own sufferings and personal experience.

CHAPTER 11

Trials and Danger

Stanton was now in the full exercise of his prerogatives as Secretary of War. He had been introduced into the Abolition Cabinet solely to bring about the deposition of M'Clellan, whose elevation in the first instance had been for a similar end. It was supposed that Stanton, in his character of *quasi* democrat—based upon the fact that, as a *dernier ressort*, he had been selected in the last days of Mr. Buchanan's Administration to fill a vacancy—would draw around him the Conservative party, which had hitherto constituted M'Clellan's strength. These political jugglers were not aware of the facts that Stanton had never enjoyed the confidence of any party; that he was viewed as an astute cunning lawyer, rather than a profound one; and that he had only received the appointment in Mr. Buchanan's Cabinet, after re peated failures to induce Southern men to take the position; and his appointment was regarded as an evidence of the weakness and un-popularity of the Administration, and entire loss of the confidence of the Southern party.

I must take occasion here to disclaim all intention of casting an imputation upon Mr. Buchanan personally, for whose ability and high moral worth I have the most profound appreciation. He was full of honours as of years, and unfit to grapple with the terrible events which crowded upon the closing period of his Administration. He had grown old in the service of his country, and cherished a holy reverence for its institutions, and would, I believe, have sacrificed his own life to have averted the doom of disruption, and sought, at least by a negative policy, to stay its progress.

By a fatality of birth, he was thrown on the wrong side when the sectional division came. But he nevertheless carries with him to the retirement of Wheatland—where I have spent many happy days—the affectionate remembrances of many of his old friends.

Stanton, however, had full confidence in his own ability to bring about these desirable results, and in his turn received the laudations of the venal hireling Northern Press—which now invariably concluded its panegyrics by styling him the 'Great Secretary,' endowing him for the time with all the attributes of Queen Elizabeth's celebrated Prime Minister Burleigh, who had for nearly three centuries enjoyed the title of the 'Great Secretary,' until Mr. Attorney Stanton came to dispute it with him.

Bennett, of the New York Herald, being more honest or more astute than his contemporaries, was more stinted in his praise, and sometimes gave a caustic analysis of the ordinances of this new god of the Abolitionists.

Amongst the first of those ordinances which emanated from the pen of the 'Great Secretary' was the one commanding all officers and departments to report to the President as the Commander-in-Chief of the Army and Navy, the responsibilities of which position, according to this royal firman, he had determined to assume; another assigning M'Clellan to the Army of the Potomac, thereby deposing him from the position of Commander-in-Chief, which he had enjoyed since he had aided so materially in consigning General Scott to the shades of private life, and ordering him very significantly to expedite his preparations for the 'On to Richmond.'

It might have been supposed that M'Clellan—young, ambitious, and with an army to back his pretensions—would, if he had not absolutely rebelled against this summary ejectment, have at least shown himself restive in submitting to the fiat of the Pennsylvania lawyer, whose skill had hitherto been displayed in the ingenious use of legal technicalities of doubtful equity, and in making 'the worse appear the better cause,' according to the size of the retaining fee. But in verity our young Napoleon showed himself imbued with a most Christian spirit; for when smitten on one cheek he meekly turned the other— thereby rebuking the expectation of friend and foe—and set himself to the performance of the duty assigned him, hoping, like Mr. Micawber, 'that something would turn up.'

To Stanton belongs the credit of having perfected that mendacious system of official reports, which emanated from the Republican War Office. It had originated under his predecessor, Cameron, who was, however, not scholar enough always to observe geographical probabilities or grammatical accuracy in the exercise of his inventive genius. Those which Mr. Stanton promulgated, were liable to no fastidious criticism of that sort; for, though equally efforts of imagination, they were nevertheless masterpieces as to literary merit, as well as from the effect they produced upon the sympathetic pulse of the New York brokers and bankers. And it was a very usual circumstance, after one of those *vermillion edicts* from the Great Secretary, to see published simultaneously, in the same paper, '*The Secretary of the Treasury, Mr. Chase, goes to New York this evening, on financial business connected with his department.*' A novel but very successful means of raising the wind.

Stanton was peculiarly fitted for the post he held as minister of a despot. Soft and deferential in his manners, to the point of servility when it suited him, he was insolent and arrogant to those whom the chapter of accidents placed in his power, though even this was tempered by a certain degree of prudence—for, like Seward, he was physically a coward. He affected great brevity of style, and an inquisitorial severity of manner, more suited to a criminal lawyer before the Old Bailey, than a cabinet minister of the nineteenth century. The public were often treated to descriptions of those audiences, and of the trembling victims who stood awe-struck before the haughty minister.

I have alluded to the adventitious means at this time resorted to, for filling the depleted Abolition coffers. It would be an erroneous idea to suppose for a moment that those able financiers, the moneyed men of New England, looked upon their transactions with Mr. Secretary Chase from any other than a business point of view, in which each party was to drive the most lucrative bargain possible. They at least did not attempt to assume the flimsy thread bare guise of patriotism. That was reserved for the people who were to be victimised, and led to the slaughter, in order that there might be a 'united Northern party.'

The old facilities and avenues of trade being closed by the war. the capital of these Wall-Street princes was lying idle, and they sought the only chance of profitable investment by playing broker to the Government, and, as the risk was great, the returns were necessarily commensurate; and Mr. Secretary Chase, in effecting his financial arrangements, did so at a cost that none but a gambler with a nation for a stake would have ventured. Enormous contracts for Government supplies also were given as additional bonus to those Wall-Street Shylocks, whose interest it became to ferment and keep up the war fever by every means in their power.

Stewart, the merchant-prince of New York, got a contract for furnishing jeans for the army, by which he made a million of dollars, and presented Mrs. Lincoln with a lace shawl, which was said to have cost three thousand dollars. The *New York Herald* described her appearance upon some occasion, with this queenly fabric around her.

I saw Mrs. Lincoln once only, and paid a sixpence for the gratification of my curiosity. I was returning from the market-place, where I had gone to purchase some flowers and shrubs, one hot summer morning at an early hour, and in passing a small shop in the avenue saw, standing before it, the Imperial coach, with its purple hangings and tall footmen in white gloves; so, yielding to the instinct of Mother Eve, I went into the shop and there beheld a little woman bargaining for some black cotton lace, very much seemingly to the disgust of the shopwoman, who left her when I entered, and came to me.

I enquired, 'Who is that?' for naturally I was curious to know which member of the family royal stood before me.

'Only Madam Lincoln.'

I asked for some trifle, deposited my sixpence, and feeling now that I had a legitimate right to look, made the most of the opportunity. She is a short, broad, flat figure, with a broad flat face, with sallow mottled complexion, light grey eyes, with scant light eyelashes, and exceedingly thin pinched lips; self-complacency, and a slightly scornful expression, characterise her bearing, as if to rebuke one for passing 'between the wind and her nobility.' Mrs. Lincoln, however, must be very tender-hearted, as she has been frequently known to express great compassion for the 'poor slaves whom God had made free, and the wicked Southerners had made this war to keep them in bondage.'

Her dress, however, was very grand; yet I do not think that Eugenie or Mrs. Davis would have selected it for that hour and occasion. The gown was composed of a rich silk, of light ground, with gaudy flowers embroidered over it, lying in voluminous folds full half a yard on the ground. Point Venise collar and sleeves, elaborately made up with pink ribands; white hat, adorned with feathers and flowers interspersed with tinsel balls; white parasol, lined with pink; white gloves, and a superb mantle of black lace, completed her costume. These items were all very deliberately noted; and, although not a very artistic description, it is nevertheless a precise inventory of Mrs. Lincoln's shopping *toilette*.

On Saturday, January 18, at two o'clock, I learned, incidentally, that I was to be removed from my own house to another prison. I was sitting in the library reading, with my little one at my feet playing with her dolls, prattling, and beguiling me almost into forgetfulness of the wickedness and persecutions which beset me, until recalled by this

111

startling intelligence.

I immediately sent for the officer of the guard, and demanded to know the facts. He told me that he had orders not to communicate with me on the subject, or to speak with me at all, but would go to the provost-marshal, General Porter, and obtain further instructions. He returned, after a short time, with written orders from that functionary, fixing the hour for my removal. Detective Allen had the ordering and regulation of the necessary arrangements; the few articles of clothing for myself and child, which I was allowed to take, were gathered together and packed, with a sentinel standing over, and examining each piece separately. Less than two hours was allowed me, before I was dragged from my home forever. A covered wagon, surrounded by a file of soldiers, was ordered by Allen to be my conveyance to my new prison. Believing that I should feel humiliated by this indignity, Lieutenant Sheldon, however, positively refused to obey this order.

Detective Allen was a German Jew, and possessed all the national instincts of his race in an exaggerated degree, besides having these inherent characteristics sharpened by Yankee association.

Miss Poole, at this time, took the oath of allegiance, and fifty dollars in gold from the Yankee Government, and went on her way rejoicing. The woman Baxley, also, applied to be released upon similar terms, which was refused, and she was sent to the Old Capitol Prison, upon which occasion I saw her for the first time.

At about four o'clock I turned my back upon what had once been a happy home; and, what was to me an additional grief, parted from my faithful maid, who had thus far stayed with me through all my trials, and served me with a fidelity and devotion not often equalled in the higher walks of life. My child wept bitterly on parting from her, and I confess that the pathetic appeals of the faithful creature, to be allowed to follow my gloomy fortunes, quite unnerved me.

The majority of the guard were drawn up in front of the house to witness my departure. Several of them had been very kind, and, on taking leave, I said, 'I trust that your next duty will be a more honourable one than that of guarding helpless women and children.'

I cast my eye up, and saw that the windows were all crowded with men, amongst whom I recognised several correspondents of the New York and Philadelphia Press eagerly watching my words and looks.

I reached the Old Capitol Prison just at dark; but, whether in anticipation of some demonstration on the part of my friends I know not, but the whole guard were under arms to receive me; a general commotion was visible in all directions, and it was evident that a great deal of interest and curiosity was felt as to the destination of 'so noted a rebel.' The receiving-room or office was crowded with officers and others, all peering at me. It was with a strange feeling of indifference that I found myself in this prison. I had already gone through so many trials, that this crowning act of villainy could only elicit a smile of scorn.

I now parted from Lieutenant Sheldon, who had entitled himself to my most grateful remembrance. His kindness to me had exposed him to the suspicion of his own Government; and it was through his instrumentality that I was now enabled to rescue some few cherished memorials from the general wreck of my effects.

So soon as I left the house, the members of the press in waiting took advantage of the opportunity to examine my apartments, and for days after the principal Abolition journals throughout the whole country contained descriptions, speculations, &c. As a sample of the unceremonious manner in which I was paraded before the public, I have thought fit to give a few extracts from some of them.

THE FEMALE TRAITORS.

Their Removal to Their New Prison Quarters—A Description of the Building, and the Accommodations for the Prisoners.

(Special Correspondence of the Press.)

Washington: Jan. 19, 1862.

On Saturday afternoon, at 5 o'clock, the female traitors confined in the Sixteenth Street prison, a description of which I gave you in a former letter, were, by order of Provost-Marshal Porter, removed to the Old Capitol Prison, where quarters had been provided for them. Before entering the carriage that was to convey them to their new quarters, the prisoners took an appropriate farewell of all their guards—Mrs. Greenhow saying to one of the soldiers, 'Goodbye, sir; I trust that in the future you may have a nobler employment than that of guarding defenceless women.' Mrs. Greenhow then advanced to Lieutenant Sheldon, who had charge of the prison quarters, and thanked him for the uniform courtesy and kindness he had shown her during her confinement; while little Rose Greenhow, who, at the request of her mother, will be imprisoned with her, threw her arms about the lieutenant's neck and embraced him.

When Rose Greenhow entered the prison at Old Capitol Hill, she naively remarked to Lieutenant Wood, 'You have got one of the hardest little rebels here that you ever saw. But,' said she, 'if you get along with me as well as Lieutenant Sheldon, you will have no trouble.' Mrs. Greenhow then, turning to her daughter, said to her, 'Rose, you must be careful what you say here.' Rose, however, did not seem to think that the caution was at all necessary, and that she would fare well in her new quarters.

The prisoners are quartered on the second floor in the north-east end of the jail.

This morning, when the rain was descending in torrents, and the sidewalks and streets were of the most impassable condition, we again visited the Sixteenth Street jail, the late quarters of the prisoners referred to. As we approached the prison we were again challenged by the guard, who this time was sheltering himself from the rain in the doorway of the building. We had seen faces at the windows of the upper stories when we entered here a few days before, but now they were gone. The form of the lieutenant, however, soon appeared at the window, and for the second time we entered the room.

The picture of Gertrude Greenhow, the deceased daughter of Mrs. Greenhow, first attracted our attention. There was the same smile there, the same strange fancy of the eye of which we have written before—so young and yet so fair—and for the moment we were entranced. Turning for the moment, and the beautiful portrait of Mrs. Moore diverted our sight; then the lieutenant welcomed us, and we took a seat with him before a bright fire glowing on the hearth.

Now that the prisoners had departed, we were invited up into the rooms formerly occupied by them. The room in which Mrs. Greenhow was lately incarcerated is situated in the second-storey back room. Besides this, Mrs. Greenhow was allowed the use of the library, the property of her husband, who was a lawyer. The library is chiefly stored with law books, interspersed with books in the French and Spanish languages. Most of the time of Mrs. Greenhow was spent in this room, which was neatly furnished, and containing, besides, a sewing machine, upon which the lady named did a great amount of sewing during her confinement.

After night set in, she employed her time in reading as well as writing, and many of the fugitive verses written by her are still preserved. She frequently remained in this room until midnight before retiring to her apartment for the night. On the desk of the sewing machine, this morning, we found standing two bottles of fluid, which were frequently used by her in her correspondence to her friends outside the prison, so as to disguise it to the eyes of the guard. The plan pursued was to interline her letters by one of the fluids, which, on the application of a second, only known to those who were in the secret, was rendered perfectly intelligible. Thus, it was that contraband information could be conveyed by her to those who aided and abetted her in her treason.

We are informed by Lieutenant Sheldon that of all the prisoners confined here, Mrs. Greenhow was the most lady-like in her manners and in her conversation. She is possessed of the finest education of any lady who has ever visited Washington; and although rather severe at times in her denunciations of the North, yet she has shown herself to be possessed of a woman's heart in her sad moments, as witness the parting from her guard on Saturday. She had a great horror of being conveyed to Fortress Monroe, as was first feared by her, and her change is the most acceptable one that she could have.

THE FEMALE PRISON AT WASHINGTON.

A correspondent of the Philadelphia 'Press' gives a description of a visit to the house on Sixteenth Street, in Washington, where female spies and rebels have been confined. He writes: —

When we visited the establishment referred to, we were admitted to the parlour of the house, formerly occupied by Mrs. Greenhow, fronting on Sixteenth Street. Passing through the door on the left, and we stood in the apartment alluded to. There were others who had stood here before us—we have no doubt of that—men and women of intelligence and refinement. There was a bright fire glowing on the hearth, and a *tête-à-tête* was drawn up in front. The two parlours were divided by a red gauze, and in the back room stood a handsome rosewood *pianoforte*, with pearl keys, upon which the prisoner of the house, Mrs. Greenhow, and her friends had often performed. The walls of the room were hung with portraits of friends and others—some on earth and some in heaven—one of them representing a former daughter of Mrs. Greenhow, Gertrude, a girl of sixteen summers, with auburn hair and light-blue eyes, who died some time since.

In the picture a smile of beauty played around the lips, and the eyes are lighted with a strange fancy, such as is often seen in the eyes of a girl just budding into womanhood.

On the east wall hangs the picture of Mrs. Florence Moore,

whose husband is now in our army, while the walls of the back room are adorned with different pictures of the men and women of our time. Just now, as we are examining pictures, there is a noise heard overhead—hardly a noise, for it is the voice of a child, soft and musical.

"That is Rose Greenhow, the daughter of Mrs. Greenhow, playing with the guard," says the lieutenant, who has noticed our distractment. "It is a strange sound here; you don't often hear it, for it is generally very quiet." And the handsome face of the lieutenant is relaxed into a shade of sadness. There are prisoners above there—no doubt of that—and maybe the tones of this young child have dropped like the rains of Spring upon the leaves of the drooping flowers. A moment more and all is quiet, and save the stepping of the guard above there is nothing heard. The Sixteenth Street gaol has been an object of considerable interest for months past, to citizens as well as visitors. Before the windows of the upper storeys were "blinded," the prisoners often appeared at these points, and were viewed by pedestrians on the other side of the way; but since the "cake affair" of New Year's Day, the prisoners have been forbidden to appear at the windows, and the excitement, instead of having been allayed, has been still further increased. . . .

The report that the cake sent to Mrs. Greenhow, on New Year's Day, came from Mrs. Douglas, to whom Mrs. Greenhow sustains the relationship of aunt, is a mistake. The cake was sent by a party well known to the Government, upon whom a strict watch is kept. . . .

These extracts will be sufficient to show in what manner I was made a *spectacle* of, in order to gratify the greedy appetites of the sensational North, and the unenviable publicity to which I was condemned. Cause enough, if no other existed, for my deep contempt and detestation of a government so lost to every instinct of propriety as to descend to that meanest of all persecutions—that of dragging my name in the slough of its own hirelings. By every principle of integrity and honour I was entitled to their protection, and they gave me such as the hyaena would give to the victim within reach of its fangs.

The dignity of my little girl was very much shocked at the part ascribed to her in the parting scene—*that of throwing her arms around the neck of Lieutenant Sheldon*—which, I need scarcely say, was without a shadow of truth, being an effort of imagination on the part of the correspondent.

Well, to continue my narrative, Mr. Wm. P. Wood, the superintendent of the Old Capitol Prison, received me with great *impressment*. He appeared fully sensible of the honour of being the custodian of '*so noted a rebel.*' The building itself was familiar to me. The first Congress of United States in Washington had held its sessions there; but it was far more hallowed in my eyes by having been the spot where the illustrious statesman John C. Calhoun breathed his last. The tide of reminiscences came thronging back upon my memory. In the room in which I now sat waiting to be conducted to my cell, I had listened to the words of prophetic wisdom from the mouth of the dying patriot.

He had said that our present form of Government would prove a failure; that the tendency had always been, towards the centralisation of power in the hands of the general Government; that the conservative element was that of States rights; that he had ever advocated it, as the only means of preserving the Government according to the Constitution; that it was a gross slander to have limited his advocacy of those principles to the narrow bounds of his own State; that he had battled for the rights of Massachusetts as well as for those of South Carolina; and that, whenever it came to pass, that an irresponsible majority would override this conservative element, that moment would the Union be virtually destroyed.

That our system was not susceptible of long duration; that no Government could stand the shock of revolution every four years, and that as our population increased the danger became more imminent; that upon this principle he had opposed the war with Mexico and the proposition for the purchase of Cuba, as all acquisition of territory was likely to bring about the agitation of the slavery question, and arouse the fanaticism of the North, which was destined, at no distant day, to set aside the constitutional restraints which now held them but feebly in check, and eventually bring about a revolution. 'I have lived,' he said, 'in advance of my time, but you in your generation will witness the fulfilment of my prophecy.'

And now scarce a decade has passed, and his prophetic warnings have been realised; and Abraham Lincoln has brought about the fulfilment of his prophecy, and written in words of blood upon the tablets of history that the '*Great Model Republic*' is a failure.

After the lapse of some half-hour, I was taken up to the room which had been selected for me by General Porter. It was situated in the back building of the prison, on the north-west side, the only view being that of the prison-yard, and was chosen purposely so as to exclude the chance of my seeing a friendly face. It is about ten feet by twelve, and furnished in the rudest manner—a straw bed, with a pair of newly-made unwashed cotton sheets—a small feather pillow, dingy and dirty enough to have formed part of the furniture of the Mayflower—a few wooden chairs, a wooden table, and a glass, six by eight inches, completed its adornment: soldiers rations being only allowed me by this magnanimous Pennsylvanian, who was doubtless driving a good trade by his patriotism.

The second day of my sojourn in this dismal hole a carpenter came to put up bars to the windows. I asked by whose order it was done, and was informed by the superintendent that General Porter not only ordered it, but made the drawings himself, so as to exclude the greatest amount of air and sunlight from the victims of abolition wrath. Wood remonstrated against the bars, saying that they had not been found necessary; whereupon Porter said, 'Oh, Wood, she (alluding to me) will fool you out of your eyes—can talk with her fingers,' &c. But to speak of myself—the door of this den is locked and barred, and the sentinels pacing up and down before it.

I had scarcely entered my cell, when this same Dr. Stewart came in, attended by his hospital steward. I received him very coldly, and he withdrew after showing himself.

On the 21st Dr. Stewart came in again, with his hospital steward, very unceremoniously—for I had no fastening on my door. He seemed determined to disturb my equanimity. I was in bed, not having arisen. The customs of our people made this seem a great outrage to me, so I told him that I trusted that his sense of delicacy would prevent his future visits to me, unless I desired his presence; that I supposed that I had been sufficiently explicit upon former occasions; that his Government had deprived me of my liberty, but that they could not force upon me civilities—and I supposed that his visit was intended as such—which I, from principle, declined to receive.

With that he spread himself like a *Basha* with three tails, discoursed fluently upon the dignity of his position, and concluded by saying it was his pleasure to come; to which I replied, 'It is mine not to receive you.'

As he went out, he said to the guard in a very loud voice, '*I am the first person who has made that woman feel that she is a prisoner, and I will yet reduce her to the condition of the other prisoners.*'

I thereupon sent for the superintendent, to make my protest against this renewed impertinence. In the course of the day, he obtained authority to exclude *Materia Medica* from my presence.

Extracts from notes kept in the Old Capitol:—

25th.—I have been one week in my new prison. My letters now all go through the detective police, who subject them to a chemical process to extract the treason. In one of the newspaper accounts, prepared under the direction of the secret police, I am supposed to use sympathetic ink. I purposely left a preparation very conspicuously placed, in order to divert attention from my real means of communication, and they have swallowed the bait and fancy my friends are at their mercy.

How I shrink from the notoriety which these dastards force upon me: for five months I have had a daily paragraph. One would think that curiosity would have been satiated; but not so. And I have the uneasy consciousness that every word I utter will appear with exaggeration in the newspapers. Even my child of eight years is deemed of importance enough to have her childish speeches recorded. Well! I bide my time, confident in the retributive justice of Heaven. Rose is subject to the same rigorous restrictions as myself. I was fearful at first that she would pine, and said, 'My little darling, you must show yourself superior to these Yankees, and, not pine.' She replied quickly, 'mamma, never fear; I hate them too much. I intend to dance and sing "Jeff. Davis is coming," just to scare them!'

January 28.—This day, as I raised my barred windows, and stood before one of them to get out of the smoke and dust, &c. the guard rudely called, 'Go away from that window!' and raised his musket and levelled it at me. I maintained my position without condescending to notice him, whereupon he called for the corporal of the guard. I called also for the officer of the guard, who informed me that I 'must not go to the window.' I quietly told him that, at whatever peril, I should avail myself of the largest liberty of the four walls of my prison. He told me that his guard would have orders to fire upon me. I had no idea that such monstrous regulations existed. Today the dinner for myself and child consists of a bowl of beans swimming in grease, two slices of fat junk, and two slices of bread. Still, my consolation is, 'Every dog has his day.'

January 30.—I wonder what will happen next. My child has been ill for several days, brought on by close confinement and want of proper food. Just now I went to the door and rapped, that being the prescribed manner of making known my wants. The guard came. 'What do you want?'

'Call the corporal of the guard,' I said.

'What do you want with him?'

'That is no business of yours; call him?'

'I won't call him.'

'You shall' (*rap, rap, rap*).

The guard;—'G—d d—n you, if you do that again I will shoot you through the door'

'Call the corporal of the guard!'

Here horrid imprecations followed. I thereupon raised the window and called, 'Corporal of the guard.' The ruffian called also, finding that I was not to be terrified by his threats. But, when the corporal came and opened the door, I was seized with laughter, for there stood the Abolitionist blubbering like a child, that *he had 'not orders to shoot the d——d Secesh woman, who was not afraid of the devil himself.'*

I sent for the officer of the guard, who was Lieutenant Carlton, of Zanesville, Ohio, and reported this outrage. He said that the guard had acted by his orders in refusing to call the corporal of the guard, and that he had no idea of allowing his non-com missioned officers to act as servants, &c. I told him that my child was ill, and I demanded the use of a servant; whereupon he told me that a servant should not be allowed me, save morning and night. I replied, 'Very well, sir. I will resort to the window, then, as my only expedient.' A servant after this was sent, but had to perform her functions with a sergeant of the guard standing over her. I told Lieutenant Carlton that I would report him to the provost-marshal, which I accordingly did, and the following is a copy of my letter:—

To General Porter, Provost-Marshal.

Old Capitol Prison: Jan. 31.

Sir,—I feel it to be my duty to make a representation of certain things done here under sanction and authority of your name.

A few days since I went to my window and leaned against the bars to escape the dust and bad odours with which it was filled, when the guard below, No. 5, called to me in a rude manner to go away, and threatened to shoot me. This morning I again went to my window, to escape the dust and atmosphere of a room without ventilation, the windows of which you well know are barred—as I am told that they evidence your mechanical skill—and the guard called to me in the same fashion, and again levelled his musket at me. A few moments since I was threatened to be fired upon through the door of my chamber, and your officer of the guard justified the outrage, and assumed the responsibility of the act.

Sir, I call your attention to these and other gross outrages, and warn you that there is another tribunal—that of the public opinion of the civilised world—to which I will appeal against your acts of inhumanity. And I now formally demand that you cause this officer, Lieutenant Carlton, to be punished for his brutality; and that you establish rules and regulations here, in accordance with the laws of humanity, and my rights as a prisoner.

I have the honour to be, &c. &c.

Rose O'N. Greenhow.

This brought no response, but I was subsequently informed that Lieutenant Carlton was temporarily placed under arrest, although he was, in the order of rotation, again in command at the prison. I can give no idea of the petty annoyances to which I was constantly exposed. I was never allowed to cross my chamber door. If a servant now entered to perform the smallest duty, the door was immediately locked and bolted, so that it was necessary to rap or call some five or ten minutes before they could get out. And when it is remembered that these servants were often negro men, who claimed perfect equality, and would tauntingly tell me that '*Massa Lincoln had made them as good as me—that they would not be called negroes, but gem'men of colour,*' some idea may be felt of the vague, undefined feeling of uneasiness that was constantly upon me.

It is but justice to the superintendent of the prison, Mr. Wood, to state that, whenever the insolence of the negroes came to his knowledge, that he invariably sent them away; and that, so far as he was able to do so, he protected the prisoners from the insolence and outrage of the guard and officers.

The rules with regard to my child were barbarously rigid. The act of commitment ran thus:—

Miss Rose Greenhow, although not a prisoner, is subject to the same rules and regulations prescribed for a prisoner.

She was in fact as much a prisoner as I was. I had never been consulted on the subject. And when occasionally, from very shame, she was allowed to go down in the yard, the child often came up cry-ing, from the effects of the brutality and indecency to which she was exposed. The superintendent was, as I have above said, disposed to be kind, but there was a constant struggle going on between him and the military authorities for supremacy, by which the comfort of the prisoner was sacrificed, and his liberty abridged. It would seem to have been purposely arranged that these respective jealousies, should result in stricter vigilance over the helpless victims.

I can conceive no more horrible destiny than that which was now my lot. At nine o'clock the lights were put out, the roll was called every night and morning, and a man peered in to see that a prisoner had not escaped through the keyhole. The walls of my room swarmed with vermin and I was obliged to employ a portion of the precious hours of candle light in burning them on the wall, in order that myself and child should not be devoured by them in the course of the night. The bed was so hard that I was obliged to fold up my clothing and place them under my child; in spite of this she would often cry out in the night, 'Oh, mamma, the bed hurts me so much.'

The portion of the prison in which I was confined was now al-most entirely converted into negro quarters, hundreds of whom were daily brought in, the rooms above and below mine being appropri-ated to their use; and the tramping and screaming of negro children overhead was most dreadful. The prison-yard, which circumscribed my view, was filled with them—for it must be remembered that these people were of both sexes, huddled together indiscriminately, as close as they could be packed. Emancipated from all control, and suddenly endowed with constitutional rights, they considered the exercise of their unbridled will as the only means of manifesting their equality.

In addition to all other sufferings was the terrible dread of infec-tious diseases, several cases of small-pox occurring, and my child had already taken the camp-measles, which had broken out amongst them. My clothes, when brought out from the *wash*, were often filled with vermin; constantly articles were stolen. Complaint on this head, of course, was unheeded. Our free fellow-citizens of colour felt them-selves entitled to whatever they liked. Several times during this period my child was reduced to a bare change of garments; and the supreme contempt with which they regarded a rebel was, of course, very edify-ing to the Yankees, who rubbed their hands in glee at the signs of the *irrepressible conflict.*

One day I called for a servant from the window. A negro man,

122

basking in the sun below, called out—'*Is any of you ladies named Laura? dai woman up dare wants you.*' And, by way of still further increasing the satisfaction with this condition of things, Captain Gilbert, of the 91st Pennsylvania Volunteers, drilled these negroes just below my window.

I protested against these infamies, and threatened to make an appeal to the United States Senate to send a committee to enquire into our present hapless condition, as they had done in the case of the negro thieves and felons confined in the gaol, many of whom had been released by *habeas corpus*, and whose cases had been deemed worthy of a senatorial report. This threat procured the instant removal of the negroes to more comfortable quarters.

CHAPTER 12

Progress of Events

The Congressional Committee of Investigation, instituted on account of Mr. Secretary Cameron's eccentric financial dalliances, was
still labouring amidst the turbid pools of corruption, whose depth they
were trying to fathom. Its researches had taken a far more extended
range than was originally intended. The newspapers, in conjunction
with Dame Rumour, sometimes lifted the screen, and gave the public
a peep at the nature of the examinations with which the committee
had charged themselves, and they were certainly of a very extraordinary character—the most remarkable being the charges against Mrs.
Lincoln of corruption, &c.

Mrs. Lincoln was said to have purchased from a New York hard
ware establishment a dinner service of china for the White House, to
be paid for by the Government, for which the dealer presented a bill
to Mr. Lincoln for the sum of 2,500 dollars; that he refused to pay
the exorbitant price, and sent for a hardware dealer of Washington to
consult as to the real value, who estimated it at about 800 dollars; that
the New York dealer still insisted on his original demand, telling Mr.
Lincoln significantly that he had better pay it without further question; that Lincoln insisting to know what he meant, the dealer finally
gave the history of the transaction, as follows: that the real price of
the china had been 800 dollars, but Mrs. Lincoln had directed him to
make out the bill for 2,500, and hand over the surplus to her.

The nature of some of these charges can be better understood by
the formal defence which the *New York Herald* thought fit to make of
her character and domestic virtues. It deprecated the attempt of the
committee to interfere with *the harmonious domestic relations* of President Lincoln and his wife said that 'she should be, like Caesar's wife,
above suspicion,'. This was very noble and praiseworthy on the part of
the *Herald*; but the committee were dealing with things as they were,
and not as they ought to be, although they afterwards came to the

conclusion that it was incompatible with the good of *public morals* that their researches should be published. It will, however, at some future day form a curious appendage to the history of the times, in the hands of some chronicler of the rise and fall of the Model Republic, which has been more recently characterised as the best Government the sun ever shone upon.

The movements of M'Clellan were now hurried, and he was forced to assume the defensive in the manner and place indicated by others. The second advance on Manassas was in accordance with this plan, and the result proved even more disastrous to the Abolition army than the first. They could no longer delude themselves as to the superiority of the fighting qualities of the enemy they had to contend with: it had been demonstrated at Manassas, and equally fatally at Ball's Bluff—where the fanatical demagogue Baker met his just doom.

And they were now to learn that this hated Southern chivalry, whom they reported at Manassas to have laid *'down' behind their trenches, too enervated to load their own guns, which was done by their negroes for them*, exceeded them quite as much in hardy endurance as in strategy and skill—all qualities essential to success; and in this instance, as if to show their contempt for the foe who had required almost eight months to recover from the last shock of arms, added insult to injury by holding them in check with wooden guns; actually introducing with success the Chinese system of warfare against these puritan propagandists of the nineteenth century.

It was at this time that I replied to the boast made by some Yankee officers of the 'total annihilation of our army'—' *We will not fight you at Manassas, but will lead you on to the Chickahominy, where we will welcome you " to hospitable graves!"'*

After the actual occurrence, this chance prophecy was published in the *New York Herald*, and other papers, as an evidence of my uninterrupted communication 'with the army at Manassas.' And the Prince de Joinville, in his apologetic letter for M'Clellan's defeat, says, '*He was forced to reveal his plans in Cabinet, and a female spy immediately sent information of them across to Beauregard, whose strategic movement was consequent upon it.*'

M'Clellan did me the honour to say that I knew his plans better than President Lincoln or his Cabinet, and had caused him four times to change them—this was a matter of public notoriety amongst the Yankees, and fully believed. But he gave me credit sometimes for more information than I possessed. I was, of course, a close observer of the smallest indications, and often drew accurate conclusions without having any precise knowledge on the subject. I was in Washington, as the Indian warrior in the trackless forest, with an enemy behind every bush. My perceptive faculties were under a painful tension, and every instinct was quickened to follow the doublings and windings of the ruthless foe who was hunting my race unto death; and, of course, no word or indication was lost upon me.

I was very often at this period intruded upon by large parties of curious Yankees, who came with passes from the provost-marshal, or governor of the district, to stare at me. Sometimes I was amused, and generally contrived to find out from these parties what was going on. One set of men came, introducing themselves as friends of Mrs. Timothy Child's—as if this would furnish a passport to a Southern woman's confidence. This party affected to be literary, one of whom was editor of a Rochester journal: informed me that I was detained on account of my talents 'as a writer,' and classed me with Mdme. de Sevigne.

Another large party came a few days after this: the women, very smartly dressed, helped themselves very unceremoniously to cake which had been just sent to my little one. A woman of this party, who claimed Boston as her residence, made quite a furious onslaught upon me, and said to me, 'Confess that it was love of notoriety which caused you to adopt your course, and you have been certainly gratified, for there is no one whom everybody has such a curiosity to see'—became very much excited, and said a great deal more. I told her that I had not supposed her object in visiting my prison was for the purpose of making a personal attack upon me, but that she did not surprise me.

And afterwards I requested the superintendent not to allow any more of these parties to have access to me; for the fish-women of Paris in the French Revolution were before my mind, and I feared that the next party might come armed with sticks or knives. The superintendent told me that numbers daily came to the prison who would gladly give him ten dollars a-piece to be allowed to pass my open door, so as to obtain a view of the indomitable rebel, as I was sometimes called in their papers. This was being 'damned to immortality.'

The disappointment of the Abolitionists at Manassas by no means diminished the zeal of the 'On to Richmond party,' although it must always be borne in mind that the most bloodthirsty and desperate of these mercenary *patriots* were, from the nature of their positions, never likely to encounter the foe whom they affected to despise. In the first Battle of Manassas, it was terrible to read the accounts of the masked batteries, and torpedoes, and infernal machines, described as buried by the rebels, who were held up to the execration of the civilised world for resorting to such unfair practices against a trusting foe, who disdained the use of any but the most orthodox means of destruction.

Poor rebels, how bitterly they were denounced! Unblushingly now these same liberators avowed to the world that they had drawn on their imaginations—in plain English, had lied most egregiously: that instead of '*the country, for the space of twenty miles, being enfiladed with masked batteries, rifle-pits, &c.*'—as they have since—only a few earthen defences, of but little strength, surmounted by wooden guns, were found; and by consequence forced to admit that the formidable defences and breastworks against which their mighty army had recoiled and fled like stricken hounds, had been formed of a small band of 'enervated Southerners,' whom they represented as an easy prey. And so they had been for long years, and the North had grown rich and intolerant upon its monopoly of their material wealth; but now they were banded together in the cause of their rights, and spirited on by the Lord of Hosts to victory.

Shrewd calculations were now entered into as to the time when this '*invincible grand army*' (for they still adhered to the name), would make its triumphant entry into Richmond. Extracts were constantly published from the *Richmond Examiner*, to prove the utter want of confidence of the populace in our President, representing him as ruling with despotic power, exposing every salient point—our exhausted resources and want of munitions of war, and other things which patriotism should have shrouded in silence, had it all been true.

The *Examiner* was also reported several times to have been suppressed by order of President Davis, on account, as they said, '*of its fearless exposure of his tyrannical government*,' and our help less condition was bemoaned by the victims of a despotism more absolute than that which they in imagination inflicted upon the Confederacy.

So convinced was I of the injury which the *Examiner* caused by exaggerating our internal differences and exposing our difficulties, that on arriving at Richmond I seriously asked the President, why, in view of the mischievous effects of this paper in giving aid and comfort to the enemy, it had not been suppressed; for that during the period of my imprisonment, I had had ample opportunity to know the important information which they derived through its columns. The reply of the President was befitting the head of a great nation—'*Better suffer from that evil which is temporary, than arrest it by a still greater one. It is a dangerous thing to interfere with the liberty of the press, for what would it avail us if we gain our independence and lose our liberty?'*

Letters were also passed about purporting to come from the ladies of our high officers and officials, regretting the erroneous judgments of their bosom lords, and all sighing after the flesh-pots of Egypt; and Mr. John Minor Botts quoted openly, as authority for our demoralised condition, and readiness to be taken into favour, if the conquering army could once get to Richmond. But there was the rub. The road to Richmond was studied on the maps, and it seemed very easy. I had the one used by the Military Committee of the Senate, with the red dotted lines which they made of the route; and thinking it might serve as a lesson to the Confederate engineers, sent it to Manassas—(I have often wondered if that might not be the identical map supposed to have been furnished by General Scott's coachman).

To their judgment, the 'On to Richmond' was *un fait accompli*; and our noble President already dragged at the wheels of the coach with purple hangings, to grace the triumph of the immortal rail-splitter. This programme was only delayed. Who could doubt its fulfilment? Mr. Secretary Chase borrowed money upon it. The bulls and bears of Wall Street kept the ball constantly in motion. Richmond was the Palestine of these modern Crusaders, and the freedom of the negro their sepulchre of Christ.

M'Clellan, by order of the '*Great Secretary*,' now made the third move in the programme of On to Richmond, by way of Yorktown. This was against his judgment; but he, however, showed himself possessed of the first requisite of a soldier—obedience to his superior. He had an effective force of 150,000 men, well appointed and disciplined—somewhat, it is true, relaxed by the *mistake* at Manassas—and eager, if we could judge from the boastful bragging tone, for the onslaught. The only opposing army at this time on the peninsula was the small but gallant band, under Magruder, of eight or ten thousand men, which he managed with such skill, by marching and countermarching, as to give the idea of fifty or sixty thousand: this estimate was constantly made by the Yankees. With this insignificant force he held M'Clellan's whole army in check for two months. Upon the principle that one Confederate was equal to five Yankees, I aided in the mystification by *inadvertently* supposing our force on the peninsula to be not less than 200,000 strong.

M'Clellan was evidently under the impression that a formidable force confronted him, and set to work to entrench himself, at a cost of $3,000,000; and demanded that reinforcements, to the amount of 50,000 men, should be sent him from Washington. Stanton haughtily replied to this requisition, in the name of poor Lincoln, by enumerating the force under his command, and ordered him to fight the battle with the army he already had; and plainly insinuated that, if he asked for any more men, they would send him instead a commanding officer. M'Clellan maintained the impossibility of his commencing offensive operations, unless reinforced.

A correspondence between him and the '*Great Secretary*' ensued, which created an active partisan warfare. M'Clellan's friends warmly espoused his cause, and asserted boldly that it was Stanton's design to sacrifice him.

Under this pressure of public feeling, which was aided by the *New York Herald*, reinforcements were sent to M'Clellan; but the order was tardily given and tardily executed. It was determined, although there were over 75,000 men behind the fortifications of Washington, that none of these could be spared, as the gaieties of the Capitol might be suddenly interrupted by a foray of the rebel *desperadoes*. How my blood tingled with satisfaction at the estimate they put upon the daring feats of our men. The gallant Ashby and his black horse cavalry were viewed with as much terror as the wild huntsman of the Black Forest.

Thirty thousand men were at last grudgingly ordered to reinforce M'Clellan—10,000 taken from each of the commands of Banks, M Dowell, and Shields. Banks accounted for his subsequent defeat by Stonewall Jackson, from having had his command weakened by this reduction, and the movement of his remaining forces impeded by the wagons, &c. consequent upon the transfer of so large a body of troops.

Meanwhile these stern alarums did not interrupt the merrymaking at the National Capitol; perhaps, at no period of its history had there been such unrestrained indulgence of revelry and mirth. The court journals gave a daily account of balls, and dinners, and routs, and exultingly proclaimed the fact that the Abolition ladies could 'dress and dance,' and 'give suppers,' 'brilliant suppers,' in spite of the withdrawal of those 'Secesh *dames* and *demoiselles*—the Greenhows, Slidells, and Clays'—and 'the foreign ministers who were wont to sympathise with these fair traitors.'

These gay doings ought to have been proof conclusive that there was 'nobody hurt,' even though the city authorities of New York and Philadelphia found their resources strained to the utmost to give bread to the thousands of destitute and starving families in their midst, and their hospitals were crowded to overflowing with wounded and dying soldiers.

The fashionable world of Abolitiondom was now put in a state of great excitement on account of the grand ball which Mrs. Lincoln had resolved to give at the White House, on February 9th. The invitations had been issued a month in advance, and the interest of the public kept alive by descriptions of the preparations as they progressed. It was got up truly upon a scale of royal magnificence. Maiard was brought on from New York to superintend the supper and its adornments; and the Chevalier Wikoff was grand master of ceremonies.

And, in order that nothing connected with the august entertainment which could enhance the general interest should be lost, the *New York Herald* published the card of invitation sent to 'Mr. and Mrs. James Gordon Bennett,' which they, however, had the good taste to decline, dreading, I suppose, the 'irrepressible conflict.' The description of the ball in its various phases, and the beautiful *toilettes*, filled many columns of the papers for days after, to the exclusion of the exciting news from the seat of war.

Mrs. Lincoln's costume received a large share of attention. She was described as being dressed in Court mourning—that is, with white and black, rose and white, and black lace intertwined and commingled, as a delicate compliment to Queen Victoria upon the death of Prince Albert. Her own son, during this heartless pageant, was lying at the point of death, and a few days after breathed his last, upon which occasion, however, she put on no mourning. Neither did she for the brother who fell afterwards, fighting in defence of his home and fireside.

These festivities at the National Capitol were intended to divert the public mind from too close a scrutiny of the policy of the Government. The superficial observer supposed that all the energy of their rulers was directed to the reduction of Richmond. M'Clellan was unsophisticated enough to suppose that he had been sent to the peninsula for the accomplishment of that end, and he addressed himself to the task with great caution and not much relish for it. He would greatly have preferred to remain in Washington during its season of festivities, enjoying the *éclat* and hero-worship of the hour.

He, however, proceeded to take the necessary measures for the advance of his army. He had the good sense never to have underrated the enemy he had to encounter; on the contrary, he magnified our force and capabilities beyond what our modesty would have allowed us to claim on our own behalf.

M'Clellan rightly judged that the only chance of success was to overwhelm us by numbers. Hence his requisition on the War Department at Washington for reinforcements, which, when conceded, *under force of the outside pressure*, were several weeks before reaching him; thus forcing him, whilst waiting for them, to extend and strengthen his original line of intrenchments and fortifications, to protect his army from the attack momentarily expected to be made by General Johnson, who had been by this delay enabled to relieve Magruder and his gallant band from the critical position they were in, for there is no doubt that had M'Clellan advanced upon them they must have been cut to pieces. They represented themselves as being somewhat in the condition of 'Admiral Hosier's army,' mere shadows, from the severe marching and flying about to which they were subjected by Magruder, in order to deceive the enemy.

During this period of digging and trenching of the Grand Army, the '*Great Secretary*' issued one of those remarkable bulletins proclaiming a great battle and a great victory at Yorktown, and, as was usual, a map and description of the seat of war appeared in all the Yankee papers.

I confess to some uneasy feeling on the subject until a friend in the War Department sent me a copy of the genuine despatch from M'Clellan, '*imploring reinforcements*' Mr. Stanton's was a financiering *ruse*, and proved very successful—for Mr. Chase was enabled thereby to effect another considerable loan.

I wrote a letter describing this same operation, which was mailed in Baltimore, and captured in the Post-office of that city, and was afterwards shown me by General Dix at the time of my mock trial before him for treason.

The Government at Washington never intended that M'Clellan should advance beyond Yorktown; he had played the role designed for him, and they were now determined to rid themselves of him, even though they should also sacrifice the army under his command. In preparation for this defeat, the transports were kept in a convenient position, and the gun-boats lay ready to cover the retreat of his forces.

The evacuation of York town by Johnson was conducted in a masterly manner: the enemy were in complete ignorance of his design until it had been entirely accomplished—held in check again by a few wooden guns. General Johnson, however, had the magnanimity to leave for their enlightenment an intelligent contraband, well posted as to his future movements and the policy and views generally of the Confederate Government.

At this time a very important character arrived at the metropolis, in the person of President Davis's negro coachman. I was not informed whether President Lincoln and his premier, Mr. Seward, invited him to dinner, but I do know that he had frequent interviews with them, the result of which was given to the curious public through the press, as conversations between the President and Mrs. Davis during their evening drives. He also said that Richmond would be evacuated on the first sign of the approach of the Abolition army, and that President Davis had had a subterranean passage made, so as to secure his own escape. These ridiculous stories were greedily swallowed, and implicit credit given to them; in truth, there was nothing too wild or extravagant for these Northern fanatics to seize hold of—and the Government offered a premium for this species of romance, as a sort of safety-valve for their own ulterior policy.

CHAPTER 13

Hopes and Fears

I became now seriously alarmed about the health and life of my child. Day by day I saw her fading away—her round chubby face, radiant with health, had become pale as marble, the pupils of her eyes were unnaturally dilated, and finally a slow nervous fever seized upon her. I implored in vain, both verbally and in writing, that a physician might be sent, and finally wrote the following letter to the provost-marshal:—

> Old Capitol Prison:
> Tuesday, February 18, 1862.

I wrote yesterday to ask that Dr. M Millen might be allowed to visit my child, who is suffering from illness brought on by a system of severity and rigorous confinement, which, as *regards children*, has no precedent in a civilised age or civilised land, unless we seek a parallel in the confinement of the children in the Temple, in the beginning of the French Revolution.

I ask, Sir, that my request may be complied with, with as little delay as possible, unless it be the intention of your government to murder my child.

> I have the honour to be, &c. &c.,
> Rose O'N. Greenhow.

A few hours after I had despatched this note, my door was rudely thrown open, and Dr. Stewart, the '*Brigand Sergeant*,' as he signed himself, unceremoniously entered, saying, 'Madam, I come to see you on official business.'

I said, 'Sir, it ought to be of a very grave character to warrant this intrusion.'

He seated himself, his hospital steward standing near the door. 'Madam, did you write a letter to the provost-marshal this day?'

'Yes, I wrote to the provost-marshal; but I have yet to learn how you, a subordinate, dare question me in regard to any correspondence I may hold with your superior.'

'Madam, I have every right: you have caused me to be rebuked by Major Allen and General Porter, for neglect of duty,' &c.

I said, 'Sir, in my letter to General Porter there was not the most distant reference to you; I asked that Dr. M Millen might visit my child, knowing him to be a man of science and a gentleman, and my note furnished no warrant for General Porter to rebuke you. As to Major Allen, his impertinence is only equalled by your own at this moment.'

He replied, 'Madam, I will believe General Porter in preference to you.'

I thereupon arose from my seat, and said, 'Sir, I have borne with you quite as long as is consistent with my self-respect, and I now desire you to quit my room, as it is no part of my plan to submit to personal insult.'

He arose also, foaming with rage, and stood confronting me—almost a giant in size—and said, 'I will not quit your room; I am here by order of Brigadier-General Porter.'

'Sir, I command you to go out; if you do not, I will summon the officer of the guard and the superintendent to put you out.'

With that he attempted to lay hands upon my child. I interposed my own person and said, 'At your peril but touch my child. You are a coward and no gentleman, thus to insult a woman.'

'I will not go out of your room, madam,' he said, this time livid and trembling with rage or fear, I don't know which.

I then went to the door and rapped—for be it remembered that he was locked and bolted in my room, that being the humane and Christian order. 'Call the officer of the guard.' The sentinel on duty being a friendly one, no time was lost in summoning him. When the officer appeared and the door was opened, it happened to be that same Lieutenant Carlton, from Zanesville, Ohio. He was very much agitated, for this man was his superior officer.

I said, 'Sir, I order you to put this man out of my room, for conduct unworthy of an officer and a gentleman, and I will report you for having allowed him to enter here'.

He nervously rubbed his hands, and said, 'I am sure Dr. Stewart will come out if you wish it.'

'Sir, I said, do your duty; order your guard to put him out.'

The sergeant, corporal, and guard—who all hated Stewart for his arrogance—were eager to obey. Whereupon this valiant Dr. Stewart actually slunk out. Strange to say, this scene filled me with uncontrollable laughter. It was farcical in the extreme—this display of valour against a sick child and careworn woman prisoner. A few hours later the kind and good Dr. M Millen came in, accompanied by an officer, but under orders not to hold any conversation with me save that which was professional.

I felt it incumbent upon me to report Dr. Stewart's visit to the provost-marshal. The following is a copy:—

To the Provost-Marshal General Andrew J. Porter.

Old Capitol Prison:

Tuesday, February 20, 1862.

Sir,—I am constrained, in consequence of the insolence and ungentlemanly conduct of Dr. Stewart, to make my complaint to you, and to ask your protection against his visits for the future.

I wrote a note to you some days since, asking that Dr. M Millen might be allowed to visit my child, who has been, and is, very ill. This Dr. Stewart came to my room yesterday morning, and obtruded himself therein, together with his hospital steward, and rudely called me to account for having written to you; said that I had caused him to be reprimanded by you and the detective called Major Allen, for neglect of duty, &c. I told him that, in my note to you, I had made no allusion to him; that I had requested the attendance of Dr. M Millen, because I knew him to be a gentleman, and I had confidence in his professional skill; and, moreover, that my note furnished you with no warrant for a rebuke to him, and that, if so, you had drawn a false conclusion, as you well knew that I had always declined his (Stewart's) professional visits.

With that he told me that he would believe you in preference to me, &c. &c. I thereupon desired him to leave my room, as I did not choose to submit to his impertinence. He refused in a rude and violent manner; said he was here by your order, and even had the audacity to approach my child to lay hands on her, which I prevented, and repeated my order that he should quit my room; and, finally, was obliged to send down for the officer of the guard and superintendent, before I could be freed from

135

his insolent intrusion.

It would occupy more time than I am disposed to engross to give you a detailed account of this man's offensive conduct, which commenced with the first days of my imprisonment, for a corroboration of which I refer you to Lieutenant Sheldon.

He claims your authority for his insolence, and I therefore respectfully demand that you will give such orders as that I may not be again exposed to it.

I have the honour to be, &c. &c.,

Rose O'N Greenhow.

General Johnson's wise and judicious falling back from Yorktown completely upset the plans and purposes of the Abolition Directory at Washington, and forced upon them an entire change of policy to suit the new emergency. Their determination with regard to M'Clellan was necessarily suspended, although not weakened in the slightest degree. But their own political existence depended upon the employment or defeat of the vast army under M'Clellan, which was now 180,000 strong. To recall him at that juncture was to have him proclaimed Military Dictator. To avoid this danger, a vigorous prosecution of the 'On to Richmond' was imperative.

Homesteads in the South were offered to that horde of barbarians, who swarmed like locusts over the fairest fields of Virginia, desolating them as they advanced, and spurred on with the hope of possession, and visions of orange groves and fair Southern wives. This is no imaginary picture. Wilson, of Massachusetts, said, few of that army, 'our boys,' as he called them, will ever return to the North; that they would have homesteads given them in the conquered country; that Congress would apportion the land into quarter sections; that they would settle and marry Southern girls. To which I replied, 'Never, sir. But our negroes will go North and marry yours, as far more fitting helpmates.'

Wilson, in this instance, proved a true prophet; but not in the sense he intended. Few of that Vandal crew ever returned to the North; but instead of homes in the sunny south, under the vine and the fig-tree, they found bloody graves amid the swamps of the Chicahominy, where their bodies lie unassoilzied, unburied, their bones bleaching in the sun, and a nation's anathema as their funeral dirge.

General Andrew Porter, the Provost-Marshal, who had distinguished himself by the most wanton invasion of the rights of the people of the district, accompanied M'Clellan to the field, followed by his bloodhounds, Allen and his gang of detectives. Porter was succeeded by a Mr. Biddle Roberts, who signed himself with as many titles as a Spanish *grandee*, and determined to convince me in the outset that I had gained nothing by the exchange.

Stanton had the grace to give an order that members of my family should visit me, without the restrictions which had been hitherto imposed.

This, however, displeased the provost-marshal and detective police, who determined to deprive me of the power of making known this concession, and took upon themselves still to refuse all passes to see me. The following is a copy of a letter which I wrote to Mrs. S. A. Douglas, which was returned to me:—

Old Capitol Prison: March 3, 1862.

My Dear Adie,—The superintendent, Mr. Wood, informed me some days since that the Secretary of War, Mr. Stanton, had ordered that Mrs. Douglas, Mr. and Mrs. Cutts, Mrs. Leonard, or any other member of my family, should have leave to visit me without a pass, or the accompaniment or presence of an officer, or anyone else, during the interview, which was to be unlimited; and I give you the words of the order, as well as I can remember, made by the superintendent in presence of the officer of the guard, and the same has been entered amongst the orders of the prison.

Rose has been very ill, brought on by the unheard-of cruelty of her incarceration. Just imagine a little child of eight years shut up for months, the only breath of air inhaled through the bars of a prison window. However, since two days we are actually allowed a half-hour's exercise in the prison-yard, where we walk up and down, picking our way as best we can through mud and negroes, followed by soldiers and corporals with bayonet in hand, ready to cry "halt!" if we turn to the right or the left. This is becoming a very tragical farce to me; and if I were not writing to so loyal a supporter of the Imperial Powers, I should say, May Heaven confound them! As it is, I shall only add, Goodbye, with my love.

Yours affectionately,

Rose O'N Greenhow.

Detective Police, for Mrs. S. A. Douglas.

This letter was detained by Captain Dennis of the detective police, who had now charge of the examination of my letters, by order of Porter Captain M Millen having fallen under his suspicion. The detective Captain Dennis pronounced Stanton a d—— fool for having given the order, and said that my letter should not go. I directed Mr. Wood to demand the return of the letter, intending to enclose it to Stanton. The following is a copy of a communication from Wood: —

Headquarters, City Police, Office of the Provost-Marshal.
Washington: April 5, 1862.
I called this day at the provost-marshal's office for Mrs. R. O'N. Greenhow's letter, addressed to Mrs. S. A. Douglas; having left the said letter two days since for examination. I find the letter still in the office, and am unable to obtain it.
William P. Wood,
Superintendent of Old Capitol Prison.
I know the above to be true,
G. R. Shiel,
Clerk at Provost-Marshal's Office.

Upon the receipt of this communication, I wrote to Stanton in the following terms: —

To Edwin M. Stanton, Secretary of War of United States.
Sir,—The superintendent of this prison informed me some days since of your considerate and humane order which I appreciate the more highly as being entirely gratuitous on your part—permitting members of my family to visit me without restriction.
I wrote a letter a few days since to a member of my family, communicating this information; and it is with great surprise that I learn that the letter has been detained by your detective police, or Provost-Marshal. I did not suppose, Sir, that even their audacity could reach this point—to hold back or suppress a letter, simply because it annunciated an order from the Secretary of War which *did not meet with their approbation.* I refrain from further comment, believing that you will properly rebuke the impertinence of your subordinates.
I have the honour to be, &c. &c.,
Rose O'N. Greenhow.

This communication I purposely sent open through the provost-marshal's office. A few hours after, I received the following:—

> Headquarters, City Police, &c.: March 5.
>
> Mrs. R. O'N Greenhow, I herewith return enclosed your letter to Mrs. S. A. Douglas, of 3rd instant. It contains improper matter, and is improperly directed.
>
> Very respectfully,
>
> S. Biddle Egberts, &c. &c.

About the beginning of February, a woman named Ada Hewit, daughter of a mechanic of Alexandria, calling herself Mrs. Morris Mason, was brought to the prison. She had, however, never been married, although the mother of two children, one of whom died a few days prior to her arrest. The immediate cause which led to her arrest was a letter written by her to Seward, claiming his protection from the attentions of Colonel Marcy (the father-in-law of M'Clellan), with whom she assumed to have established previously very amicable relations. Seward, after consultation with M'Clellan, had her incarcerated, in order to avoid a *family* scandal.

Mrs. William Henry Norris, of Baltimore, was also confined at the Old Capitol as a prisoner. She was a most excellent lady; was detained about two weeks, and was released upon parole through the influence of the Hon. Reverdy Johnson. The new regulations allowing half an hour in the prison yard had only gone into operation a few days before Mrs. Norris left, so that it was but a brief pleasure that I enjoyed in her society.

On March 6th, General Wordsworth called to see me in his character of Governor of the District, the first appointment of the kind made by Abraham the First. Consequently, the Provost-Marshal became simply chief of police, without other authority. A subordinate officer, Major Doster, was appointed to the place.

General Wordsworth was gentlemanly and kind, and seemingly recognised the right of a prisoner to be treated with humanity and respect. He appeared greatly surprised to hear of the system pursued towards myself and child, and ordered that I should enjoy, as a right, the usual exercise allotted to other prisoners; also, that my child should have the privilege of going outside the walls, accompanied by an officer. But it was one thing to make humane laws, and another to have them executed. The love of tyranny had become too strong a passion within those walls to be easily abolished; any appeal required two or three days to reach the proper quarter; each subordinate officer took upon himself to interpret the rules; and corporals and sergeants assumed the airs of their chiefs, and had to be daily instructed, for, alas! we were only rebels, and inhaled the air by sufferance.

The vexations and annoyances on this head were unceasing. The most brutal of the officers with whom I was brought in contact was Captain Gilbert, of the 91st Pennsylvania Volunteers (the same who had drilled the negroes), and Lieutenant Carlton, of Zanesville, Ohio. The most humane and kind were Captain Higgins and Lieutenant Miller, of New Jersey. These gentlemen merit the consideration of every prisoner for the reluctance with which they obeyed the harsh orders of their superiors; and, if the chances of war ever throw them in our midst, I should deem it a privilege, by every means in my power, to ameliorate their condition.

One day, on going down in the yard, the market-cart of the superintendent had just come in. My friend Charlie, who drove it, said, 'Will you take a ride?' I immediately got in—the other female prisoners following my example—exclaiming, 'I am off for Dixie!' and Charlie drove rapidly around the yard. It is impossible to describe the panic and confusion which ensued. All the prisoners rushed to the windows to enjoy the scene. The officer of the guard, Captain Gilbert, also rushed out, crying with might and main, 'Stop that wehickle!' The guard were doubled all around the yard, and, I believe, were actually preparing to fire upon us. After driving around the enclosure two or three times, we drew up in front of our redoubtable captain, who verily believed that an escape had been meditated, and that his timely intervention had alone frustrated it.

March 10.—The greatest dismay and anxiety was felt at Washington on account of the extraordinary prowess of the *Merrimac*, or the *Virginia*, as she had been newly christened. The War Department forbade the publication of her glorious achievements: one entire edition of a Baltimore paper was suppressed, from having contained a graphic account of the engagement. In spite of these vigilant efforts, it became widely spread; and Mr. Seward even awoke to the conviction that there was '*something the matter,*' and recommended to the Governors of the north-eastern States the subject of their coast defences. The Chamber of Commerce of New York hastily convened to take into consideration the harbour defences of that city. Each night the Abolition Government at Washington retired with the dread anticipation of seeing in the morning *the Norfolk Turtle* lying off the Potomac, ready to shell the White House. The Abolitionists hastily sent off their families, and a special train waited several days, with steam up, ready to bear off Lincoln and his Cabinet.

Quite an excitement was created throughout the prison, about this time, by the arrest of a woman in male attire. She was apprehended at the hotel of a man named Donnelly, in Washington, who, unfortunately for her, died a few days prior to her arrival. Her object had been to go to Richmond with the proffer of a projectile which her husband, who was in England, had invented, the model of which she had in her trunk. Donnelly was to have forwarded her over.

She was very handsome, and was a woman of some cultivation and scientific attainments. She was a keen observer, and both spoke and wrote well. Her room was adjoining mine; and, although there was a double door between, I was enabled to converse and pass communications through the keyhole. This had been arranged by a skilful use of the penknife by the gentlemen who had been removed for this prisoner, in order that we might in turn avail ourselves of each other's facilities in sending communications out of the prison.

Mrs. M Cartney was the name of this person, and, apart from her *costume*, there was nothing about her but was calculated to inspire respect, as her conduct was marked by great modesty and propriety. She was a monarchist in politics, had supreme contempt for the Abolition Government, and sneeringly enumerated its lawless acts in support of her thesis—that sooner or later all republican forms of government resolved themselves into unlimited despotisms. I was not tempted to controvert this position, being, as it was, entirely in accordance with my own experience of this '*most perfect Government the sun ever shone upon.*' She demanded her freedom, as there was no proof against her; and, for want of *proof*, she was, after a few weeks' imprisonment, discharged. I admired her spirit and independence, and wish her well wherever she may be.

This lady laid before the Government the most horrible outrage committed in that Old Capitol Prison—too dreadful, too revolting, to be mentioned here. She also wrote to Miss Dix, with whom she was well acquainted, describing the foul act, which caused Mr. Under-Secretary of War Watson to come to the prison under pretext of an investigation, which shifted the crime and responsibility from one set of officers and men to another, and was, in fact, a humbug, gotten up by the Superintendent Wood for the purpose of clearing himself, and allaying the excitement consequent upon the dark deed.

CHAPTER 15

Renewed Anxieties

On the 22nd of April, the Honourable Mr. Ely came to call upon me, and seemed magnanimously bent on serving me in some way. He said that he had been well and kindly treated at Richmond (where he had been as a prisoner since the Battle of Bull Run), and he had come to see what he could do for me. I told him that the only service I could receive from him was, to ascertain from his government the reasons for my detention, after the notification I had received, and what they intended to do. On the 26th he again called upon me. He told me that General Wordsworth informed him '*that the order for my detention had been given by M'Clellan, who objected to my release on the grounds that I knew his plans better than Lincoln, &c., and that he did not wish me sent South at this time.*'

Ely brought with him a New York paper, commenting harshly upon his visit to '*a lady who had done the national cause so much injury, and hoping that he would not repeat it, as his patriotism would be damaged by it in the public estimation,*' &c. He told me that this paper was brought to his seat by a member of Congress, with a friendly admonition against the '*repetition of the imprudence.*' Ely said that he took out the pass he had, and said, I am going to see Mrs. Greenhow at this moment, and will do all I can to resist this fanatical persecution, *for they did not treat me so at Richmond.*' On taking leave he asked me for my *carte de visite* (which I gave him), and said, 'Madam, I will call again to see if I can be of use,' &c. &c.

I replied, 'No; you will be refused a pass. They are afraid lest my fearless denunciations of their infamies may open the eyes of their followers, and make them question the orthodoxy of Abolitionism.'

I subsequently learned, through a message from Ely, that my prediction had been verified; for, on application again for a pass to visit me, it had been refused—and this was the last I heard of the Honourable Mr. Ely.

The tedium of my prison life at this time was greater than I can depict, and I now also began to realise the fact that my physical health was being gradually undermined by want of exercise and want of proper food. A feeling of lassitude was stealing over me, and a nervous excitability which prevented me from sleeping. My child's health was failing alarmingly also. I had nothing to read, and even the newspapers were served or not, according to the caprice of my jailors, and were very sure to be withheld whenever they contained Southern news.

My room swarmed with vermin, which the warm weather now caused to come out in myriads from their hiding-places; and, although at this time allowed the half-hour exercise in the prison yard, I could not regard it as relaxation, for the yard was filled with the stolen negroes, who lay about, obstructing the walk, or engaged in boisterous practical jokes during the while, in utter disregard of social distinction, and even ventured to seat themselves on the same bench. And I must also add that the association with the women prisoners was but a shade less obnoxious than that of this degraded servile class. Each day brought some collision between them and the guard, which was mortifying to me in the extreme.

The guard were at this time often extremely insolent, and questioned the slightest rule of privilege, so that it was necessary to make constant appeals to the officer on duty. One day, on going down, the guard very rudely placed his musket before me, and said, 'You shall not go down that way, and ordered me to go by a dirty back stair, which was not the usual route. I immediately sent for the officer of the guard, Lieutenant Miller, who passed me down. Sometime after the woman Baxley, and the one *calling herself Mrs. Morris*, or *Mason*, attempted to go down, and were also stopped by the guard, with whom they entered into an angry contest, and resolved in defiance to force their way through them.

Morris was pushed into a corner, and held there by a bayonet crossed before her, whilst the more daring of the two, Baxley, seized on the musket that obstructed her passage, and attempted to pass under it. The guard cursed her. She struck him in the face, which caused his nose to bleed, and he knocked her down and kicked her. Attracted by the commotion, I went up, under escort of Lieutenant Miller, when this statement was given to me and to the officer by the women, amidst sobs and cries—the guard, also, who witnessed it, giving substantially the same account. Thus, it will be seen that I must have suffered much from this humiliating association.

Captain Higgins came up to speak with me on the subject, greatly mortified at the occurrence, and said that he would punish the guard if he could have any justification in doing so. I told him that I thought it was a case which he could not take cognisance of, as he could only regard it as a fight between a prisoner and a guard, in which the prisoner was the aggressor. Captain Higgins then implored those prisoners to have no words with his guard, but to appeal to him in case of insolence or disrespect, and that they should be summarily punished.

At this time, I occasionally saw members of my family, who were admitted to see me under the special order to that effect from Secretary Stanton, although the privilege was necessarily used with great caution, as all who were known to be my friends were in consequence put under the surveillance of the detective police. The health of my child troubled me greatly. All her buoyancy was gone, and she would now lie for hours upon my lap with—'Mamma, tell me a story;' and, with a heavy heart, I have often beguiled her with wild and improbable legends, until she would fall into feverish slumbers in my arms.

Finally I resolved to make another appeal in behalf of my family physician being permitted to visit her, and wrote to General Wordsworth on the subject, stating her condition, &c. General Wordsworth, upon the receipt of my note, and the endorsement by the Superintendent of the alarming condition of the child, gave orders that Dr. Miller (who was himself under surveillance) should have a special order to visit me.

Dr. Miller, upon visiting me, found the condition of the child critical, and represented to the general the necessity of her having more nutritious food, also air and exercise; and thenceforward she was taken out very generally for a short time each day by one or other of the officers. Captain Higgins, Lieutenant Miller, and Lieutenant Holmes, were each very kind to Rose; they seemed to be ashamed of the persecution which could go so far as to threaten the life of a little child of eight years.

Several Federal officers were at this time confined as prisoners for various offences. One Dr. Cox, a surgeon in the regular United States Army, was arrested for disloyalty to the Government and sympathy with the rebels. I had a great deal of conversation with this officer through the keyhole of his door, the room being the same which had been occupied by Mrs. M'Cartney. He was the son of Dr. Cox, of Philadelphia, and a man of cultivation. After some weeks of imprisonment, his resignation, which had been previously tendered, was accepted, and he was liberated on parole. The others were mostly German officers taken up for stealing (or peculation, the term brought in vogue by Cameron), one the chief of Carl Schutts' staff.

A Mr. Morton, ex-Lieutenant-Governor of the State of New York, was a prisoner by order of Seward, whose deadly animosity he had excited. Poor man! he was most inhumanly treated, and was gradually dying from the effects of it. The keenest sympathy of all the prisoners was excited on his behalf. He was allowed communication with no one, not even his wife; and when his half-hour of exercise in the prison yard came round, everyone was driven in as if he had been stricken with the plague, and a solitary walk prescribed, in sight but out of reach of communion with the guards even.

I frequently sent out letters for him; but as he was in solitary confinement it was very difficult, and required the cooperation of several persons. The process was this: when Morton went down in the yard, he would watch his opportunity to bow to me—I having been previously notified that he was below. If I had an opportunity to communicate outside, I would hold up a letter—if not, would shake my head; and bitterly would my heart ache when I would see the desponding manner with which the poor fellow would let his head fall upon his breast when I would give the negative signal. By means of a string he would pass his letter to Captain Pliny Bryan, C.S.A., who would pass it by a similar process to Dr. Cox, U.S.A., from whom it would reach me.

My anxiety was at this time intense to receive correct information from the Confederacy. Things of vast importance were transpiring; and although I had long since discarded all faith in Yankee accounts of current events, being well satisfied of their mendacious character, I knew too well the power and malignity of the Government arrayed for the purpose of crushing us, to lull myself into a false security or even momentary forgetfulness of the perils which threatened us on all sides. In spite of our continued successes, gloom hangs over our devoted land. What matters it that we repulse the Vandals at every point?

The Battle of Shiloh, where the brave and accomplished Sidney Johnson fell, and which would have decided the fate of Europe, was scarcely felt by the invaders, who take no account of human life so long as their shattered ranks are filled up by the outcasts of civilised Europe, and so long as greedy speculators and contractors are reaping harvests in *greenbacks*.

The fate of New Orleans at this time made me weep tears of

blood. Oh! better that she had buried her whole population under her smoking ruins, than to have been given over a bloodless victory to the invaders; and from my soul I pray that heavy retribution may fall upon the dastards in the dark tragedy!

May 1.—The Abolition General, Butler, is in command of New Orleans. This man is, perhaps, better fitted to execute the wholesale order of Messrs. Seward & Co.—of devastation, rapine, and murder—than any other who could have been selected. He was a Northern democrat; had been a member of the Charleston Convention, where he exerted all his faculties in widening the breach and inflaming sectional animosities. He advocated the dissolution of the Union as one of the inevitable necessities of Lincoln's election, and no man hurled bolder defiance at the Abolition party, or denounced the unconstitutionally of their measures in more unequivocal terms. He proclaimed the doctrine of the inalienable rights of the South, and counselled resistance as the last measure of self-protection. This man remained in the councils of the Southern party up to a late hour, and heartily concurred in the justice of the doom of the miscreant John Brown.

One of the first administrative acts which emanated from Brigadier-General Butler as military Commander of New Orleans was the Order No. 28, commanding that the whole female population of that city should be subjected to outrage and infamy, *as common women of the town.* Comment hereupon would be out of place. The shuddering abhorrence with which the whole civilised world received its annunciation is the best record of this man's crimes to nations yet unborn.

Another of those Northern democrats, Caleb Cushing, who had been President of the Charleston Convention, asked me, at the time that the Virginia Convention was in cession, 'if I thought that the ordinance of secession would be passed.' I said 'Yes,' as I knew that certain measures were in contemplation by the Abolition Government which would make it imperative—alluding to the call for 75,000 men then being urged upon Lincoln.

He replied, 'I am very glad to hear it. I feared that Virginia would decide upon "armed neutrality;" and the South, in my opinion, has no other alternative in this crisis, in order to maintain her own dignity and independence, but to secede. Her Northern friends and supporters have a right to expect that she will not back down,' &c.

Further conversation on this head followed, and I was so much impressed with his strong Southern views and sympathies, that I almost

146

forgot that this man had once written and printed puffs eulogistic of himself.

A few months later, when the fanatical Abolition war fever was at its height, Caleb Gushing asked to be appointed Brigadier-General in the Abolition army, in order to aid in the subjugation of a people whom he had recommended *to resort to arms, as the only means left to them for the preservation of their rights, and to drive the invader from their soil.* O consistency! thou art a jewel unknown to Northern placemen. Lincoln refused him the appointment, not having confidence in the stability of this last *act of faith*—so I was informed by Senator Wilson, of Massachusetts.

This was the gloomiest period of my life. Time dragged most heavily. I had absolutely nothing to occupy myself with. I had no books, and often no paper to write on, and those who approached me appeared entirely oblivious of the mental as well as physical wants of a prisoner. My imprisonment seemed destined to be indefinitely prolonged. Hope even had fled, and left me chafing against my prison bars, with the iron of the despot eating into my soul.

I contrived to elude the vigilance of my gaolers, which was now greater than ever, and send a note to the Honourable James M. Bayard, United States Senator from Delaware, with a request that he would ascertain what was to be my fate, for the doubt and uncertainty which hung over me was more trying to me than the darkest reality.

Mr. Bayard, in pursuance of my request, went to General Wordsworth, the military Governor of the district, and was told by him 'that M'Clellan had countermanded the order for sending me South, and protested against it on the ground that I knew his plans better than Lincoln, having caused him four times to change them, and demanded that I should be held a prisoner for the war'—thus repeating substantially the old story. Mr. Bayard also obtained a pass to visit me, by reason of his having been a classmate of Wordsworth's.

Meanwhile, every species of annoyance was put upon me. My friends, on calling at the provost-marshal's, were often informed that *I had been gone South some several weeks*, and their newspapers published characteristic paragraphs about me: sometimes that I vehemently protested against leaving Washington; at others, that I had made a full confession of my treason. In answer to a paragraph that went the rounds on this head, and which was copied into the *Baltimore News Sheet*, I wrote the following:—

Sir,—I wish to correct a statement which has been copied into your paper. I have made no confession of treason, or treasonable correspondence; neither was I subjected to an examination intended to bring to the light my sources of information. I but claim the right which our fathers did in '76 to protest against tyranny and oppression.

Very respectfully,

Rose O'N. Greenhow.

★★★★★★★★★★

This note accidentally found its way into some books sent by me to the President's house, and was returned to me with the following gratifying note from the President:

Richmond: May 26, 1863.

Dear Madam,—The enclosed was found on the floor of my residence, and is returned to its owner. Accidentally I have thus been made acquainted with another of the many bitter trials to which your free spirit was subjected while your person was in the power of a vulgar despotism.

Very respectfully and truly yours,

Jefferson Davis.

★★★★★★★★★★

Extracts from my notes in Old Capitol Prison:—

Saturday, May 10.—This day at five o'clock the Yankees formally took possession of Norfolk, our troops having evacuated it in the forenoon. Direful events seem rapidly chasing each other. At first, I did not credit it, the Yankee papers having for the last ten days heralded the important event. The *Virginia*, the noble *Virginia*, also destroyed! I would rather have lost both of my hands than to be obliged to write this fact as *un fait accompli*. The exultation of the Yankees and their insolence are beyond all description. Strange, no feeling of despondency is in my heart. My confidence in the ultimate result—the achievement of our independence—is strong as the faith planted on the Rock of Ages; and even in this dark hour the star of hope rises steadily beyond the gloom, guiding us on to victory and to empire.

These great calamities have been permitted in order to arouse our people to a full sense of their peril, and to corresponding measures of resistance against our ruthless invaders. Altogether this has been a dark day in the prison. It may perhaps be well to say that my notes are principally in cipher. Captain Bryan and Harry Stewart are going to escape tonight—the attempt to be made when the guard whom they have bribed comes on at midnight. I long for the morrow, and the All's well! A presentiment of evil weighs me down. I have a raging nervous headache. I have just bidden them both goodbye, and given Bryan my pistol. This continued anxiety is killing me.

Sunday Morning, May 11.—I was aroused at a little after five by the report of a rifle, and a cry enough to startle the dead: Harry Stewart had been shot by the guard whom he had bribed. Being disappointed in the attempt at night, Bryan had given it up. But poor impetuous confiding Harry Stewart was induced by the guard, when he came on again at five, to renew the attempt. Dr. Cox and the other Yankee officers confined in the room above heard the plot between the guards to murder him; the man who was in his pay saying to the other, 'When he gets fairly out of the window I will cry "Halt!" and fire at the same time; you hold your fire until he is down, and then give it to him.'

The agreement by Stewart had been to give the man fifty dollars after he got down. The supposition was that they thought to rob him as they carried him round to the prison entrance. His friends, however, defeated this by drawing him up into his room. His leg was dreadfully shattered, making amputation necessary; but he was so much prostrated by loss of blood previous to the operation that he could not rally from the effects of the chloroform, but died between three and four o'clock.

On the evening of the 12th an examination took place in the prison, ostensibly for the purpose of establishing the fact of the bribery, and Dr. Cox and the other Yankee officers made the statement above; and it is inexplicable why the victim had not been warned by them of the murderous plot.

My own evidence was taken, having been cognisant of the whole affair, and hearing the agreement with the guard. I was asked if I would aid a prisoner in an attempt, &c. I answered 'Yes.' I considered it a point of honour to render any aid in money or otherwise. The woman calling herself Morris certified that I had furnished the means, through my sister, Mrs. Leonard, for the escape, &c., thereby causing the arrest and detention of my sister for several days. She demanded to be brought before the Secretary of War, when the Assistant-Secretary Watson informed her that the charge had been made against her by this woman; at the same time, he released her from custody. I saw my sister but once afterwards, when she left the city as no longer a safe place for her.

149

My child is so nervous from a repetition of these dreadful scenes that she starts and cries out in her sleep. Horrors like this will shatter the nerves of the strongest.

13th.—The murderer has been released from custody, promoted to a corporal, and put again on duty on this post. I sent for the officer of the guard, and remonstrated against it as an outrage and insult to every prisoner, and that, if allowed to remain, he would probably be killed before the day was over. He was in consequence sent away.

May 14.—The sky of our destiny is brightening. The successes of the gallant Ashby and Jackson have inspired the Yankees with wholesome dread, and they again apprehend a descent on Washington. But they watch me more closely in consequence. When will this end? I am nearly starved. I had a fowl served up to me today (or rather a small piece of one), which must have been the cock which crowed thrice to wake Peter; we could not get our teeth through it. Rose cried heartily, for she was very hungry. Captain Bryan, and the other gentlemen below, have just smuggled me a supper. I should starve but for the considerate kindness of these gentlemen.

May 15.—Last night the wildest panic prevailed. The long roll was beat; the guard doubled round the prison; and the rumbling of artillery and tramp of men, yelling and cursing as they marched, kept us all on the *qui vive*. Yet even amidst our wild hopes mingled dread, for we believed that our brutal guard would endeavour to wreak their vengeance upon us in the event of an attempt at rescue: threats to that effect had often been vaguely uttered.

The panic was caused by a number of mules breaking their *coral*, and coming across the Long Bridge. The clatter of their hoofs alarmed the pickets, who fled in great terror, communicating the panic in their route, that Jackson, Ashby, and Stuart were in hot pursuit, with a mighty army.

Oh, that it had been true! that our hosts could sweep over their lands, and leave behind the desolating footprint of war! for as yet this people have known none of its horrors, but made mighty profit thereby. Their manufacturing interests are revived with renewed energy in the furnishing of implements of war, clothing, and other supplies for their vast armies in the field, whilst Mr. Chase complacently duplicates *greenbacks*, chuckling over the issue of each additional million as a step nearer to national bankruptcy, and the absolute despotism which is to rise out of the ruin of the old system.

Heaven speed them in their work! and may no ray of common sense stay their onward march!

How farcical now seem the boasted Government of our fathers, the Declaration of Independence, and the Constitution of the United States!—almost as much so as the Constitution of the kingdom of Lilliput, and which the first rude shock has scattered to the winds. That profound and thinking men should now believe in the permanence of a system based upon such feeble security as the integrity of the governing power is still the wonder.

I can only hope that the experience of the past will guide our own people in the formation of a government which will be eternal, with no element of disruption in it.

May 17.—We are all in good spirits. Accounts are received daily of skirmishes, in which our people are always successful. The Yankees are in continual dread of Jackson's advance on Washington.

May 18.—A senatorial committee have just visited the prison. I cannot understand precisely the object of it, although certainly not meant for the benefit of the prisoners. Wood is very uneasy. Wilson, of Massachusetts, was brought by him to see me, and in the course of conversation told me that I was, up to that period, the most important prisoner taken; that he had, nevertheless, advised my being immediately sent South, but 'that Seward, M'Clellan, and the *rest*' thought differently; that I would soon, however, be set free, as the rebellion would be crushed out in a little while, as Richmond had already fallen. I told him that, if Richmond fell, it would bury the Abolitionists under its ruins, and rise from its ashes the capital of a mighty empire.

I do not venture to repeat the whole of my conversation with this Abolition leader, for all the bitterness and contempt which I felt for his race was thrown into it. In the course of the interview, I had the satisfaction of seeing the jealousy and division amongst themselves, which I welcomed with joy, as the *avant-courier* of the bitter retribution—in the shape of civil war at the North—which is to terminate the national existence of that corrupt and debased people. The progress of events is slow but sure, for they now groan under the yoke of absolute despotism, although all outspoken expression of discontent is suppressed.

The leaders are, however, aware of its existence, and hope to avert the catastrophe by a vigorous invasion of the South, and the employment of all the evil passions of their race in that unholy crusade.

151

May 19.—There is again a talk of removing me to another prison. Since the murder of Harry Stewart, all my friends are interdicted from visiting me; and as I will not associate with the women prisoners, I am in absolute solitude. The hope of being released has quite unsettled my prison routine, and I find it very difficult to fix my mind on anything but the unutterable weariness of my lot. When will it end? I shrink with terror from the contemplation of the indefinite future, and try to fix my mind upon the heroic deeds of my countrymen—for in them indeed is my trust, my only hope.

May 21.—Mr. Wood came to me just now, and told me, if I would write him a note asking him to recover my papers, that he thought he could get them. I question it very much; nevertheless, —I will do it: so I addressed him the following note:—

> Mr. Wood, Superintendent, etc. etc.
>
> Old Capitol Prison: May 21.
> Sir,—Believing that the "decree" for my release of your *Revolutionary Commission* will be acted upon some time before the millennium, I therefore most respectfully beg that you will use every exertion to obtain the restoration of my papers, seized some nine months ago, when I was first made a prisoner by order of this *invincible Government*.
> Very respectfully,
>
> Rose O'N. Greenhow.

To this demand I received the following reply:—

> Mrs. Greenhow,—If you will be kind enough to dispense with the God and Liberty style in your *pronunciamento*, and give me a plain *power* of attorney to receipt for your papers, I shall use every power to obtain them; and I shall be happy to restore them to you (the proper person to have them).
> W. P. Wood.

To this I answered Mr. Wood:—

> To make reference to God, or Liberty either, behind the bars of this prison, to its *admirable administrator*, would be—knowing *your peculiar views*—in as bad taste as writing in a dead language. As to my papers, they may even remain where they are until I shake off the chains of tyranny.
> Very respectfully,   Rose O'N. Greenhow.

In order to make the above intelligible, I must state that this man was an *infidel*—that he derided Christianity, and exercised his astute reasoning powers in the analysis of those mysteries which our dull materialism was not destined to fathom, *as proofs of the absurdity of a faith founded upon theories and traditions so wild and vague as to be rejected when submitted to the test of reason.* He also rejected the evidence of the Bible in support of Christianity, and denied its sacred character. His text-book was the writings of Paine; and if anyone asked him for a book to read, he was sure either to give them, as a great favour, a folio volume of his own writings, collected in the form of a scrap-book, with the ideas of Paine intensified or diluted, or else, as a special mark of grace, the works of that *infidel*; for, apart from other peculiarities patent to every prisoner, his desire to make proselytes to his own *want of faith* was the ruling passion of his soul.

He was vindictive, cunning, and ambitious, repelled with warmth any claim to being considered a gentleman, and yet, strange to say, was by no means devoid of some generous inspirations; for I have known him to perform acts of great magnanimity and generosity. Stanton was his patron, to whom he seemed bound by strong ties. So, it will be readily seen that he neither feared God nor man, and that William P. Wood, Abraham Lincoln, and the Emperor of Russia were the most irresponsible absolute despots on earth.

23rd.—My existence is now a positive blank. Day glides into day with nothing to mark the flight of time, and hope paints no silver lining to the clouds which hang over me. Wood tantalises me each day with expectation of something which never happens. In a fit of vexation, I ordered him not to address himself to me save in his official capacity. I almost wish I had not done it; for the chattering of a monkey would even break pleasantly on the monotony of my life.

May 25.—Today, as I walked in the prison yard, a prisoner captured at Front Royal, Virginia, threw at my feet a small piece of paper containing intelligence which made my heart leap with joy. I eagerly devoured its contents, which were that a battle had been fought on the 23rd and 24th at Front Royal, in which we had gained a great victory, having driven the Yankees from the town, and taken 1,470 prisoners, besides a large quantity of stores, which we very much needed. All honour to the brave Jackson, who is now the special terror of the Yankees!

26th.—Great excitement prevails here. The Abolitionists are again sending off their families. Last night I put my candle on the window, in order to get something out of my trunk, near which it stood, all unconscious of committing any offence against prison discipline, when the guard below called out, 'Put out that light.' I gave no heed, and only lighted another; whereupon several voices took up the cry, adding, 'D—n you, I will fire into your room.' Rose was in a state of great delight, and collected all the ends of candle to add to the illumination. By this the clank of arms and clatter of feet, in conjunction with a furious rap at my door, and demand to open it, announced the advent of corporals and sergeants.

My door was now secured inside by a bolt which had been allowed me. I asked their business. Answer—'You are making signals, and must remove your lights from the window.'

I said, 'But it suits my convenience to keep them there.'

'We will break open your door if you don't open it.'

'You will act as you see fit, but it will be at your peril.'

They did not dare to carry out their threat, as they knew that I had a very admirable pistol on my mantelpiece, restored to me a short time since, although they did not know that I had no ammunition for it. The guard, meanwhile, were doubled around the prison on every post, and the 'All's well' cried throughout the night. I subsequently explained to the officer of the guard the absurdity of the whole proceeding, which he had the good sense to admit. An order, however, came from the provost-marshal to capture my pistol, which was accordingly done with reluctance by Lieutenant Miller. I relate this as one of the absurd events which were constantly occurring, sometimes in a far more offensive form.

27th.—Oh, how weary I am! I have not had even the newspapers for several days. An odd volume of *Silvio Pellico* has helped me to beguile the heavy hours; but the similarity of my own fate with that of other victims of tyranny does not diminish my sense of suffering. The heat is intense, with the sun beating down upon the house-top and in the windows; the stench terrible; and hunger gnawing at one's vitals; for, alas! I cannot eat the food set before me. My child is looking pale and ill. 'He who entereth here leaves hope behind' is written in letters of blood over the portal of Lincoln's prison. But even in this bitter cup there is a sweet drop of consolation: it is that the gulf is widening between the two races; each victim immolated by the tyrant but makes the barrier more impassable. That thought sustains me in the dread ordeal.

28th.—The Yankee papers this morning are certainly trying to cover a defeat under extravagant boastings. Mr. Stanton is again exhibiting his skill in his peculiar line in aid of Mr. Chase's Wall-Street gambling. Have just had a telegram from below that a battle has been fought at Winchester, where the Yankees were defeated with great loss by Stonewall Jackson. This news was brought in by some prisoners just arrived; also, that our great and good President is in perfect health, the Yankees having reported him in a critical state. The wish was father to the thought. May angels guard him, for his country's sake!

29th.—Alarm here on the increase. Jackson supposed to be *en route* for Washington. Yankee sentinels very humble and conciliatory. Banks states that his defeat was caused by the War Department taking away 10,000 men to reinforce M'Clellan, &c.

30th.—A long dull day, with tantalising rumours of my being sent to Fort Warren. Wood says I am certainly to be sent away, and advises me to hold myself in readiness. Alas! my faith in Yankee human nature is long since gone.

Saturday, May 31.—At two o'clock today Wood came in with the announcement that I was to start at three o'clock for Baltimore. It being impossible to be ready at that hour, the time was extended to five o'clock. There was a terrible scene between Wood and the woman Baxley last night; she raved and screamed throughout the night. I could not sleep, so have a dreadful nervous headache with which to begin my journey. I do not pretend to understand the merits of the case. In justice I must state how very kind Captain Higgins, Lieutenant Miller, and Mr. Wood have been today. Captain Higgins carried me throughout the prison, to say 'Goodbye' to my companions in captivity. I exhorted them all to bear up bravely under their misfortune—not that they needed it, for all burned to be free, to share in the glorious struggle now going on. God grant that they were, for many a stout arm would strike a blow for freedom!

After taking leave of these kind friends, Captain Higgins introduced Lieutenant ——, who was, by order of the War Department, to be the chief of my escort. He had six men detailed to accompany him, making quite a military display, dressed in full uniform, with sword and carbine in hand. Outside of the prison the whole guard were drawn up under arms, besides a mounted guard of twelve men, also with swords and carbines. Before entering the carriage, I turned to the officer and said, 'Sir, ere I advance further. I ask you, not as Lincoln's officer, but as a man of honour and a gentleman, are your orders from Baltimore to conduct me to a Northern prison, or to some point in the Confederacy?'

He replied, with politeness and promptness, 'On my honour, madam, to conduct you to Fortress Monroe, and thence to the Southern Confederacy, in proof of which I show you my order for transportation,' &c.

Satisfied on this head, I entered the carriage. The woman Baxley, and the one calling herself Mrs. Morris, Mason, &c., were sent at the same time. The superintendent who accompanied, and the officer and guard, as also the mounted escort, followed the carriage, with carbines and drawn swords, to the depot. Arrived there, a large force was in attendance to prevent communication with sympathising friends. These precautions, however, failed, for many a word was stealthily whispered, and many a hearty 'God bless you!' spoken. A separate car was taken for the prisoners and guard.

Arriving at Baltimore, the car in which I was was kept back until all the passengers had left the depot—a strong military guard being here also in attendance. I was put into a carriage with my child, the other prisoners in another, and was driven (with the officer inside of the carriage with me, and the guard on the box) to the Gilmer House, the officer and guard jealously watching to prevent communication. Apartments being prepared, I was taken to mine. Sentinels were stationed at the different doors to prevent communication, all intercourse being prohibited. My name had been put in the register. The detective Baker, by order of General Dix, had it erased, as they did not wish it known that I was in that rebel city.

General Dix, being telegraphed to go to Washington, left early on Sunday morning; consequently Mr. Wood took upon himself to relax the rigorous interdict, and allowed me to see some kind and sympathising friends; and my soul expanded once more under the genial influences of a kindred race.

At five o'clock on the afternoon of Sunday, June 1, the officer of the guard announced that all was in readiness to depart for the boat, which had been detained for the purpose of conveying me to Fortress Monroe. A large number of persons had by this assembled to offer congratulations. The good news had reached *our friends* that a battle had been fought, and that skirmishing was still going on, at Seven

Pines, near Richmond, in which we had defeated the Yankees with heavy loss. This, of course, was the brightest augury that could have greeted me.

The 'goodbye' was spoken, and many friends followed to the boat. Upon reaching it a guard was stationed around, who, with bayonet in hand, repulsed every attempt of any but the prisoners to go on board, such being the orders. General Dix and suite being expected, the boat was detained for them several hours. During all that time, an eager crowd surrounded the approaches to the wharf, and, regardless of the angry and rude repulse of the military, continued to assemble. So far as the eye could reach handkerchiefs were waving, and the tearful eye and hearty 'God bless you!' which responded from all sides, regardless of the bayonets of the tyrant, told that the hearts of the people of Maryland, however repressed and downtrodden, beat in unison with their brethren of the South.

General Dix arriving about eight o'clock, the signal was given to weigh anchor, and I was fairly *en route* for the capital of the Confederacy. General Dix, after a few moments, came to pay his respects to me, and in very kind terms expressed his congratulations, &c. I was deeply Chagrined at the rude conduct of the *two women* towards General Dix, and rebuked it by my manner as well as I could. The boat reached the wharf at Fortress Monroe at an early hour on the morning of June 2. General Dix and suite went ashore here for the purpose of relieving General Wool, who had made himself so obnoxious to the people of Norfolk and its vicinity, on account of his harshness and cruelty, that the Abolition Government deemed it politic to replace him by one whose kind and conciliatory conduct had been deeply appreciated by the people of Baltimore. I regretted the exchange, for I did not wish the bitter pill of national degradation to be sugar-coated. The fiercer the rule, the more certain the retribution to follow.

No orders had been given to provide refreshments, but the captain of the boat, who was a most gentle manly person, prepared at his own cost a most ample luncheon, together with some iced champagne; and I had the pleasure of proposing the health of President Davis and the success of the Confederate cause under the bristling guns of the enemy, and my toast drunk by all present, several visitors having been added to the number on board. The officer of the guard behaved very well, and discreetly got out of hearing.

Meanwhile an *aide-de-camp* of General Wool, accompanied by the provost-marshal, Colonel Jones, came on board to make arrangements for forwarding me on my journey. Colonel Jones asked me where I wished to go. I replied, 'To the capital of the Confederacy, wherever that might be.' He told me that it was still Richmond asserting that that city had not fallen, as had been published at the North, but that it would be in their hands before I got there. I said I would take the chances, and only asked that no time might be lost. Colonel Gay fell into conversation with me, and I gleaned some very interesting facts from him. He was in a short time summoned away, and, I was told, put under arrest, *for having been too communicative.*

About four o'clock in the afternoon I was called upon to be in readiness to go on board of the boat which had been chartered to take me to City Point, and marched through the broiling sun to the place where she lay. Sometime after the boat got under way, but made no great progress. Night coming on, and the river (the James River) being difficult of navigation, the buoys having all been taken up by our people, the captain was afraid of running aground, so lay to until daylight. On the morning of the 3rd, about seven o'clock, we came in sight of the glorious achievements of the *Virginia*, the wreck of the *Congress* and other vessels destroyed by her. The *Monitor* lay down the stream at a short distance, and I had a good view of the low black ugly thing. At this point the captain again anchored, and an officer went off in a small boat to get instructions from the commander of the *Monitor* for landing me.

After an absence which seemed endless, a large-sized boat put off from her, in which I, with the other prisoners, embarked, and were taken alongside of the *Monitor*, an officer from that boat coming on board, in command of the party to City Point. I was under intense excitement, for, after nearly ten weary months of imprisonment, I was in sight of the promised land. In a short time, we reached the shore, and my foot pressed the sacred soil. I had worn on my shoulders from Fortress Monroe, in the folds of a shawl, a large battle-flag, which had been made by myself and other prisoners whilst in prison for General Beauregard. I felt strongly tempted to unfold it and cast it to the breeze, as a parting defiance to the Yankees; but I remembered that the same means might be useful again.

I was received by Colonel Ash and other Confederate officers, whose bold and soldierly bearing contrasted most strikingly with the Vandal race whom I had seen, I hope, for the last time.

I was conducted under escort of those gentlemen to Petersburg, where I was received with every demonstration of kindness and respect. General Ransom, the Commander of the Department, came to call upon me, and took charge of the arrangements for my departure to Richmond, and sent Colonel Ash to escort me. I arrived in Richmond on the morning of the 4th, and was taken to the best hotel in the place, the Ballard House, where rooms had been prepared for me. General Winder, the Commandant of Richmond, came immediately to call upon me, so as to dispense with the usual formality of my reporting to him.

On the evening after my arrival our President did me the honour to call upon me, and his words of greeting, 'But for you there would have been no Battle of Bull Run,' repaid me for all that I had endured, even though it had been magnified tenfold. And I shall ever remember that as the proudest moment of my whole life, to have received the tribute of praise from him who stands as the apostle of our country's liberty in the eyes of the civilised world.

It would swell these pages far beyond my prescribed limits if I were to enter upon a description of the exciting scenes which met my eye on my arrival at Richmond. All was warlike preparation and stern defiance and resistance to the invader. The result of the battles before Richmond is well known, and exhibits to the world the capabilities of a people in the defence of their rights.

The proud triumphant foe, with every advantage of numbers, &c., in his favour, who flaunted his banner before our capital, threatening us with annihilation, was defeated and driven for shelter behind his gunboats. The scene of their insolent triumph was changed into a charnel-house, with the very air rank and pestiferous with the effluvia from their half-decomposed bodies, where they lay as a warning monument to tyrants for all future time. This is a fruitful theme for abler pens than mine.

My intention is, in the succeeding chapter, to touch upon the causes which have effected the disruption of the Federal compact between North and South, as an exemplification of the evil consequences which flow from usurpation.

CHAPTER 16

Man Incapable of Self-Government

In this, my concluding chapter, I shall touch upon a subject which properly does not come within my text, and I approach it with a gravity commensurate with its importance.

It is not my purpose to elucidate the causes which have brought about the downfall of the American Republic. I do not pretend to the character of a publicist, or that of a philosophical historian. But as an attentive, and, I trust, impartial observer, I think I can correct some grave misconceptions of the events which have gained credence.

In the first place, slavery, although the occasion, was not the producing cause of the dissolution. The cord which bound the sections together was strained beyond its strength, and, of course, snapped at the point where the fretting of the strands was greatest.

The contest on the part of the North was for supreme control, especially in relation to the *fiscal* action of the Government. This object could not be fully attained by a mere *numerical majority. A majority of States was also necessary.* To secure this majority, and thus complete the *political ascendency* of the North, the policy of '*no more Slave States*' was formally set forth.

A political party was formed, whose sole principle was the exclusion of slavery from the territories. There was no moral sentiment involved in this. It did not alter the *status* of slavery. It made not a human being free; nor did it propose to do so. 'Sir,' said Mr. Webster in the Senate, 'this is not a moral question: it is a question of political power.' Lord Russell has more recently corroborated this bold assertion, by saying, that '*this was a struggle on one side for supremacy, and on the other for independence.*'

On the other hand, the Southern States, struggling for equality, and seeking to maintain the equilibrium of the Government, insisted upon the rights of their citizens to enter and live in the new territories upon terms of equality with the men north of Mason and Dixon's line. They contended for the right of extending their social institutions, not to propagate slavery—not to make a single human being a slave that would otherwise be free—but simply to preserve the equilibrium of power between the two sections.

It is true that the anti-slavery fanaticism was brought to bear; and it is also true that there followed a rancorous agitation which divided churches, rent asunder political parties, diminished and embittered the intercourse of society, and unfitted Congress for the performance of its constitutional duties, and resulted in the estrangement of the Southern people from their Northern connection. But this estrangement was not an active or stimulating motive, and manifested itself rather in the want of any general anxiety to restrain the movement for disunion.

Equally unfounded is the allegation that the secession of the South originated in the exasperation of a defeated party, and hostility to the successful candidate. The personal character of Mr. Lincoln, and his political opinions (except so far as they represented that 'armed doctrine' which menaced the equality of the Southern States, and was contrived for their oppression and degradation), had not formed with the Southern people the subject of either interest or enquiry. They knew that there were in the Constitution important checks which would furnish them with ample means of protecting themselves against the hostile purposes of the existing incumbent, and even of repairing such violations of the fundamental law as might during his term of service be beyond their control.

The stern protest of the Southern people, free from all party violence and recklessness, indicated a thorough knowledge of the extent and depth of the grievances inflicted upon them; and subsequent events have proved that they had both wisdom and heroism adequate to evolve the proper remedy, and firmly to apply it. They regarded it as the first step towards the overthrow of American representative liberty. Even considering the Northern theory of government to be true—*viz.* that the Union was one consolidated Republic—it is essential that the central authority derive its powers and draw its force from all the parts of the entire nation, so that by their reciprocal independence they can counteract the tendency of any one part to usurp the sovereignty of the whole.

When the North assumed the government over the South, as its own exclusive possession, it sought to establish an unmitigated tyranny. For liberty, true civil liberty, cannot exist where *rights* are on one side of a geographical line, and the *power* on the other.

The Southern people are law-abiding, long-suffering, tenacious in their attachments, and opposed even to a fault to innovations; but where the alternative was presented of an overthrow of their political liberty, or a change in their Federal relations, they did not hesitate.

To prove that they were fully justified, I will cite the testimony of ex-President Fillmore, a Northern statesman, never charged with Southern or pro-slavery sympathies:—

'We see a political party presenting candidates for the Presidency and Vice-Presidency, selected for the first time from the Free States alone, with the avowed purpose of electing those candidates by the suffrage of *one part of the Union only, to rule over the whole of the United States.* Can it be possible that those who are engaged in such a measure can have seriously reflected upon the consequences which must inevitably follow in case of success? *Can they have the madness or folly to believe that our Southern brethren would submit to be governed by such a chief magistrate?'*

After inveighing with great earnestness against a course so monstrous, he adds: 'These are serious but practical questions, and in order to appreciate them fully, it is only necessary to turn the tables upon ourselves. Suppose that the South, having a majority of the electoral votes, should declare that they would only have slaveholders for Presidents, and should elect such by their exclusive suffrages to rule over us at the North. *Do you think that we would submit to it?* (Cries of "No, never!") *No, not for a moment. And do you believe that our Southern brethren are less sensitive upon this subject than you, or less jealous of their rights?* If you do, let me tell you that you are mistaken. And, therefore, you must see that, if this sectional party succeeds, it leads inevitably to the destruction of this beautiful fabric reared by our forefathers, consolidated by their blood, and bequeathed to us as a priceless blessing.'

I call especial attention to the following views, not only on account of their intrinsic value, but from the notoriety which attaches to the author as the *interested advocate* of the Lincoln Government. I doubt if the annals of revolution furnish a more flagrant instance of political apostasy. But I will appeal from Philip drunk to Philip sober.

The following is a portion of the letter by the Hon. R. J. Walker, entitled 'An Appeal for the Union,' setting forth the enormity of the pretensions of the Abolition party, and the consequences certain to succeed their assumption of the control of the Government.

Letter From the Hon. Robert J. Walker,
Entitled 'An Appeal for the Union'.
Hon. Charles Shaler and others, Democratic Committee, Pittsburgh, Pennsylvania.

New York: Tuesday, Sept. 30, 1856.

We are approaching the close of a momentous struggle. On the one side is arrayed the Democratic party. It exists in every State, and over its united columns float the flag of the Constitution and of the Union. On the other side is found a sectional and geographical party, composed exclusively of the States of the North. The father of his country clearly foresaw the danger of such a party, and warned us against its fatal tendency, in his affectionate farewell address. But his solemn appeals and prophetic forebodings are swept from our memory, amid the wild uproar of geographical strife and sectional prejudice.

For the first time in our history, such a geographical party is now formed. It is composed exclusively of the States of the North, and is arrayed in violent hostility against the Southern section of the Confederacy. It draws a line, clear and distinct, between the North and the South, and wars upon the people and institutions of the latter. It declares the institutions of the South so degraded and infamous, that Congress must exclude them from all that vast territory acquired by common blood and treasure, and which is the joint inheritance of all the States of the Union. Louisiana (including Kansas and Nebraska) was acquired by Jefferson and saved by Jackson. But the South are no longer held worthy to inherit any portion of that territory, acquired by the illustrious patriot of Virginia, and saved by the immortal hero of Tennessee.

So, too, with all the vast region acquired in the war with Mexico. Two gallant sons of Virginia, Scott and Taylor, were the leaders of those brilliant campaigns. The blood of the South was poured out in copious libations, and mingled freely with the blood of the North, upon the many and well-fought fields of Mexico. Beside the gallant sons of the North an heroic regiment of South Carolina was swept by the deadly fire of the Mexican forces. Leader after leader, column after column, of that regiment fell mortally wounded, yet the survivors never wavered, and their arms were crowned with victory.

Yet no son of Carolina, or of all the South, is held worthy to

163

possess any, the smallest portion of all that territory acquired from Mexico. From the whole coast of the Pacific the South is already excluded, and now the platform of the Sectional party of the North is this: The universal Wilmot proviso—no slave territory, and no more Slave States north or south of the line of the Missouri Compromise.

There shall be no division of the common territory, but the North must have the whole. There are fifteen Southern and sixteen Northern States, seven organised Territories, and a vast region yet to be organised. The North must have all these, and all our future acquisitions. No matter what may be the voice or vote of the people of the Territory, or when becoming a State. You shall have no voice or vote in the matter, but the North, commanding a Northern majority in the Electoral College and in Congress, must have the whole.

But it is said the North has the majority, and the South must submit. Has then the South no rights, or does she hold them merely at the mercy of a Northern majority? Has the South no claims on the justice of the North, and is it not unjust to exclude the South from all the common territory of the Union? But this is not a mere question of justice, but of constitutional power. *The Constitution was framed and ratified by the States, each voting and acting for itself alone. Thus, we became 'United States;' a Confederacy, not a central Republic—a Confederacy receiving all its power from the States, through an instrument called by them the Constitution, granting therein only certain specified powers, and reserving all others.* It is clear, then, that Congress can exercise such powers only as are granted by the Constitution, and that all their laws, not based upon the delegated powers, are founded on usurpation, and are absolute nullities.

Now, the Constitution delegates no power to establish or abolish slavery in States or Territories. Such is the opinion of the South, and of a large minority (if not a majority) of the North. But it is said, the North claims that such power in the Territories is granted to Congress by the Constitution. The South denies the existence of any such power. How is the question to be decided? Most clearly, not by the North, or the South, but, as a disputed question of constitutional law, by the Supreme Court of the United States.

Now, before the repeal of the Missouri Compromise, the South proposed to carry that line to the Pacific, although it gave them but three degrees and a half on that ocean, leaving twelve degrees and a half to the North. That measure passed the Senate, but was voted down in the House by a Northern majority. Thus, the North seized the whole coast on the Pacific, nearly equal to our entire front on the Atlantic. The South yielded, but uniformly thereafter most justly regarded the Missouri Compromise as repudiated by the North, rejected by their votes, and denounced by their addresses.

The South next proposed to submit the disputed question of the power of Congress over slavery in the Territories to the adjudication of the Supreme Court of the United States. That measure, known as the Clayton Compromise, also passed the Senate, and was voted down in the House by a Northern majority. This most wise and patriotic measure submitted this question to the supreme judicial tribunal created by the Constitution, clothed by it with full authority to expound that instrument, and to restrain Congress within the limits of the specific granted powers.

But this peaceful and final arbitrament of this question, proposed by the South, was rejected by the North.

The so-called 'Republican' party does not adopt the restoration of the Missouri Compromise, but distinctly repudiates that measure, and declares there shall be no Slave Territory and no more Slave States, anywhere or under any circumstances, admitted to the Union, however clear or unanimous may be the will of the people of such State or Territory, or how far South the location. The very question, then, on which this party rests is sectional: its candidates are sectional, and, anticipating no electoral vote from the South, it looks for success exclusively to the North. Nay, more: it assumes the exclusive right of the North to decide this question, and rejecting all division of the common territory by any line, it claims the whole for the North, discards the vote of the people of the Territory, either before or in becoming a State, and rejects also the arbitrament of the Supreme Court of the United States.

It is conceded that, under the Constitution of the United States, slaves are property; and whether they may or may not be held as such in the Territories is the great disputed question of constitutional law. It involves rights of property, and as such is peculiarly a judicial question. *But the Supreme Court of the Union is to be superseded by the popular suffrage of the North, and these rights of property are thus to be decided. Such a doctrine is not only sectional, aggressive, and belligerent, but agrarian and revolutionary. It is an overthrow of the Constitution, of all its guarantees, and of every Conservative principle on which it is founded. Such a government would not be a Constitutional Republic, but an elective despotism. But it is said the North are the majority, and such is their will. Sic volo, sic jubeo, stat pro ratione voluntas.*

But the votes and will of the French people made Napoleon the Great first their Consul, and then their Emperor; and the votes and will of the French people made Napoleon III. first their President, and then clothed him with the imperial purple. Such was the will of the people; but with us the Constitution is the supreme law, and so declared in that instrument, as framed and ratified by the people of each State. That Constitution, after withholding all but the specifically granted powers, distributes their exercise between the legislative, executive, and judicial authorities.

It rendered paramount to Congress the decree of the Supreme Court of the United States. It gave to that Court the power to expound the law, and especially that supreme law called the Constitution. But this Court is superseded by the refusal of the North to submit this question to its decision, and the substitution of the will of a Northern majority. If constitutional guarantees and judicial decisions are thus to be overthrown through the vote of the people by Congress, why not also in the States by the State Legislatures, and the doctrine established that all rights of property in the Territories are held subject to the will of the people in the election of Congress; and all rights of property in the States to the will of the people in the election of State Legislatures? If the Constitution is to be disregarded, judicial tribunals superseded, and questions involving rights of property decided at the ballot-box by the people in one case, why not in all others?

The doctrine, if asked to be applied to one species of property in Kansas today, may be extended to all property everywhere tomorrow. It may be extended to lands, houses, rents, vessels, railroads, debts, stocks, and all other property, and may subject them all to division or confiscation by the decision of the people at the ballot-box. If it is right for the North, by the vote of the majority, to deprive the South, who are a minority, of all rights in the common territory of the Union, and to supersede judicial tribunals on disputed points of constitutional law involving rights of property, will not the same principle apply to the State Legislatures in each of the States, and the tenure of all property be decided by the people at each successive election? The truth is, the Black 'Republican' party is revolutionary and agrarian; it involves principles which must strike down the tenure of all property in every State as well as in every Territory of the Union. It discards the peaceful arbitrament of the Supreme Court of the United States—the great Conservative feature of our institutions; it overthrows the Constitution and all its guarantees, and substitutes in their place an elective despotism, by which a majority of the people may abolish, divide, or confiscate all property at each successive election. It is said the majority of this tribunal are from the South, and therefore the North cannot trust them with the decision of this great constitutional question.

It is but a majority of one, and that one the venerable Chief Justice, born and ever residing in the most conservative of all the States of the South, bordering upon the North, with but very few slaves, from which the Institution of Slavery is rapidly disappearing; with its great river, the Susquehanna, leading into the heart of Pennsylvania and traversing large portions of the State of New York; a State, three-fourths of whose trade and intercourse, by bays and rivers, by railroads and canals, is with the Free States of this Confederacy.

But if such a tribunal cannot be trusted, in executing the functions assigned to it by the Constitution, because it numbers from the South a majority of one, performing its high duties after full argument upon both sides, deep investigation and research, calm and deliberate, uninfluenced so far as humanity can be by passion or prejudice, enlightened and incorruptible, far surpassing any other judicial tribunal upon earth for its talents, wisdom, and legal knowledge—familiar with the Constitution, accustomed for many years to close examination of all its provisions, and to hear them constantly discussed on both sides by the great and distinguished jurists of our country—if such a tribunal cannot be trusted, because it holds accidentally at this time a majority of one from the South, can such a question be more wisely referred to the popular suffrage, where the North has a majority of fifty-four in the House of Representatives, and fifty-six in the Electoral College, and that majority constantly and rapidly augmenting?

Will this controversy be more wisely decided by the people of the North, a single geographical section, inflamed by sectional passion and prejudice, impelled by newspaper editors, and hustings orators, and political priests, with or without knowledge, with or without patriotism, with or without sincere religion, with or without fanaticism, with or without mature investigation, with or without selfish aspirations? Day by day, from the press, the hustings, the bookstore, the pulpit, the lecture-room, the schoolhouse, the theatre, the library, the author's closet, the painter's brush, and the power of song, the North now is, and long has been, trained and educated to hate the South, to despise their institutions, to trample upon their rights, to lacerate their feelings, to calumniate their character, to forget all their noble deeds in war and in peace, and all their generous qualities and high intellectual endowments, and to dwell only upon their faults, which are the lot of our common humanity.

Nor is this all. A direct appeal is constantly made to the local interests of the North, to the spirit of avarice and love of power and domination, which unfortunately exist, more or less, in every age and country; and the North are told that it is their interest to monopolise for ever, for themselves and their children, the whole of the common territory of the Union. Under these circumstances, is the popular suffrage of the North that calm, wise, enlightened, unprejudiced, disinterested tribunal to which should be assigned the decision of the great question involved in this controversy? *In a matter involving the rights, interests, and property of the South, the North is asked to be the sole judge in its own case, and to decide this matter in its own favour, by its own exclusive suffrage.*

No man respects popular suffrage more than myself: universal suffrage in this country, on all merely political questions, within the limits of the Constitution. But on judicial questions, involving rights of property of incalculable value, our fathers, in founding the Government, for the welfare and safety of all, discarded the French idea of their elective despotism of 1852, or

168

of their popular assemblage of 1789, unrestrained by conservative checks or constitutional guarantees, and deciding through the popular vote upon rights of property.

Division and confiscation, followed by sack, by plunder, and the guillotine, were there the inevitable consequence; and similar doctrines would soon produce here the same dreadful catastrophe. No man respects the press and the pulpit more than myself. In discharging their appropriate functions, they are the highest vocations upon earth, the one for time, the other for eternity. No one deems more useful than myself addresses to the people from the hustings by able orators on political questions. But judicial questions, involving rights of property, requiring impartial investigation, should not be decided by popular suffrage, and especially when, as in this case, the suffrage of one section of the Union, incited by interest, passion, or prejudice, is asked to decide for itself, and in its own favour, by its own exclusive electoral vote, against another great section of the Confederacy. But this so-called Republican platform is not only revolutionary and agrarian, but by forming a sectional and geographical party, arraying the North against the South, and assailing the bulwarks of the Constitution, it exposes the Union to imminent peril. It is the Constitution that makes the Union, and the subversion of the Constitution is the overthrow of the Union. It is revolution, because it changes in fact our form of government. The parchment upon which the Constitution is written may still remain, the empty forms may still be administered, but even these will soon follow, until not a fragment remains of the Government formed by the patriots and sages of the Revolution.

If there are those that believe that the Union can long be preserved, when the Constitution shall have been subverted, and the supreme judicial tribunal of the Union expunged or obliterated, their delusive hopes, their dreams of dominion and power, will soon vanish. We have now not only a sectional and geographical party, based upon a sectional issue, and realising all the fears of the illustrious Washington, but we have a party advocating doctrines agrarian and revolutionary, subjecting all property to division or confiscation, and expunging the supreme judicial tribunal.

I indulge in no menaces against the Union. I make no predictions on a subject of such fearful import. *But this I can say, that the South will not and ought not to submit to degradation; they will not be despoiled by the North of all rights in the common territory; they will not surrender their constitutional guarantees; they love the Union,* but it is the Union of the Constitution, the union of equals with equals, and not of sovereign States of the North with subject States—say rather, conquered provinces of the South. Rather than submit to this, they will adopt the last alternative—*Separation*—and will then exclaim:

Thy spirit, INDEPENDENCE, let me share,
Lord of the Lion heart and Eagle eye:
Thy steps I'll follow with my bosom bare,
Nor heed the storm that lowers along the sky.

Indeed, it is a most remarkable fact, that while in their native Africa the race has made no progress, while in the mock Republic of Hayti or brutal despotism of Soulouque, in Jamaica and the British West Indies, the emancipated slaves have retrograded to barbarism, while even in our own North the free black race is generally found in the gaols, or poor-houses, or hospitals, the asylums of the deaf and dumb, the blind or insane, or in pestilent alleys or cellars, amid scenes of destitution and infamy, yet in Africa alone, a colony of emancipated slaves, born and raised in the much-abused South, and trained and manumitted by Southern masters, we find the only hope of the African race, and the only success they have ever achieved out of bondage.

When anyone ventures to admonish the people of the danger of sectional or geographical parties, he is now denounced as a traitor or disunionist. Washington, Jefferson, Madison, Monroe, Franklin, Hamilton, Jackson, Clay, and Webster, all warned the people of the danger to the Union of sectional and geographical parties. But we who repeat these warnings are the true friends of the Union; and those who disregard these admonitions, and form sectional and geographical parties, are the enemies of the Constitution and the Union.

No, my countrymen, if, in the madness of sectional passions and geographical prejudice, you overthrow the Constitution framed by Washington and the sages of the Revolution, you can never provide adequate substitutes. Those who have achieved our country's ruin can never regather the scattered fragments of the

170

Constitution, and rebuild the sacred edifice. No, it will be war, civil war, of all others the most sanguinary and ferocious. The line which separates the North from the South will be known in all history as the line of blood.

It will be marked on either side by frowning fortresses, by opposing batteries, by gleaming sabres, by bristling bayonets, by the tramp of contending armies, by towns and cities sacked and pillaged, by dwellings given to the flames, and fields laid waste and desolate. No mortal hand can lift the veil which conceals the unspeakable disasters of such a conflict. No prophet vision can penetrate the dark abyss of such a catastrophe. It will be a second fall of mankind, and while we shall be performing here the bloody drama of a nation's suicide, from the thrones of Europe will arise the exulting shouts of despots, and upon their gloomy banners shall be inscribed, as they believe never to be effaced, their motto,

Man is incapable of self-government.

Nor let it be supposed by the North that superior numbers will give them the victory over the South, or exempt them from the calamities of such a conflict. The financial and industrial ruin of the North would be great and overwhelming. The annual products of the South have now reached at least thirteen hundred millions of dollars, and a much larger portion of this is surplus for export than in the North. Thus, the total exports abroad of the whole country, of our own products and manufactures (excluding specie), for the year ending 30th June, 1855, were $192,751,000, of which there were from the North $67,626,000, and from the South $125,124,000, cotton alone being $88,143,000, thus showing the export of the South nearly double that of the North. But in the table of these Northern exports is $5,857,000 of cotton piece goods. Now these were made out of 40,000 bales of Southern cotton, costing (at $50 a bale) $2,000,000, furnished by the South to the North, to be deducted from the Northern and added to the Southern export, making a difference in this article alone in favour of the South of $4,000,000.

In the same manner, in the table of Northern exports, are found spirits of molasses, $1,448,000; manufactured tobacco, $1,486,000; spirits of turpentine, $1,137,000; and a vast number of other articles, of which the raw materials are chiefly from the

171

South, amounting (including cotton) to at least $10,000,000, to be deducted from the Northern and added to the Southern export, making the former $57,626,000, and the latter $135,124,000, or vastly more than double. Thus, it is that the South furnish vastly more than double those exports which constitute the basis of our exchange and commerce, which build up our commercial marine (the cradle of our navy), and employ our shipping, more than doubling our tonnage, and enabling us ultimately to command the commerce of the world.

So also, as to the articles not exported abroad. Those of the South being almost exclusively raw products, and those of the North, to a great extent, manufactures, the raw materials furnished by the South to the North must be deducted from the Northern product, and added to that of the South.

The population of the Free States at the last census was 13,434,922, and that of the South, 9,664,656. The annual products of the South now reach at least $1,300,000,000, which furnish the means of employment to more than three millions of the people of the North. This arises in various ways. In supplying so vast a portion of the freight and passengers for transportation abroad and coast wise, on the ocean, lakes, bays, and rivers, railroads and canals, and which bring back the return cargoes, the timber must be cut, the iron and other materials furnished, the vehicles of commerce built, the railroads and engines constructed, the crews and hands employed, the shipments and reshipments made, the stores occupied, the merchandise sold, furnishing profit, employment, and wages to thousands at the North.

Then, too, the farmers, workmen, and other parties of the North and North-west, in supplying manufactures and provisions to the South, increase the number to millions. Indeed, it would be impossible to enumerate all the multiplied ramifications of the business of the North connected with the South that give employment to Northern capital and Northern labour.

Now, by a dissolution of the Union and civil war, there would be total non-intercourse between the North and the South, an absolute prohibition of all imports or exports, which would necessarily throw the trade of the South into other channels. This, we have seen, would throw out of employment more than three millions of the people of the North, including the families connected with them, most of whom would be reduced to absolute indigence. It would not be the case with them of low profits, low compensation or salaries, or low wages, but of none, because the business that gave them employment would have ceased. As these millions, thus reduced to want, would be unable as hereto fore to make their former purchases, many thousands more in the North would, to a vast extent, lose their business and employment, and thus extend the disaster so as to affect most injuriously the whole people of the North.

The northern railroads, vessels, and steamers, would lose their freight and passengers passing to and from the South; the Northern stores connected with this trade would be closed, the Northern vessels lie idle at the wharves, the Northern manufactures no longer reach the markets of the South, nor the cotton be furnished in return; the shipyards and engine-works thus employed would be discontinued; the Northern farms would cease to supply breadstuffs and provisions to the South these they would raise themselves at home, in lieu of that portion of their cotton heretofore supplied to the Northern market.

Their own exports would be shipped abroad in their own or foreign vessels, from their own ports; and to the same points, in the same manner, would be brought back the return cargoes. Indeed, such a cessation of business, of intercourse, of wages and employment, produced by civil war between the North and the South, would cause here a perfect paralysis.

Commerce would perish; credit would decay; all property, real and personal, would rapidly depreciate in value; good debts to banks and others would become worthless; wages or salaries would cease or decline; stocks would sink to a nominal value; confidence would vanish; all available means would take the form of specie, which would be hoarded and seek its usual hiding-places as in all times of convulsion. To crown the disaster, more than three millions of people at the North, receiving no wages or employment, must live. They must have houses, food, and raiment. But how to be obtained?

Would it be by the new agrarian doctrine of submitting rights of property to the decision of the ballot-box? Would it be by division and confiscation? Would the anti-rent doctrine become universal? or is this too tedious a process? Would riots prevail? Would plunder and pillage close the disaster? But crimes, tumults, taxes, misery, deaths, government, state, city, and county debts, at enormous rates of interest, and emigration of persons and capital to other countries, would all increase, while liberty itself would expire in the conflict, and the bayonet, as in Europe, take the place of the ballot-box. The gaols and poor-houses would be multiplied, sieges and battles prevail, and thousands perish in fraternal strife. The taxes to support those who could not support themselves, and to maintain large and costly armies in the field, would be incalculable.

Look at Europe. Her armies, now numbering nearly four millions of men (greater than our whole voting-population), trample down the rights and interests of the people and consume their substance, while European government debts have nearly reached ten thousand millions of dollars. But at least they have suppressed the guillotine, and possess what they call *Law and Order*. But would we have even these, until military usurpation had closed the drama of blood and violence, and written the last sad epitaph of human liberty? The picture is darkly shadowed, but it is by the pencil of truth, and the gloomy reality would be darker still. My soul shrinks from the contemplation of scenes like these, and my pen would refuse to perform its office in describing them, if a solemn sense of duty did not compel me to give these warnings, ere *it is too late*, and exert all my feeble efforts to prevent the ruin of my country. Now, these efforts may possibly accomplish something; after the election, my humble voice would be unheard or unheeded in the tempest of passion that would sweep the country.

Let those of the North who tell you there is no danger shrink from the fearful responsibility they have assumed ere the evil day shall come upon us. They tell us there is no danger that they have heard this cry before, of danger to the Union but there is no peril. None in 1820, none in 1833, none in 1850, and the warnings of Washington were a delusion. Why, then, did they call Henry Clay the great pacificator, and announce that thrice he had saved his country? How saved he the Union, if it never was in danger? But it was imperilled, and it was saved by measures adopted by the votes of the North and the South.

But now the union between the North and the South, so far as the votes for the sectional candidates of the so-called (Republican party are concerned) is already dissolved; for no man anticipates a solitary electoral vote for those candidates in any State of the South, but this controversy is to be settled exclusively in favour of and by the exclusive vote of the North; and the rights, wishes, and interests of the South are to be wholly disregarded.

Beware, nay countrymen, ere it is too late, how you adopt these perilous counsels. Give no vote that puts the Union in the slightest peril—make no such fearful experiment. Friends of the Union, of all parties, our enemies have combined; they have fused, and under their united efforts, the pillars of the Constitution and of the Union are rocking to their base, and we may have assembled in November next for the last time under our country's flag, and as citizens of a common Union. The enemies of the Union have united, and why should we be separated?

The flag of the North 'American' party, as they call themselves, is trailing in the dust, and is replaced by the Black 'Republican' standard. Your leaders have surrendered the American flag and taken in exchange the African banner. They have capitulated at discretion; they have surrendered your candidates and principles, and demand your votes for the candidates and platform of the Black 'Republican' party. Friends of the Union, come and unite with us to save the Union! Come, without any surrender of principle on your part or ours, to the rescue of our country. Come, my brother, give me your hand; let us save the country first, and then settle, at some future election, the administrative measures about which we now differ. Come, in the name of our common country, now in the agony of an approaching convulsion! Come, in the name of the Constitution and of the Union, now subjected to imminent peril! Come, in memory of the commingled blood of the North and the South, poured out on the battlefields of the Revolution! Come, in the name of the liberties of the world, which would be crushed by the fall of the American Union!

Respectfully, your fellow-citizen,

R. J. Walker.

As my object is to give a simple record of events, I do not propose to attempt the vindication of the Institution which has been the fruitful theme of reproach and denunciation amongst the opponents of Southern independence.

The English writers who discuss this subject seem to confine themselves to the consideration of the abstract principle of slavery, and entirely overlook the facts and circumstances of the case. Few institutions of government or society could stand such a test.

If the question were simply whether it would not be better for the South to have four millions of intelligent, industrious, and valiant freemen in the place of four millions of African slaves, it would be neither so delicate nor difficult of solution. But the question which taxes the practical statesmanship and philanthropy of the Southern people is of a far graver character. It is this. Two races—one civilised, the other barbarous—being locally intermingled, what does the good of society require—the freedom or servitude of the barbarous race? The South, believe that the freedom of the blacks, under such circumstances, would result certainly in their final extermination, and that servitude is best adapted to their intellectual and. moral condition.

The antagonism of race is as fixed and immutable as any other law of nature, and has been exemplified in the history of the world wherever the opposing elements have come in conflict. The North American Indians were a race of warriors, with far higher intellectual capabilities than the negro, and not inheriting that *unutterable prejudice* against *amalgamation* which exists against the negro. But at the same time, there being no motive of interest in the superior race to protect them, they have been driven from their hunting-grounds, which at no distant period embraced half of the North American continent, to a few acres on the confines of civilisation, which they inhabit by the sufferance of the dominant race.

In support of the usages of civilisation in favour of this law of race, I can cite an example which comes within my own immediate knowledge, and which is uninfluenced by the fanaticism and demagogism which attach to the negro question. In California, there are between sixty and seventy thousand Chinese, being about one-seventh of the whole population. They are a civilised, industrious, and most useful people. Yet they cannot be naturalised, cannot bear witness in court, cannot intermarry with the white race, or exercise a single right of citizenship, except *pay taxes.*

The wisdom of the policy of the South in regard to this *inherited responsibility* is abundantly vindicated by the very aspect which the Institution of Slavery now presents to the world.

For thirty years its enemies have unceasingly assailed it by every agency of mind and heart. The pulpit, the press, hostile legislation, secret societies, armed robbers, have all been employed to excite discontent and insurrection in the Southern States.

Their agitations have split the aspiring structure of the American Government from turret to foundation-stone. They have caused the most bloody and implacable war known to modern history; and yet the *Institution of Slavery* survives it all, firm and unimpaired.

Nowhere on earth, not even in happy England, rejoicing in peace, does there exist between the various classes of society such harmony, such sympathy, as the South exhibits in the midst of her trials. Surely the condition of such a social commonwealth must rest upon the solid foundation which supports all civil institutions—the good of the whole State.

But we are asked, 'Do not your statutes withhold any legal enforcement to the marriage relations amongst slaves?' I beg my readers to have this objection properly stated. It should be borne in mind that we have not taken from them any rights which they had ever recognised or conferred among themselves. The race, as we found it, was destitute of any such institution, or even the knowledge of it. Nevertheless, it is true that our laws are justly chargeable with the reproach of not having secured to them this blessing of civilisation. But what the law has failed to do, religion and usage have effected. The institution of marriage does exist among slaves, and is encouraged and protected by their owners.

The statesmen of the South, when free from the embarrassment of their fanatical enemies, should lose no time in protecting all the domestic ties by laws forbidding the separation of families. That such legislation is not inconsistent with the Institution is proved by the fact that some of the South-Western States have long since removed this evil by statutory enactments.

In point of fact, there is a greater amount of separation in families and rending of domestic ties during one year in the United Kingdom of England, Scotland, and Ireland, than takes place in ten years among the negroes of the South.

The South, however, does not feel herself called upon to vindicate this or any other of her institutions before the bar of the world: and, I think, English philanthropists may safely leave to Southern statesmen the removal of such abuses as cling to this in common with all other human institutions. Ameliorations will continue to be adopted as this class of Southern society increases in its fitness to receive and enjoy them.

In the meantime, I commend to the Abolition agitators of Great

Britain the policy in which their puissant Government has taken refuge—Non–intervention.

Mrs. Greenhow

By W. G. Beymer

These pages record the story of the woman who cast a pebble into the sea of circumstance—a pebble from whose widening ripples there rose a mighty wave, on whose crest the Confederate States of America were borne through four years of civil war.

Rose O'Neal Greenhow gave to General Beauregard information which enabled him to concentrate the widely scattered Confederate forces in time to meet McDowell on the field of Manassas, and there, with General Johnson, to win for the South the all-important battle of Bull Run.

Mrs. Greenhow's cipher despatch—nine words on a scrap of paper—set in motion the reinforcements which arrived at the height of the battle and turned it against the North. But for the part she played in the Confederate victory Rose O'Neal Greenhow paid a heavy price.

During the Buchanan administration Mrs. Greenhow was one of the leaders of Washington society. She was a Southerner by birth, but a resident of Washington from her girlhood; a widow, beautiful, accomplished, wealthy, and noted for her wit and her forceful personality. Her home was the rendezvous of those prominent in official life in Washington—the "court circle," had America been a monarchy.

She was personally acquainted with all the leading men of the country, many of whom had partaken of her hospitality. President Buchanan was a close personal friend; a friend, too, was William H. Seward, then Senator from New York; her niece, a granddaughter of Dolly Madison, was the wife of Stephen A. Douglas. It was in such company that she watched with burning interest the war clouds grow and darken over Charleston Harbor, then burst into the four years' storm; she never saw it end.

Among her guests at this time was Colonel Thomas Jordan, who,

179

before leaving Washington to accept the appointment of Adjutant-General of the Confederate Army at Manassas, broached to Mrs. Greenhow the subject of a secret military correspondence. What would *she* do to aid the Confederacy? he asked her. Ah, what would she not do! Then he told her how someone in Washington was needed by the South; of the importance of the work which might be done, and her own especial fitness for the task. And that night before he left the house he gave her a cipher code, and arranged that her despatches to him were to be addressed to "Thomas John Rayford."

And so he crossed the river into Virginia and left her, in the Federal capital, armed with the glittering shield, "Justified by military necessity," and the two-edged sword, "All's fair in love and war";—left her, his agent, to gather in her own way information from the enemy, her former friends, where and from whom she would.

It was in April, '61, that she took up her work; in November, Allan Pinkerton, head of the Federal Secret Service, made to the War Department a report in which he said—in the vehement language of a partisanship as intense as Mrs. Greenhow's own:—

'It was a fact too notorious to need reciting here, that for months ... Mrs. Greenhow was actively and to a great extent openly engaged in giving aid and comfort, sympathy and information; ... her house was the rendezvous, for the most violent enemies of the government. .... where they were furnished with every possible information to be obtained by the untiring energies of this very remarkable woman; ... that since the commencement of this rebellion this woman, from her long residence at the capital, her superior education, her uncommon social powers, her very extensive acquaintance among, and her active association with, the leading politicians of this nation, has possessed an almost superhuman power, all of which she has most wickedly used to destroy the government. ...

'She has made use of whoever and whatever she could as mediums to carry into effect her unholy purposes. ... She has not used her powers in vain among the officers of the army, not a few of whom she has robbed of patriotic hearts and transformed them into sympathizers with the enemies of the country. ... She had her secret and insidious agents in all parts of this city and scattered over a large extent of country. ... She had alphabets, numbers, ciphers, and various other not mentioned ways of holding intercourse. ... Statistical facts were thus obtained and forwarded that could have been found nowhere but in the national archives, thus leading me to the conclusion that such evidence must have been obtained from employees and agents in the various departments of the government.'

Thus, she worked throughout the opening days of the war. Washington lay ringed about with camps of new-formed regiments, drilling feverishly. Already the press and public had raised the cry, "On to Richmond." When would they start? Where would they first strike? It was on those two points that the Confederate plan of campaign hinged. It was Mrs. Greenhow who gave the information. To General Beauregard at Manassas, where he anxiously awaited tidings of the Federal advance, there came about the 10th of July the first message from Mrs. Greenhow. The message told of the intended advance of the enemy across the Potomac and on to Manassas *via* Fairfax Courthouse and Centreville.

It was brought into the Confederate lines by a young lady of Washington, Miss Duval, who, disguised as a market-girl, carried the message to a house near Fairfax Court-house, occupied by the wife and daughters (Southern born) of an officer in the Federal Army. General Beauregard at once commenced his preparations for receiving the attack, and sent one of his *aides* to President Davis to communicate the information and to urge the immediate concentration of the scattered Confederate forces.

But still the Federal start was delayed, and the precise date was as indefinite as ever. It was during this period of uncertainty that G. Donellan, who, before joining the Confederates, had been a clerk in the Department of the Interior, volunteered to return to Washington for information. He was armed with the two words "Trust Bearer" in Colonel Jordan's cipher, and was sent across the Potomac with instructions to report to Mrs. Greenhow. He arrived at the very moment that she most needed a messenger. Hastily writing in cipher her all-important despatch, "Order issued for McDowell to move, on Manassas tonight," she gave it to Donellan, who was taken by her agents in a buggy, with relays of horses, down the eastern shore of the Potomac to a ferry near Dumfries, where he was ferried across. Cavalry couriers delivered the despatch into General Beauregard's hands that night, July 16th.

And the source of Mrs. Greenhow's information? She has made the statement that she "*received a copy of the order to McDowell.*" Allan Pinkerton was not wrong when he said that she "had not used her powers in vain among the officers of the army."

At midday of the 17th there came Colonel Jordan's reply:—

'Yours was received at eight o'clock at night. Let them come; we are ready for them. We rely upon you for precise information. Be particular as to description and destination of forces, quantity of artillery, etc.'

She was ready with fresh information, and the messenger was sent back with the news that the Federals intended to cut the Manassas Gap Railroad to prevent Johnson, at Winchester, from reinforcing Beauregard. After that there was nothing to be done but await the result of the inevitable battle. She had done her best. What that best was worth she learned when she received from Colonel Jordan the treasured message:—

'Our President and our general direct me to thank you. We rely upon you for further information. The Confederacy owes you a debt.'

When the details of the battle became known, and she learned how the last of Johnson's 8,500 men (marched to General Beauregard's aid because of *her* despatches) had arrived at three o'clock on the day of the battle and had turned the wavering Federal Army into a mob of panic-stricken fugitives, she felt that the "Confederacy owed her a debt," indeed.

In the days immediately following Bull Run it seemed to the Confederate sympathizers in the city that their victorious army had only to march into Washington to take it. Mrs. Greenhow wrote:—

"Everything about the national Capitol betokened the panic of the Administration. Preparations were made for the expected attack, and signals were arranged to give the alarm. . . . I went round with the principal officer in charge of this duty, and; took advantage of the situation. . . . Our gallant Beauregard would have found himself right ably seconded by the rebels in Washington had he deemed it expedient to advance on the city.

"A part of the plan was to have cut the telegraph wires connecting with the various military positions with the War Department, to make prisoners of McClellan and several others, thereby creating still greater confusion in the first moments of panic. Measures had also been taken to spike the guns in Fort Corcoran, Fort Ellsworth, and other important points, accurate drawings of which had been furnished to our commanding officer by me."

Doubtless it was these same drawings concerning which the *New York Herald* commented editorially a month later:—

". . . We have in this little matter (Mrs. Greenhow's arrest) a clue to the mystery of those important government maps and plans which

182

MRS GREENHOW AND HER DAUGHTER

the rebels lately left behind them in their hasty flight from Fairfax Courthouse, . . . and we are at liberty to guess how Beauregard was so minutely informed of this advance, and of our plan of attack on his lines, as to be ready to meet it at every salient point with overwhelming numbers.

Poor Mrs. Greenhow—from the very first doomed to disaster. Her maps and plans (if these, indeed, were hers) were allowed to fall into the enemy's hands; despatches were sent to her by an ill-chosen messenger, who, too late, was discovered to be a spy for the Federal War Department; her very cipher code, given her by Colonel Jordan, proved to be an amateurish affair that was readily deciphered by the Federal War Office. She never had a chance to escape detection. Concerning the cipher, Colonel Jordan wrote to Confederate Secretary of War Judah P. Benjamin, October, '61 (the letter was found in the archives of Richmond four years later):—

"This cipher I arranged last April. Being my first attempt and hastily devised it may be deciphered by any expert, as I found after use of it for a time. . . . That does not matter as of course I used it with but the lady, and with her it has served our purpose. . . ."

It had, indeed, served their purpose, but in serving it had brought imprisonment and ruin to the woman.

When the War Department began to shake itself free from the staggering burden placed upon it by the rout at Bull Run, almost its first step was to seek out the source of the steady and swift-flowing stream of information to Richmond. Suspicion at once fell upon Mrs. Greenhow. Many expressed their secession sentiments as openly as did she, but there was none other who possessed her opportunities for obtaining Federal secrets. Federal officers and officials continued their pleasant social relations with her, and she was believed by the War Office to be influencing some of these. Thomas A. Scott, Assistant Secretary of War, sent for Allan Pinkerton and instructed him to place Mrs. Greenhow under surveillance; her house was to be constantly watched, as well as all visitors from the moment they were seen to enter or to leave it, and, should any of these visitors later attempt to go South, they were immediately to be arrested.

The watch on the house continued for some days; many prominent gentlemen called—men whose loyalty was above question. Then on the night of August 22nd, while Pinkerton and several of his men watched during a hard storm, an officer of the Federal Army entered the house. Pinkerton removed his shoes and stood on the shoulders of one of his men that he might watch and listen at a crack in the shutters. When the officer left the house, he was followed by Pinkerton (still in his stocking feet) and one of his detectives. Turning suddenly, the officer discovered that he was being followed; he broke into a run, and the three of them raced through the deserted, rainswept streets straight to the door of a station of the provost marshal. The pursued had maintained his lead and reached the station first; he was its commanding officer, and instantly turned out the guard. Allan Pinkerton and his agent suddenly found that the quarry had bagged the hunters.

The angry officer refused to send word for them to Secretary Scott, to General McClellan, to the provost-marshal—to anyone! He clapped them into the guard-house—"a most filthy and uncomfortable place"—and left them there, wet and bedraggled, among the crowd of drunken soldiers and common prisoners of the streets. In the morning, when the guard was relieved, one of them, whom Pinkerton had bribed, carried a message to Secretary Scott, by whom they were at once set free. In his report Allan Pinkerton says:—

"...The officer then (immediately after Pinkerton was put under arrest) went upstairs while I halted and looked at my watch. Said officer returned in twenty minutes with a revolver in his hand, saying that he went up-stairs on purpose to get the revolver. The inquiry arises, was it for that purpose he stayed thus, or for the more probable one of hiding or destroying the evidence. of his guilt obtained of Mrs. Greenhow or furnished to her? . . ."

This report goes no further into the charge, but that very day, August 23rd, within a few hours of his release, Allan Pinkerton placed Mrs. Greenhow under arrest as a spy.

Of the events of that fateful Friday Mrs. Greenhow has left a graphic record, complete save that it does not tell why such events need ever have been, for she had been warned of her proposed arrest—warned in ample time at least to have attempted an escape. The message which told of the impending blow had been sent to her, Mrs. Greenhow tells, by a lady in Georgetown, to whom one of General McClellan's *aides* had given the information. The note said also that the Hon. William Preston, Minister to Spain until the outbreak of the war, was likewise to be arrested.

To him Mrs. Greenhow passed on the warning, and he safely reached the Confederate Army. But Mrs. Greenhow—why did she stay? Did escape seem so improbable that she dared not run the risk of indubitably convicting herself by an attempted flight? Did she underestimate the gravity of her situation and depend upon "influence" to save her? Or was it. after all, some Casabianca-like folly of remaining at her "post" until the end? Whatever the reason, she stayed.

Day after day she waited for the warning's fulfilment. Though waiting, she worked on. She told a friend long afterward:—

"'Twas very exciting. I would be walking down the Avenue with one of the officials, military or state, and as we strolled along there would pass—perhaps a washerwoman carrying home her basket of clean clothes, or maybe, a gaily attired youth from lower Seventh Avenue; but something in the way the woman held her basket, or in the way the youth twirled his cane, told me that news had been received, or that news was wanted—that I must open up communications in some way. Or as we sat in some city park a sedate old gentleman would pass by: to my unsuspecting escort the passer-by was but commonplace, but to me his manner of polishing his glasses, or the flourish of the handkerchief with which he rubbed his nose, was a message."

Days full of anxious forebodings sped by until the morning of the 23rd of August dawned, oppressively sultry after the night of rain which had so bedraggled Allan Pinkerton and his detective. At about eleven o'clock that morning Mrs. Greenhow was returning home from a promenade with a distinguished member of the diplomatic

185

corps, but for whose escort she believed she would have been arrested sooner, for she knew she was being followed. Excusing herself to her escort, she stopped to inquire for the sick child of a neighbour, and there they warned her that her house was being watched. So, then, the time had come! As she paused at her neighbour's door, perhaps for the moment a trifle irresolute, one of her "humble agents" chanced to be coming that way; farther down the street two men were watching her; she knew their mission.

LITTLE ROSE GREENHOW

To her passing agent she called, softly:—

"I think that I am about to be arrested. Watch from Corcoran's corner. I shall raise my handkerchief to my face if they arrest me. Give information of it."

Then she slowly crossed the street to her house. She had several important papers with her that morning; one, a tiny note, she put into her mouth and destroyed; the other, a letter in cipher, she was unable to get from her pocket without being observed; for the opportunity to destroy it she must trust to chance. As she mounted the short flight of steps to her door, the two men—Allan Pinkerton and his operative, who had followed her rapidly—reached the foot of the steps. She turned and faced them, waiting for them to speak.

"Is this Mrs. Greenhow?"

"Yes," she replied, coldly. As they still hesitated, she asked, "Who are you, and what do you want?"

"I have come to arrest you," Pinkerton answered, shortly.

"By what authority? Let me see your warrant," she demanded,

bravely enough except for what seemed a nervous movement of the fluttering handkerchief. To the detectives, if they noticed it, it was but the tremulous gesture of a woman's fright. To the agent lingering at Corcoran's corner, it was the signal.

"I have no power to resist you," she said; "but, had I been inside of my house I would have killed one of you before I had submitted to this illegal process." They followed her into her house and closed the door.

"It seemed but a moment," she tells, "before the house became filled with men, and an indiscriminate search commenced. Men rushed with frantic haste into my chamber, into every sanctuary. Beds, drawers, wardrobes, soiled linen—search was made everywhere! Even scraps of paper—children's unlettered scribblings—were seized and tortured into dangerous correspondence with the enemy."

It was a very hot day. She asked to be allowed to change her dress, and permission was grudgingly given her, but almost immediately a detective followed to her bedroom, calling, "Madam! Madam!" and flung open the door. She barely had had time to destroy the cipher note that was in her pocket. Very shortly afterward a woman detective arrived, and "I was allowed the poor privilege of unfastening my own garments, which one by one were received by this pseudo-woman and carefully examined."

Though wild confusion existed within the house, no sign of it was allowed to show itself from without, for the house was now a trap,

THE OLD CAPITOL PRISON

baited and set; behind the doors detectives waited to seize all who, ignorant of the fate of its owner, might call. Anxious to save her friends, and fearful, too, lest she be compromised further by papers which might be found on them when searched, Mrs. Greenhow sought means to warn them away. The frightened servants were all under guard, but there was one member of the household whose freedom was not yet taken from her—Mrs. Greenhow's daughter, Rose, a child of eight. It is her letters which have supplied many of the details for this story. Of that day, so full of terror and bewilderment, the memory which stands out most clear to her is that of climbing a tree in the garden and from there calling to all the passers-by: "Mother has been arrested! Mother has been arrested!" until the detectives in the house heard her, and angrily dragged her, weeping, from the tree.

But in spite of the efforts of the "humble agent" who had waited at Corcoran's corner for the handkerchief signal, in spite of the sacrifice of little Rose's freedom, the trap that day was sprung many times. Miss Mackall and her sister, close friends of Mrs. Greenhow, were seized as they crossed the threshold, and searched and detained. Their mother, coming to find her daughters, became with them a prisoner. A negro girl—a former servant—and her brother, who were merely passing the house, were induced to enter it. and for hours subjected to an inquisition.

Night came, and the men left in charge grew boisterous; an argument started among them. Mrs. Greenhow tells—with keen enjoyment—of having egged on the disputants, pitting nationality against nationality—English, German, Irish, Yankee—so that in the still night their loud, angry voices might serve as a danger signal to her friends. But the dispute died out at last—too soon to save two gentlemen who called late that evening, a call which cost them months of imprisonment on the never-proved charge of being engaged in "contraband and treasonable correspondence with the Confederates."

Soon after midnight there came the brief relaxing of vigilance for which Mrs. Greenhow had watched expectantly all day. She had taken the resolution to fire the house if she did not succeed in obtaining certain papers in the course of the night, for she had no hope that they would escape a second day's search. But now the time for making the attempt had come, and she stole noiselessly into the dark library. From the topmost shelf she took down a book, between whose leaves lay the coveted despatch; concealing it in the folds of her dress, she swiftly regained her room. A few moments later the guard returned to his post at her open door.

She had been permitted the companionship of Miss Mackall, and now as the two women reclined on the bed, they planned how they might get the despatch out of the house. When Mrs. Greenhow had been searched that afternoon her shoes and stockings had not been examined, and so, trusting to the slim chance that Miss Mackall's would likewise escape examination, it was determined that the despatch should be hidden in her stocking; and this—since the room was in darkness save for the faint light from the open door, and the bed stood in deep shadow—was accomplished in the very presence of the guard. They planned that should Miss Mackall, when about to be released, have reason to believe she was to be searched carefully, she must then be seized with compunction at leaving her friend, and return.

Between three and four o'clock Saturday morning those friends who had been detained were permitted to depart (except the two gentlemen, who, some hours before, had been taken to the provost-marshal), and with Miss Mackall went in safety the despatch for whose destruction Mrs. Greenhow would have burned her house.

But though she had destroyed or saved much dangerous correspondence, there fell into the hands of the Federal secret service much more of her correspondence, by which were dragged into the net many of her friends and agents. A letter in cipher addressed to Thomas John Bayford in part read:—

"Your three last despatches I never got. Those by Applegate were betrayed by him to the War Department; also, the one sent by our other channel was destroyed by Van Camp."

Dr. Aaron Van Camp, charged with being a spy, was arrested, and cast into the Old Capitol Prison. In a stove in the Greenhow house were found, and pieced together, the fragments of a note from Donellan, the messenger who had carried her despatch to Beauregard before Bull Run. The note introduced:

"Colonel Thompson, the bearer, . . . (who) will be happy to take from your hands any communications and obey your injunctions as to disposition of same with despatch."

The arrest of Colonel Thompson, as of Mrs. Greenhow, involved others; it was all like a house of cards—by the arrest of Mrs. Greenhow the whole flimsy structure had been brought crashing down.

Of the days which followed the beginning of Mrs. Greenhow's imprisonment in her own house, few were devoid of excitement of some sort. After a few days Miss Mackall had obtained permission

189

to return and share her friend's captivity. It was she who fortunately found and destroyed a sheet of blotting-paper which bore the perfect imprint of the Bull Run despatch! The detectives remained in charge for seven days; they examined every book in the library leaf by leaf (too late!); boxes containing books, china, and glass that had been packed away for months were likewise minutely examined. Portions of the furniture were taken apart; pictures removed from their frames; beds overturned many times.

Mrs. Greenhow tells:—

"Seemingly I was treated with deference. Once only were violent hands put upon my person—the detective, Captain Denis, having rudely seized me to prevent me giving warning to a lady and gentleman on the first evening of my arrest (which I succeeded in doing)."

She was permitted to be alone scarcely a moment:—

"If I wished to lie down, he was seated a few paces from my bed. If I desired to change my dress, it was obliged to be done with open doors. . . . They still presumed to seat themselves at table with me, with unwashed hands and shirtsleeves."

Only a few months before this the President of the United States had dined frequently at that very table.

Her jailers sought to be bribed to carry messages for her—in order to betray her; their hands were ever outstretched. One set himself the pleasant task of making love to her maid, Lizzie Fitzgerald, a quick-witted Irish girl, who entered keenly into the sport of sentimental walks and treats at Uncle Sam's expense—and, of course, revealed nothing.

On Friday morning, the 30th of August, Mrs. Greenhow was informed that other prisoners were to be brought in, and that her house was to be converted into a prison. A lieutenant and twenty-one men of the Sturgis Rifles (General McClellan's bodyguard) were now placed in charge instead of the detective police. The house began to fill with other prisoners—all women. The once quiet and unpretentious residence at 398 Sixteenth Street became known as "Fort Greenhow," and an object of intense interest to the crowds that came to stare at it—which provoked from the *New York Times* the caustic comment:—

"Had Madam Greenhow been sent South immediately after her arrest, as we recommended, we should have heard no more of the heroic deeds of Secesh women, which she has made the fashion."

Had the gaping crowds known what the harassed sentries knew, they would have stared with better cause. They sought to catch a glimpse of Mrs. Greenhow because of what she had done; the guards' chief concern was with the Mrs. Greenhow of the present moment. For during the entire time that she was a prisoner in her own house Mrs. Greenhow was in frequent communication with the South. How she accomplished the seemingly impossible will never be fully known.

She tells of information being conveyed to her by her "little bird"; of preparing "those *peculiar, square* despatches to be forwarded to our great and good President at Richmond"; of "tapestry-work in a vocabulary of colours, which, though not a very prolific language, served my purpose"; and she gives, as an example of many such, "a seemingly innocent letter," which seems innocent, indeed, and must forever remain so, since she does not supply the key whereby its hidden meaning may be understood.

Then there is the story of the ball of pink knitting-yarn, a story which, unlike the yarn ball, was never unwound to lay its innermost secrets bare. Now and then the prisoners passed one another when being marched for their period of exercise in the garden or back into the house again; and it was thus that Mrs. Greenhow one day met Mrs. Philips in the hall. Behind each stalked an armed guard; the ladies might not pause even long enough to bid each other good day. But as she passed on into the house, Mrs. Philips called, "I found your ball of pink yarn in the shrub-bush under your window, and tossed it into your room." Pink yarn! Women talk!—not worth a soldier's heed, and the sentries gave it none.

Out in the garden Mrs. Greenhow restlessly paced up and down; for the first time the brief half-hour seemed too long; for the first time, too, she was glad to be marched back to her room again. Yes! there on the floor in a band of sunlight lay the pink ball—safe. As she dropped it carelessly into her work-basket the guard watched her narrowly, then again languidly seated himself at her door. That is all of the story—except that the ball of pink yarn was wound around a little roll of paper, a cipher message from the South.

By such means she was able to outwit her many guards—though not as invariably as at the time she believed that she had done. Allan Pinkerton reports to the War Department, with a mixture of irritation and complacency:—

"She has not ceased to lay plans, to attempt the bribery of officers having her in charge, to make use of signs from the windows of her house to her friends on the streets, to communicate with such friends and through them as she supposed send information to the rebels in

191

ciphers requiring much time to decipher—all of which she supposed she was doing through an officer who had her in charge and whom she supposed she had bribed to that purpose, but who, faithful to his trust, laid her communications before yourself."

But Mrs. Greenhow evidently made use of other channels as well, for the copy of her first letter to Secretary Seward safely reached the hands of those friends to whom it was addressed, and by them it was published in the newspapers, North and South, thereby showing to all the world that a tendril of the grapevine telegraph still reached out from "Fort Greenhow." It was not this alone which made officialdom and the public gasp—it was the letter itself. In tone it was calm, almost dispassionate—a masterly letter. The blunt Anglo-Saxon words which set forth in detail the indignities which she suffered from, the unceasing watch kept over her came like so many blows. She pointed out that her arrest had been without warrant; that her house and all its contents had been seized, and that she herself had been held a prisoner more than three months without a trial, and that she was yet ignorant of the charge against her. The letter was strong, simple, dignified, but it brought no reply.

The heat of midsummer had passed and autumn had come, and with it many changes. Miss Mackall was one day abruptly taken away and sent to her own home; the two friends were never to meet again. Other prisoners were freed or transferred elsewhere, and yet others came—among them a Miss Poole, who almost immediately sought to curry favour by reporting that little Rose, who for some time had been allowed to play, under guard, on the pavement, had received a communication for her mother; and the child was again confined within the four walls.

"This was perhaps my hardest trial—to see my little one pining and fading under my eyes for want of food and air. The health and spirits of my faithful maid also began to fail."

The attempt of several of the guard to communicate information was likewise reported by Miss Poole, and the thumbscrews of discipline were tightened by many turns. The kindly officer of the guard, Lieutenant Sheldon, was ordered to hold no personal communication with Mrs. Greenhow; the guard was set as spies upon one another and upon him; they, too, were forbidden under severe penalty to speak to her or to answer her questions. An order was issued prohibiting her from purchasing newspapers, or being informed of their contents. At times it seemed as though her house, and she in it, had been swal-

THE BARRED WINDOW LOOKED OUT UPON THE PRISON YARD

lowed, and now lay within the four walls of a Chillon or a Château d'If; it was added bitterness to her to look about the familiar room and remember that once it had been home!

Miss Mackall had been making ceaseless efforts to be allowed to visit her friend, but permission was steadily denied. Then the news sifted into "Fort Greenhow," and reached its one-time mistress, that Miss Mackall was ill, desperately ill; for the first time Mrs. Greenhow ceased to demand—she pleaded to see her friend; and failed. Then came the news that Miss Mackall was dead.

Among those friends of the old days who now and then were allowed to call was Edwin M. Stanton, not yet Secretary of War. Mrs. Greenhow endeavoured to engage him as counsel to obtain for her a writ of *habeas corpus,* but he declined.

Friends—with dubious tact—smuggled to her newspaper clippings in which the statement was made that "Mrs. Greenhow had lost her mind," and that "it is rumoured that the government is about to remove her to a private lunatic asylum."

She wrote:—

193

"My blood freezes even now, when I recall my feelings at the reception of this communication, and I wonder that I had not gone mad."

When the Judge-Advocate, making a friendly, "unofficial" call, asked, "To what terms would you be willing to subscribe for your release?" she replied, with unbroken courage:—

"None, sir! I demand my unconditional release, indemnity for losses, and the restoration of my papers and effects."

The day after Christmas Mrs. Greenhow wrote two letters. The one, in cipher, was found in the archives of the Confederate War Department when Richmond was evacuated; it was deciphered and published in the Official Records —

"December 20th

"In a day or two 1,200 cavalry supported by four batteries of artillery will cross the river above to get behind Manassas and cut off railroad and other communications with our army whilst an attack is made in front. For God's sake heed this. It is positive. . . ."

The grape-vine telegraph lines were still clear both into and out of "Fort Greenhow."

The other was a second letter to Secretary Seward—a very different sort of letter from the first, being but a tirade on the ethics of the Southern cause, purposeless, save that:—

"Contempt and defiance alone actuated me. I had known Seward intimately, and he had frequently enjoyed the hospitalities of my table."

Unlike its worthy predecessor, this letter was to bear fruit.

On the morning of the 5th of January, a search was again commenced throughout the house. The police were searching for the copy of the second letter. But, as in the first instance, the copy had gone out simultaneously with the original. When Mrs. Greenhow was allowed to return to her room she found that the window had been nailed up, and every scrap of paper had been taken from her writing-desk and table.

It was this copy of the second letter to Secretary Seward which sent Mrs. Greenhow to the Old Capitol Prison.

It was published as the first had been, thereby clearly showing that Mrs. Greenhow was still able to communicate with the South almost at will in spite of all efforts to prevent her. It was the last straw. The State Department acted swiftly. On January 18th came the order for Mrs. Greenhow to prepare for immediate removal elsewhere; two hours later she parted from her faithful and weeping maid, and she and the little Rose left their home forever. Between the doorstep and the carriage was a double file of soldiers, between whom she passed; at the carriage—still holding little Rose by the hand—she turned on the soldiers indignantly. "May your next duty he a more honourable one than that of guarding helpless women and children," she said.

Dusk had fallen ere the carriage reached the Old Capitol; here, too, a guard was drawn up under arms to prevent any attempt at rescue. The receiving room of the prison was crowded with officers and civilians, all peering curiously. Half an hour later she and the child were marched into a room very different from that which they had left in the house in Sixteenth Street. The room, 10 x 12, was on the second floor of the back building of the prison; its only window (over which special bars were placed next day) looked out upon the prison-yard. A narrow bed, on which was a straw mattress covered by a pair of unwashed cotton sheets, a small feather pillow, dingy and dirty, a few wooden chairs, a table, and a cracked mirror, furnished the room which from that night was to be theirs during months of heart-breaking imprisonment.

An understanding of those bitter days can be given best by extracts from her diary:

"*January 25th.*—I have been one week in my new prison. My letters now all go through the detective police, who subject them to a chemical process to extract the treason. In one of the newspaper accounts I am supposed to use sympathetic ink. I purposely left a preparation very conspicuously placed, in order to divert attention from, my real means of communication, and they have swallowed the bait and fancy my friends are at their mercy.

January 28th.—This day as I stood at my barred window the guard rudely called 'Go 'way from that window!' and levelled his musket at me. I maintained my position without condescending to notice him, whereupon he called the corporal of the guard. I called also for the officer of the guard, . . . who informed me that I must not go to the window. I quietly told him that, at whatever peril, I should avail myself of the largest liberty of the four walls of my prison. He told me that his guard would have orders to fire upon me. I had no idea that such monstrous regulations existed. Today the dinner for myself and child consists of a bowl of beans swimming in grease, two slices of fat junk, and two slices of bread. . . . I was very often intruded upon by large parties of Yankees, who came with passes from the provost marshal to stare at me. Sometimes I was amused, and generally contrived to find out what was going on. . . .

Afterward I requested the superintendent not to allow any more of these parties to have access to me. He told me that numbers daily came to the prison who would gladly give him ten dollars apiece to be allowed to pass my open door.

March 3rd.—Since two days we are actually allowed a half-hour's exercise in the prison-yard, where we walk up and down, picking our way as best we can through mud and negroes, followed by soldiers and corporals, bayonets in hand. . . . Last night I put my candle on the window, in order to get something out of my trunk near which it stood, all unconscious of committing any offense against prison discipline, when the guard below called, 'Put out that light!' I gave no heed, but only lighted another, whereupon several voices took up the cry, adding, 'Damn you, I will fire into your room!' Rose was in a state of great delight, and collected all the ends of candles to add to the illumination. By this the clank of arms and patter of feet, in conjunction with the furious rapping at my door, with a demand to open it, announced the advent of corporal and sergeant.

My door was now secured inside by a bolt which had been allowed me. I asked their business. Answer, 'You are making signals, and must remove your lights from the window.' I said, 'But it suits my convenience to keep them there.'—'We will break open your door if you don't open it.'—'You will act as you see fit, but it will be at your peril!' They did not dare to carry out this threat, as they knew that I had a very admirable pistol on my mantelpiece, restored to me a short time since, although they did not know that I had no ammunition for it."

The candles burned themselves out, and that ended it, save that next day, by order of the provost marshal, the pistol was taken from the prisoner.

But it was not all a merry baiting of the guards—there was hardship connected with this imprisonment. In spite of the folded clothing placed on the hard bed, the child used to cry out in the night, "Oh, mamma, mamma, the bed hurts me so!" The rooms above were filled with negroes. "The tramping and screaming of negro children overhead was most dreadful." Worse than mere sound came from these other prisoners: there came disease. Smallpox broke out among them, also the lesser disease, camp measles, which latter was contracted by the little Rose. She, too, had her memories of the Old Capitol; in a recent letter she wrote:—

"I do not remember very much about our imprisonment except that I used to cry myself to sleep from hunger. . . . There was a tiny closet in our room in which mother contrived to loosen a plank that she would lift up, and the prisoners of war underneath would catch hold of my legs and lower me into their room; they were allowed to receive fruit, etc., from the outside, and generously shared with me, also they would give mother news of the outside world."

Thus, the days passed until Mrs. Greenhow was summoned to appear, March 25th, before the United States Commissioners for the Trial of State Prisoners.

Of this "trial" the only record available is her own—rather too flippant in tone to be wholly convincing as to its entire sincerity. Her account begins soberly enough: the cold, raw day, the slowly falling snow, the mud through which the carriage laboured to the office of the provost marshal in what had been the residence of Senator Guin—

". . .one of the most elegant in the city; . . . my mind instinctively reverted to the gay and brilliant scenes in which I had mingled in that house, and the goodly company who had enjoyed its hospitality."

There was a long wait in a fireless anteroom; then she was led before the Commissioners for her trial.

"My name was announced, and the Commissioners advanced to receive me with ill-concealed embarrassment. I bowed to them, saying: 'Gentlemen, resume your seats. I recognise the embarrassment of your positions; it was a mistake on the part of your government to have selected gentlemen for this mission. You have, however, shown me but scant courtesy in having kept me waiting your pleasure for nearly an hour in the cold."

The prisoner took her place at the long table, midway between the two commissioners, one of whom, General Dix, was a former friend; at smaller tables were several secretaries; if there were any spectators other than the newspaper reporters, she makes no mention of them. The trial began:—

"One of the reporters now said, 'If you please, speak a little louder, madam.' I rose from my seat, and said to General Dix, 'If it is your object to make a spectacle of me, and furnish reports for the newspapers, I shall have the honour to withdraw from this presence.' Hereupon both commissioners arose and protested that they had no such intention, but that it was necessary to take notes. . . ."

The examination then continued:

"In a strain in no respect different from that of an ordinary conver-

sation held in a drawing-room, and to which I replied sarcastically, . . .
and a careless listener would have imagined that the commission was
endeavouring with plausible arguments to defend the government
rather than to incriminate me. . . ."

The other commissioner then said:

"'General Dix, you are so much better acquainted with Mrs.
Greenhow, suppose you continue the examination?' I laughingly said,
'Commence it, for I hold that it has not begun.'"

Mrs. Greenhow's account makes no mention of any witnesses either for or against her; the evidence seems to have consisted solely
in the papers found in her house. The whole examination—as she
records it—may be summed up in the following questions and an-
swers:—

'You are charged with treason.'

'I deny it!'—

'You are charged, madam, with having caused a letter which
you wrote to the Secretary of State to be published in Richmond.'—

'That can hardly be brought forward as one of the causes of my
arrest, for I had been some three months a prisoner when that
letter was written.'—

'You are charged, madam, with holding communication with
the enemy in the South.'—

'If this were an established fact, you could not be surprised at it;
I am a Southern woman.'—

'How is it, madam, that you have managed to communicate, in
spite of the vigilance exercised over you?'—

'That is my secret!'

And that was practically the end, save that the prisoner said she
would refuse to take the oath of allegiance if this opportunity to be
freed were offered her.

April 3rd the superintendent of the Old Capitol read to her a copy
of the decree of the Commission: she had been sentenced to be exiled.
But the days passed and nothing came of it. Tantalised beyond endurance, she wrote that she was "ready" to go South. General McClellan,
she was then told, had objected to her being sent South at this time.
(Federal spies—secret-service men, who, under Allan Pinkerton, had
arrested Mrs. Greenhow—were on trial for their lives in Richmond;
it was feared that, were she sent South, her testimony would be used

against them.) The diary continues:—

Day glides into day with nothing to mark the flight of time. The heat is intense, with the sun beating down upon the house-top and in the windows. . . . My child is looking pale and ill. . .

Saturday, May 31st.—At two o'clock today (Prison Superintendent) Wood came in with the announcement that I was to start at three o'clock for Baltimore."

The end of imprisonment had come as suddenly as its beginning.

Disquieting rumours had been reaching Mrs. Greenhow for some time in regard to removal to Fort Warren. Was this, after all, a mere Yankee trick to get her there quietly? She was about to enter the carriage that was to bear her from the Old Capitol, when, unable longer to bear the suspense, she turned suddenly to the young lieutenant of the escort: "Sir, ere I advance further, I ask you, not as Lincoln's officer, but as a man of honour and a gentleman, are your orders from Baltimore to conduct me to a Northern prison, or to some point in the Confederacy?"

"On my honour, madam," he answered, "to conduct you to Fortress Monroe and thence to the Southern Confederacy."

Her imprisonment had indeed, ended. There was yet the Abolition-soldier guard—on the way to the station, on the cars, in Baltimore, on the steamer; there was yet to he signed at Fortress Monroe the parole in which, in consideration of being set at liberty, she pledged her honour not to return north of the Potomac during the war; but from that moment at the carriage-door she felt herself no longer a prisoner.

To the query of the provost marshal at Fortress Monroe she replied that she wished to be sent "to the capital of the Confederacy, wherever that might be." That was still Richmond, he told her, but it would be in Federal hands before she could reach there. She would take chances on that, was her laughing rejoinder. And so, she was set ashore at City Point by a boat from the *Monitor*, and next morning, June 4th., she and little Rose, escorted by Confederate officers, arrived in Richmond. And there:—

"On the evening of my arrival, our President did me the honour to call on me, and his words of greeting, 'But for you there would have been no Battle of Bull Bun,' repaid me for all I had endured."

Could the story be told of the succeeding twenty-seven months of Mrs. Greenhow's life, much of the secret history of the Confederacy might be revealed. It is improbable that the story ever will be told.

Months of effort to learn details have resulted in but vague glimpses of her, as one sees an ever-receding figure at the turns of a winding road. Her daughter Rose has written:—

"Whether mother did anything for the Confederacy in Richmond is more than I can tell. I know that we went to Charleston, South Carolina, and that she saw General Beauregard there."

Then came weeks of waiting for the sailing of a blockade runner from Wilmington, North Carolina; quiet, happy weeks they were, perhaps the happiest she had known since the war began. She was taking little Rose to Paris, to place her in the Convent of the Sacred Heart, she told her new-made friends. One morning they found that she and little Rose had gone. A blockade-runner had slipped out during the night and was on its way with them to Bermuda.

Many have definitely asserted that Mrs. Greenhow went to England and France on a secret mission for the Confederacy. No proof of this has ever been found, but the little which has been learned of her sojourn in Europe strongly supports the theory of such a mission there. The ship which bore them to England from Bermuda was an English man-of-war, in which they sailed "at President Davis's especial request." Then there were President Davis's personal letters to Messrs. Mason and Slidell, requesting them that they show to Mrs. Greenhow every attention.

In France she was given a private audience with Napoleon III.; in London, presented to England's Queen. A letter written to her by James Spence, financial agent of the Confederates in Liverpool, shows her to have been actively engaged in support of the interests of the South from her arrival in England. But of any secret mission there is not a trace—unless her book, *My Imprisonment, or the First Year of Abolition Rule in Washington,* may thus be considered. The book was brought out in November, 1863, by the well-known English publishing-house of Richard Bentley & Son; immediately it made a profound sensation in London—particularly in the highest society circles, into which Mrs. Greenhow had at once been received. *My Imprisonment* was a brilliant veneer of personal war-time experiences laid alluringly over a solid backing of Confederate States' propaganda. Richmond may or may not have fathered it, but that book in England served the South well. (Many of the passages in this article have been quoted from Mrs. Greenhow's own narrative.)

None who knew Mrs. Greenhow ever forgot her charm; she made friends everywhere—such friends as Thomas Carlyle and Lady Franklin, and a score more whose names are nearly as well known today. She was betrothed to a prominent peer.

All in all, this is but scant information to cover a period of more than two years. Only one other fact has been obtained regarding her life abroad, but it is most significant in support of the belief that she was a secret agent for the Confederacy. In August, 1864, Mrs. Greenhow left England suddenly and sailed for Wilmington on the ship *Condor*. Though her plans were to return almost at once, marry, and remain in England, the fact that she left in London her affianced husband, and her little Rose in the Convent of the Sacred Heart in Paris, while she herself risked her life to run the blockade, seems strong evidence that her business in the Confederate States of America was important business, indeed.

The *Condor* was a three funnelled steamer, newly built, and on her first trip as a blockade-runner—a trade for which she was superbly adapted, being swift as a sea-swallow. She was commanded by a veteran captain of the Crimean War—an English officer on a year's leave, blockade-running for adventure—Captain Augustus Charles Hobart-Hampden, variously known to the blockade-running fleet as Captain Roberts, Hewett, or Gulick.

On the night of September 30th, the *Condor* arrived opposite the mouth of the Cape Fear River, the entry for Wilmington, and in the darkness stole swiftly through the blockade. She was almost in the mouth of the river, and not two hundred yards from shore, when suddenly there loomed up in the darkness a vessel dead ahead. To the frightened pilot of the *Condor*, it was one of the Federal squadron; he swerved his ship sharply, and she drove hard on New Inlet bar. In reality the ship which had caused the damage was the wreck of the blockade-runner *Nighthawk*, which had been run down the previous night. The *Condor's* pilot sprang overboard and swam ashore.

Dawn was near breaking, and in the now growing light the Federal blockaders which had followed the *Condor* were seen to be closing in. Though the *Condor*, lying almost under the very guns of Fort Fisher— which had begun firing at the Federal ships and was holding them off—was for the time being safe, yet Mrs. Greenhow and the two other passengers, Judge Holcombe and Lieutenant Wilson, Confederate agents, demanded that they be set ashore. There was little wind and there had been no storm, but the tiderip ran high over the bar, and the boat was lowered into heavy surf. Scarcely was it clear of the tackles ere a great wave caught it, and in an instant, it was overturned. Mrs.

Greenhow, weighted down by her heavy black silk dress and a bag full of gold sovereigns, which she had fastened round her waist, sank at once and did not rise again. The others succeeded in getting ashore.

The body of Mrs. Greenhow was washed up on the beach next day. They buried her in Wilmington—buried her with the honours of war, and a Confederate flag wrapped about her coffin. And every Memorial Day since then there is laid upon her grave a wreath of laurel leaves such as is placed only upon the graves of soldiers. Long ago the Ladies' Memorial Society placed there a simple marble cross, on which is carved:—

Mrs. Rose O'Neal Greenhow. A Bearer of Despatches to the Confederate Government.

MRS. GREENHOW AND THE TWO OTHER
PASSENGERS DEMANDED TO BE SET ASHORE

www.ingramcontent.com/pod-product-compliance
Lightning Source LLC
Chambersburg PA
CBHW021055090426
42738CB00006B/348